Advance Praise for
Recycling Reality

"Take a serious dose of wanderlust, mix in an obsessive curiosity about life, sprinkle it all with masses of talent, and you have Nicky Almasy's life. From Cartel-controlled Mexico, Britpop London, and a couple of decades roaming Asia, Recycling Reality captures multiple unique times and places, always seen with Almasy's hyper-observant eye."

— Paul French, author of *Midnight in Peking*

"A stunning meditation on the photojournalist life on the road by a fellow photography superstar."

— Christopher Makos, Andy Warhol's personal photographer

"Almasy eloquently and insightfully captures life behind the lens - from gangsters at the Mexico borderlands to vampire-fearing medics in Southeast Asia to the explosive energy of Shanghai during a fascinating and pivotal moment in its unique history. An engrossing read."

— Ned Kelly, Editor, That's Shanghai

RECYCLING REALITY

Mexico to Asia through a Photojournalist's Lens

NICKY ALMASY

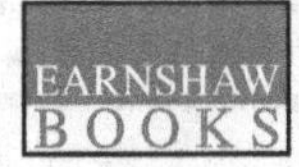

Recycling Reality

Nicky Almasy

ISBN-13: 978-988-8769-69-8

Cover design by Zoltan Jenei

BIOGRAPHY / AUTOBIOGRAPHY

EB174

Published by Earnshaw Books Ltd. (Hong Kong)

Smudging Borderlines

'OK, IT'S a box then.'

I came to the final, bitter conclusion of how I might make it across the U.S. border, as I marched out into the unfriendly night of Tijuana, one of the most dangerous cities on the planet, in northern Mexico, bordering California. I was aware of its reputation and half knew what I was getting myself into by succumbing to its unpredictable street laws, but right now I felt its poisonous grasp unmistakably tightening around me, and I realized there was no escape.

'There's no way back from this,' I recall vividly thinking, as I followed a group of unknown men out of the small hotel to their pick-up truck that would take me to the coyotes, the people smugglers who would get me across the Mexican-American border.

I will say it before you do: I was young and stupid. Determined for sure. Either way, the incident was to mark the end of a whole era of immaturity, once and for all carving a distinct line between two periods of my life. I should have known better, of course. But the unmistakable, sinister omens became apparent way too late. Even though it was actually just a few hours since I'd arrived in this godforsaken desert city.

Tijuana is notorious for its culture of aggression, and from my first steps there, I found it reeking of machismo and crime; its streets dotted with illegal pharmacies, questionable plastic surgeries, dodgy bars and small hotels. This assortment created a cesspool for wrongdoing, the ideal setting in which all manner of illegal activities thrived. And, to put it mildly, this was just scratching the surface. The city is known as an invisible battlefield for drug cartels, with corrupt politicians and police in their grip. Everyone looks suspect in Tijuana. If I close my eyes and think of its streets, all I see are suspicious cops, shady characters and the endless pharmacies. It was as if the town's entire existence was to supply illegal and cheap pharmaceutical drugs to the pill-popping nip-and-tuck wrecks and celebrities of nearby California, just a few miles across the border.

The second sign was minor, yet telling. My host, who was the mastermind behind the following mess, arrived at our rendezvous wearing no shoes. He was completely barefoot. And within one minute of getting into his car, near a downtown shopping mall, the police pulled us over and, in the middle of the parking lot, frisked us for drugs. It happened so fast that I couldn't even properly greet the guy. The city welcomed me with a proper shake-down. It was a surreal arrival and in those anxious moments, I couldn't fathom what was happening. Never before or ever since had the entire contents of my luggage been laid out, humiliatingly, on a street pavement, with three police officers rummaging though my belongings like preoccupied raccoons. But strangely, there was a noticeable absence of disapproval from the passers-by witnessing my shame, in stark contrast to what I'm sure I would have felt in any other city — and I knew why: everyone was familiar with such a situation; everyone was guilty in this town. This was the drill. It was routine around here.

Seconds later, one of the officers rose up and held up my head-cold medicine and some innocent over-the-counter painkillers. He shook the little bottle in front of my eyes as if I'd been caught red-handed with some illicit narcotic or a shopping bag full of cocaine.

'What are these, sir?'

Everyone had a hard-on for medicine in this godless place, it seemed. Their questions did me a favor, unwittingly giving me a crash course, outlining just how rotten things were in this paranoia-filled border town. My volunteer tour guides to hell—the Tijuana police force.

Here's the background to the story. A year earlier, I'd been leading a decent life in New York, living in Queens and working on Manhattan's Upper East Side. But my time there was unexpectedly interrupted when I needed to return home to Hungary because of personal issues. In my haste, I made the mistake of leaving the US with my visa having expired, thus making it impossible to apply for a new one for me to return. The life I'd left behind in New York City was somewhat fabulous to me, and in my consideration—at least back then—it was worth anything to reclaim it. After living in London for almost a decade, I returned to my home country for a short period of time before choosing New York City as my next target for continuing my urban explorations.

My arrival in the US had been inauspicious enough. It had started with a somewhat desperate search, rummaging through meaningless, temporary dead-end jobs at different joints across the rigid grid of Manhattan; washing dishes in the East Village, serving coffee in Soho, being a food-runner in a Midtown restaurant—the everyday stuff one has to go through to get ahead in the the merciless job-machine of the Big Apple.

It wasn't plain sailing. Memorably, I was once fired from a restaurant on my very first day, just hours after starting.

'Bro, you want to come out for a cigarette?' asked the Russian head-waiter, in a quiet moment when there were no guests to serve.

'Nah, man,' I replied. 'I'm new. I'll just clean the kitchen before we get busy again.'

But he was insistent. 'C'mon bro, no one cares. Just come out for one before you go downstairs. I want to get to know you.'

Since I was working directly under him, I reluctantly succumbed. I thought it was the right thing to do, to start off on a friendly footing. But the moment I lit the cigarette, the restaurant boss rushed out, remonstrating angrily: 'Smoking outside on your first day, when we should be preparing the kitchen?! Get the fuck out of here. You're fired!'

And that was that. As this little scenario unfolded within a matter minutes, and I never saw either of those guys again, to this day I'm not sure if I'd walked into a trap, whether it had been a deliberate act from the head-waiter or just an unfortunate coincidence. Either way, in a strange twist of fate, I had so much to thank him for, later on, for ejecting me from that particular place. At the time, though, I was utterly crestfallen, and I took to walking the New York City streets aimlessly. It was one of those tipping points when you feel that everything is pointless, that you'll never succeed and that you just want to give up. I felt so beaten and down that I felt I didn't have the strength to restart, or even to face people again in the effort to do so. But such feelings didn't last long. Only a young mind can switch so quickly and feel so invincible. In the moment of my dejection, I decided: I just don't care, I'll carry on anyway. I was in America. In New York City! I wasn't about to give up and squander the opportunity. Further still, I wasn't prepared to wait another day for things to improve. I decided there and then: I will change everything now.

It was just after lunchtime, so I headed straight back to the agency in Queens through which I had secured the job in the first place. For a few bucks, they organized restaurant jobs for illegal workers, for Mexicans, Russians, Eastern Europeans, anyone who arrived in town without the appropriate visa, and as I was on a single-entry tourist one—and even that was soon to expire—I was left with no choice other than to rely on illegal work agencies such as this. Here, all you had to do was bide your time in a waiting room, chat for a few minutes to a consultant, and soon enough you were given an address and could head out again, to a random venue in the city and get to work.

I was given the address of a restaurant called Balitore, situated on the posh Upper East Side of Manhattan, on the corner of 3rd Avenue and 92nd Street. I had to be there at 4:30pm, the time they opened. Upon arriving, a nice Italian-American guy named Charlie greeted me. He was elegantly dressed, with a bald head, dark skin and a striking pair of eyes darting up and down all over me. Moving quickly like a panther, he showed me around the elegant, cosy joint. It was instantly appealing. There were about thirty tables and the place had a classy decor, with beautiful black-and-white photographs of wild horses on its walls, and a spacious open area overlooking the busy traffic of 3rd Avenue, as it swept upwards to Harlem. I noticed instantly that Charlie addressed me with respect. Within minutes, I felt I was now on a better track, that I had stumbled upon the right place. It was such a striking contrast to the treatment I'd endured at other restaurants, so that all of a sudden I was grateful to the Russian head-waiter who'd gotten me fired just a few hours ago.

This was also the day that I became known as Nicky, the name I use to this day.

'Can you start immediately?' asked Charlie.

'Yes, absolutely,' I replied.

'That's the spirit! What's your name?'

I hesitated for a moment. My given name is Tibor, which is particular to Eastern Europe. I'm affectionately known as Tibi, but neither version has an equivalent in English, and it often caused confusion. People would forget it, mispronounce it, and keep asking me to repeat it. In that moment, I decided that it was time for a change—I would choose a new name for myself, something that was easily recognizable to the English-speaking world, and one that required no explanation or repetition. Instinctively, I opted for Nicky; to my mind this sounded similar enough to Tibi, with the repeated 'i' sounds, so that it didn't feel as if I was rejecting my identity.

'Nicky,' I said. 'My name is Nicky.'

'Alright, Nicky,' said Charlie, looking straight into my eyes. 'You'll be our food-runner.' He placed a hand on my shoulder. 'I want you to go down to the kitchen, introduce yourself to the chef, Al, and his team, and get straight to work. We'll get busy around six o'clock. Now, go!'

And with that, I joined the staff of Balitore, a busy Irish-Italian joint that catered for the wealthy clientele of Manhattan. Initially, I had no idea what a treasure I'd actually stumbled upon. All I knew, and all that mattered, was that I was working again and that I'd found myself embraced by the restaurant's kind-hearted community of managers and staff. The place quickly became a home. I worked hard, often pulling double-shifts, and they seemed to greatly appreciate it. I was rewarded with a sense of trust and, of course, with financial stability. I started to earn a decent wage from tips—easily a hundred dollars a day—and thus Balitore pretty much transformed my experience in New York.

However, the ultimate reward from my efforts only became apparent later. The staff kept referring to 'Gabriel', one of the bosses, who would soon be returning from a few months of film shooting in Europe. He was an actor, they said, and a very successful one. I didn't have the time to pay much attention to it, but I kept hearing about him, and at that point I still had no idea who the owners of the restaurant were. I was just happy fitting in and doing my job. And then, one day, Irish Hollywood star Gabriel Byrne, walked through the door of Balitore. He was alone. He looked smart in his suit. He greeted everyone kindly and sat down at one of the tables overlooking the avenue. One of the managers ran up to him: 'Oh, the prodigal son returns, finally!' And then, to me: 'Nicky, the boss is here now. Can you prepare some green tea?'

I was surprised. It turned out that the 'Gabriel' they'd kept referring to was in fact one of my favorite actors, Gabriel Byrne. And now he was my boss! This could only happen in New York City, I thought. Recovering quickly, I told myself to act cool and casual around him. From that day, he came to the restaurant often, usually alone, and sat at his preferred table overlooking the traffic, sipping his favorite green tea.

I remember the first moment when he came up to me, resting his hand over my shoulders: 'What's your name again? Oh, Nick, right? Nick, can you do me a favor, can you please turn the air-conditioning down a bit?'

Little things like this, which I found unbelievable at first, became casual everyday occurrences. I soon discovered that the restaurant was named after his father's home village of Ballitore in County Kildare, Ireland.

With Gabriel Byrne as the restaurant's owner, not surprisingly, there was no shortage of Hollywood stars booking to dine. It turned out that Gabriel was co-owner with Michael Tadross, producer of the Die Hard movies, among many other Hollywood hits. When in town, the Tadross family often came for dinner and, as his son was into music, especially rap, I often found myself engaged in conversation in the kitchen with Tadross Jr. With the return of Gabriel, the small restaurant turned into an A-list haven. Gabriel's fellow Irish movie star and friend, Liam Neeson popped in from time to time. One evening, we had a party with

Macaulay Culkin. He parked his limo right outside Balitore, and did a limbo dance between the car and the restaurant. This was during a difficult phase in his life when the fame and fortune he'd earned as a child actor in the Home Alone movies had clearly got the better of him. His eyes were swimming in delirium, and he was obviously already high on drugs and alcohol—he seemed completely oblivious of his surroundings. I remember him accidentally sweeping all the drinks off his table as he misjudged an arm gesture to make a particular point. The few words I exchanged with him left a strange impression on me; meeting him was like meeting Mickey Mouse, something far removed from reality, far removed from an actual person.

That year, the two Matrix sequels premiered within a few months of each other. In New York City, giant posters marked the releases, and one night the Balitore was host to a bearded Keanu Reeves, who walked in with a friend. He was the polar opposite of Macaulay Culkin, so down-to-earth and normal that you could barely associate him with the guy on the posters. There was also a music-related aspect to Balitore; at the bar, there was Nikki with whom I was on great terms. She was the girlfriend of Julian Casablancas, frontman of the hugely feted New York band, The Strokes. Ultimately, getting to know Gabriel Byrne, being on friendly terms with the Tadross family and everyone in that circle didn't dazzle me at all. On the contrary, it sobered me with its reality—it was as if such celebrity and riches were within arm's reach. I admired the casual nature of it, and this mindset eventually led me to view such status—something that had been hitherto unfathomable—entirely differently.

But it wasn't only the Hollywood stars that defined my beloved New York experience. I now belonged to a great community, full of inspiring people with whom I could hang out, through unforgettable times. We used to go to galleries, clubs and concerts, catching great shows all across the city. Apart from renting my own place on the other side of the river in Astoria, Queens, I became the house-sitter for a few months for one of the managers of Balitore. The property in Harlem where I stayed, located in a small side street, was later used as a set for Martin Scorsese's TV show, Boardwalk Empire. Through such experiences, my life in New York City turned into a dream-like existence. And so, when I had to unexpectedly leave, due to the emergency back home, I desperately wanted to return. At any cost. This was why, once the reality of my error of having left the US with an expired visa became apparent, I grew even more determined to get back to New York, whatever it took, however unorthodox, however illegal, to get back to where I felt I belonged.

I cast my net widely when exploring the options. While back home, I came across a guy who said he knew people who knew an easy route into the US across the Mexican border. I was friendly with his family, and considered them trustworthy, but I didn't realize that, as an individual, this guy wasn't. All I had to do, he said, was to make my way to Tijuana via Mexico City, and my re-entry into the US would be assured. He claimed to know exactly where the border guards were the most obliging and, once some money had exchanged hands, they'd let me through. Easy! Stupidly, I took this fiction at face value, and went for it. I was so desperate to get back to my old life, to my friends in New York, that I ignored the obvious obstacles in my way. My plan was, once I'd crossed the Mexican border, to make my way to San Diego, and from there up the East Coast, back to my happy life in New York City.

But in Tijuana, things went wrong. My contact, the man with no shoes, informed me right after the police shake-down that the situation had changed, and that further complications had arisen that meant we couldn't cross the border at the moment. I began to despair. We'd spoken on the phone twenty-four hours prior to this and he hadn't mentioned any potential problems. Suddenly, my world started to collapse around me. I felt vulnerable and at the mercy of Tijuana's mean streets. I'd left everything behind back home. I'd put all the expenses for this trip on one card, and had made this long journey to the other side of the world into what now seemed to be the pits of hell. I stood there with no option but to attempt another way, any way, to get back to the US. To add more weight to the situation I'd arrived on a one-way ticket. I hadn't bought a return, either to Mexico City, or to Europe. This had raised questions at Mexico City airport and I'd had to explain why I was boarding a flight to Tijuana with no obvious intention of flying back. My mumbled answer was something about planning to travel around inside Mexico.

I was exhausted. I'd been flying for two entire days to reach this godforsaken destination. I couldn't think straight. I saw everything through the fog of tiredness, not the best state in which to make important decisions, let alone ones that might actually endanger my life. But the man with no shoes had other ideas. He said he knew a couple of people who, in turn, knew some coyotes—illegal people smugglers—around the border. But first, he suggested that I find a hotel, somewhere for me to rest and a base for us to make plans. At that point I had US$1,600 in cash with me. Some of this was earmarked to pay for the cross-border trip and the rest for traveling expenses through the US from the West Coast to the East Coast.

The hotel was an extra expense I hadn't counted on. Mr. No Shoes had assured me that my border crossing would happen immediately, as soon as I arrived in Tijuana, so I hadn't needed to factor in accommodation. But we soon found a hotel. It wasn't hard. The streets of Tijuana are rich with quick solutions. I paid for two nights and during that day, I hardly left the hotel, barely ate anything, and even though I was totally exhausted, I was unable to sleep because of the constant worry. And then, to exacerbate the situation, that very same afternoon the barefoot man vanished. When I tried to call his mobile, it was switched off. In the tiny, windowless hotel room I felt like a caged animal, pacing up and down the same few square meters, not knowing what to do. I couldn't believe how I'd allowed myself to get swindled this way. Still no sleep over the third day. Needless to say, I didn't dare ring home to confide in my family—they would have been flabbergasted, and very worried to learn about my predicament. Cognizant of the precarious nature of my plan, I had kept them in the dark about my planned illegal border crossing.

No-shoes man eventually resurfaced after an entire day's absence. Although he looked like a proper drug addict, deranged and shaking, talking nonsense, I just wanted to chain myself to him, as he was my only contact in this perilous place, and I couldn't afford to be left alone again. By then, I was feeling quite deranged myself from the lack of sleep. He explained himself by saying that during his no-show the previous night he'd been ensconced in a nearby hotel working on how to remedy my situation—and, reassuring me, he announced that he had already located the right people to get me over the border. But we had to go straight away, that night. In any normal situation, to a person with a clear mind, this sense of urgency should have raised further alarm bells. But with my judgement clouded, I reasoned that I was in so deep already that there was nothing for it but to throw whatever caution I had left to the wind. The sensible thing would have been to get on a bus back to Mexico City as soon as possible. But, desperately believing that it would be better to emerge from this experience in New York with my nerves battered and torn, rather than to retreat in the name of safety, I decided to risk it. Despite an assurance of an immediate increase in my personal security, I knew that if I retreated, I wouldn't be able to resist branding myself a quitter and a loser. Deep inside, however, I'd already given up on a good outcome to all of this. Everything seemed so rushed and so, so obviously wrong.

I had little choice but to agree that he should leave me alone in the hotel again, while he went off to make the arrangements. So, as before, I paced about my hotel room, eagerly anticipating his return. At this point I was even further away than ever from sleeping. I was on edge, drifting in a half-awake delirium, only slightly distracted by the vacuous Hollywood TV shows that flickered in the background, coloring the hotel room in blueish, alien hues. I watched the screen without really seeing anything; any show that I happened to be familiar with took on a whole new meaning. The very idea of America now seemed surreal and distant, even as the TV taunted me with images of a world, my world, seemingly out of reach on the other side of the border fence that I had came so close to passing through. The contrast did nothing but highlight the terrible situation I'd gotten myself into and how low I felt.

Eventually, late into the night, Barefoot Man returned and told me to pack my bags at once: his people were waiting for me downstairs. They were ready to go. I was briefed about the deal while I packed: I had to pay $1,000 up front. And… I might have to spend the night hiding inside a box in the car, if I didn't mind. He offered no further details and I didn't ask. The fact that I agreed so readily proves to me now just how far at this point I had drifted from my true self; I had already sunk so low, down into the rotten guts of Tijuana, that I didn't care. I just wanted to get this over with.

'OK,' I said. Adding with a twist of bitter humour, 'It's a box then. Let's get the fuck out of here.'

He smiled and said, 'Yeah, that's the spirit!'

A pick-up truck was waiting for me outside in the dark. The man with no shoes said goodbye briefly and wished me luck. I could tell that he was nervous about this, too. He'd probably came up with this solution overnight and latched on to the first person, anyone, who could help right his wrong, remedy the situation, and just get rid of me. There were several men in the truck. Who were they? I had no idea. They seemed friendly enough, and reassured my man that 'the boy will be safe. It's all easy anyway.' But as soon as he was out of sight and the engine started, my companions fell silent. Their behavior changed dramatically and a sinister air weighed heavy inside the truck as we drove. We travelled to a desert-like area without another word uttered, as a wall of dust billowed behind us on the bumpy road. When I dared to ask questions they told me to shut up. They became rude and aggressive. 'Enough with the questions. Just follow us,' they commanded through their teeth, full of malevolence and menace.

We arrived at a house with all the lights out, its backyard opening straight onto the desert. We got out and they led me towards the back of the property in a hurried march—I now started to feel as if I was being kidnapped. We continued on foot, increasing the pace as we walked. They led me through small dusty paths fringed by wild plants until we reached a high wall that I gathered to be part of the border between the United States and Mexico. It rose above us in the dark, significant and sinister. At this point, I knew there was no way back. I couldn't do anything now; I certainly couldn't change my mind about this adventure—it was too late. The air was tense around us, and my hosts were clearly growing ever more hostile, like some kind of executioners, remaining eerily silent. There, as I was marched through the dark in hurried steps I recall telling myself almost without emotion, 'This is your last journey. You know that, right? This is where it all ends, no mistake.'

It was just after midnight when we cut through an area filled with the metal skeletons of car wrecks stacked one on top of each other. It was like an automobile Stonehenge, shimmering balefully in the moonlight. We made our way through, moving faster and faster to an unknown destination. To my shock, as we wove through the cars, they came to life: people were living in them. I saw shadows of desperate lives staggering about, talking and shouting in the darkness. Years later, I saw this place, or one just like it, in a movie. Although the scene was shot in broad daylight, the image shook me to my core, dredging up forcibly buried memories.

As we marched out of this tiny village of wrecks, the path led into another desert zone, like a glade. In the middle of it the orange glow of a huge bonfire illuminated the hellish surroundings and I caught sight of what looked like junkie tribesmen gathered around it. Some were dancing. When I got closer to the fire I noticed that the ground was littered with empty bottles and used syringes — we had run into a herd of drug addicts living in the middle of the desert. I was told to sit down among them for a while. I didn't dare to look around and certainly didn't make eye contact with anyone. Someone offered me a drink but I refused. My sense of dread and peril was growing deeper by the minute, as did my grim realization that I was now in big trouble, and that for sure this wasn't going to end well.

Only now, with fifteen years' hindsight, have I regained my nerve to the point where I am able revisit these events properly in my head, and actually try and put a name to the location where all this went down. For many years, I buried it all deep down, mostly out of a sense of shame at my own stupidity, but partly because of the personal trauma it caused. Judging from the satellite image I found on Google Maps, I reckon the venue for these miserable events must have been the northern and outer fringes of either Zona Norte or Libertad. I say outer fringes, because it was a desert area with sand dunes neighboring the border wall—we walked for a long time away from any houses. Like retrieving information from a damaged hard disc lost for fifteen years, it's hard to recall data in my mind about what happened next. As with the moment of an accident that could have been prevented, the brain tries hard to delete the details, burying them deep in the subconscious. It took time for me to find and retrieve the data.

I hadn't been sitting around the bonfire long when my coyote companions returned, and we resumed our hurried walk along the towering Mexican-American border wall. Again, only this time more desperately, I started to ask questions.

'Where are we going? What do I have to do? Is there another car waiting for me?'

The response was again aggressive, and I was told to just shut up. It quickly dawned on me that there were in fact no more cars waiting, no more roads ahead. The coyotes were in fact looking for a good spot to beat me up, to take my money and throw me over the wall as prey to the US border police—getting rid of me altogether by dumping me on the other side. As we marched ahead, the sand dunes became very steep, almost reaching the height of the wall. When we reached a peak, everyone stopped.

'The money! Give me the money!' someone shouted, as if there was a sudden urgency.

As soon as I reached into my pockets, they grabbed it from my hands, and that's when I received the first blow. They punched me, again and again. When I fell, they kicked me repeatedly as

I tried to crawl away. The shock was so great that, thankfully, I can't recall any pain. The unlikeliness, the location, the absurdity and the danger of the situation was on a much higher level than my pain response.

I don't remember if it was near the top of the wall where this nightmare scenario unfolded, or whether there was a hole, a crack in the wall just halfway up, but I do recall they forced me over the edge and the next thing I knew I was crash landing from a considerable height and tumbling down into a narrow ditch which was, fortunately, filled with sand. I knew instantly that I was in no-man's-land, in between the two high bordering walls between Mexico and the United States. I heard cars passing at a distance, from what must have been a highway on the San Diego side. The sand broke my fall and I was fortunate to only end up with bruises. But any actual injuries were the last thing on my mind as I struggled to cope with the trauma of what had just happened.

I began climbing up the steep ditch, but within a few minutes I could hear sirens in the distance, before two or three US patrol police cars swept into view in a cloud of dust. I later reasoned that my movement, my fall, must have been detected on a camera somewhere. There I was, as surely no one ever believes they'll find themselves, quivering with raised hands in front of agitated policemen, blinking in the flashing crossfire of torchlights, blue sirens and the blinding reflectors from the top of their cars. The police were forceful and aggressive as they pushed me against one of the cars — but I could instantly tell that they were surprised that I wasn't another Mexican trying to gain illegal access to the US, but that I was, like them, Caucasian. They questioned me on the spot about how I happened to be there, and I recall my fear when recounting details of the event. After all, it was entirely possible that right next to us, on the other side of the wall, my attackers were just meters away, listening. I told the police that I'd been attacked on the Mexican side and thrown over the wall, but I was sensible enough — finally — to keep to myself my original, and patently ridiculous, plan to get into US unofficially.

There was no way out, it seemed. They told me I had broken immigration law and I was about to be taken into custody and transported to a prison nearby until such a time when they could deal with me. They opened one of the police truck's back doors, to reveal a cage, like for traveling pets, only bigger. We stood there for a moment in the flickering blue light, everyone silent. And then I did the impossible.

'No!' I protested. 'I can't go to prison. Don't you understand? I was attacked!'

There was a short silence again as they looked at each other. Moments ago, I'd been pushed up against the police car by two officers to be interrogated. And now, to top it all, here I was, resisting arrest. I'm sure the only thing stopping them from manhandling me into their mobile jail was their evident surprise that I was white and not the usual Mexican would-be illegal alien.

At this point they asked me for my passport. There was more confusion when they saw that I was from Europe. Why was I here on the US side of the wall? Why was I even at the border in the first place? Thinking on my feet I told them I had been traveling around Mexico, but had got drunk in a bar and got mixed up with the wrong people. They looked at me, not sure whether to believe me or not. One of the officers pointed up to the physical border towering over us and said, 'I'll give you one option. If you can climb back up the wall and make your way over to the Mexican side again, we'll let you go.' No laughter followed from the others, but he was obviously toying with me. It was impossible to climb back. However, with a San Diego prison crammed with criminals in mind, I looked up at the wall that must have been four to five meters high, and began to climb.

I remember picking out the rusty metal splinters from under my nails and fingertips for weeks afterwards. Like an animal, I wanted to maul my way out of the situation. Anything but prison. Anything but prison with, who knows, ten others in a cell? I fell back, then started again, no matter how impossible it seemed. The policemen weren't laughing, but I felt their amusement as they watching the desperate process. Then one of them said to the others,

'Listen, stop this,' he said. 'He looks like a decent guy. Let's give him a chance.'

The others, hesitant and perhaps mindful of the inevitable paperwork that my case would generate, looked at each other and finally agreed.

'Listen, son,' said the friendliest of the officers. 'Come with us to the edge of this fence. There's a one-way gate back.' They put me in the car and drove me to a section where there was a long open-air corridor with a turnstile. I assumed it led back to Tijuana. They stopped.

'I tell you what,' the officer said. 'You walk towards that gate. Can you see it?' His voice was commanding, as if imploring me to not let him down and take advantage of his leniency. 'If you move just one inch left or right, I'll shoot you, and I'll be kneeling on your back within a second. You understand?'

I nodded, and began to walk slowly straight without looking back. But there was a problem: as I walked I saw that the corridor split into two separate paths ahead. The policemen were already too far away to ask, so I took one of the paths at random. Immediately, I heard shouts from behind me. I stopped and closed my eyes. It was the wrong gate. But there was no gunfire, no one racing to kneel on my back. I retraced my steps and took the other path. I reached the gate and I went through. Within a few steps, I was back in Mexico.

There, as I began walking back through downtown Tijuana, I had a moment to take stock of my physical condition as I caught my reflection in a shop window. My fingertips were bleeding, and my clothes were torn. I was all dirty, and I ached everywhere from the fall and from the coyotes' beating. I walked back towards the centre of town and found the hotel I'd stayed at—thankfully, I had already paid for a second night in advance. I recall walking through the deserted streets, but I have no recollection of entering the hotel. I do remember arriving at my room and discovering that one of my bags was still on the floor, full of my stuff. The man with no shoes had promised he'd send it on after me. As if. I stood there in shock. What had just happened? Why did I do all that? Where was I, really? A torrent of questions flooded my mind, but I was too traumatized to fathom the situation or to somehow make sense of the events that had just taken place. This was now my fourth day without any sleep. It was the early hours, but I felt I compelled to try and find the guy who'd handed me over to the coyotes, the man wearing no shoes.

I went down to the reception and told them I was in trouble and asked if I could make a phone call. They obliged, but I wasn't surprised to discover that my mans's mobile was switched off. I went back to the room and fell asleep from exhaustion, but only for what must have been an hour. I woke up with a thought that felt like another punch in my stomach. Those coyotes know where I am! They picked me up from here! They might have heard my encounter with the police through the border wall and know that I had returned to the hotel. My still only tissue-thin sense of security at having reached the relative sanctuary of the hotel vanished in an instant, and I was thrown into a panic. Was I paranoid from the exhaustion, from the shock, from the sleep deprivation or was my concern real? Did the people smugglers have a reason to come back here and find me, or were they laying low, staying away? I had no way of telling, but now I was in fear. In the early hours of the morning, I called the no-shoe man one more time. Nothing. Once again, I found myself pacing up and down in that small hotel room. I was stuck in Tijuana and I'd have to vacate the hotel at noon. What then? I kept trying the man's phone and then, miraculously it seemed, just before the midday check-out time, he answered. He listened to my horror story in silent shock. 'OK,' he said. 'I'll be there soon.' And with that, he hung up.

I was actually surprised when, true to his word, he turned up a few hours later. He took me to a tiny bar nearby and I remember he bought me a beer and a shot of vodka, which helped with my head a bit. He sat me down and said: 'Listen, I have an idea. There are these guys, they can take you through the beach, but you have to be in water for a while and…'

'Are you out of your fucking mind!!?' I heard myself screaming at him, cutting him off. 'Can you see the state I'm in? I have nothing left. No money, no energy. I haven't slept for days. I got beaten up because of you. Are you trying to kill me?!' My question was serious. 'I'll tell you what you'll do,' I told him in a bland insomniac frenzy of a rant, as I prepared to corner him to prevent him from leaving the tiny, poorly lit bar. I felt suddenly emboldened. After all, there was nothing else to lose. 'This is all your fault,' I said, accusing him. 'You told me to come here and that everything was prepared. You told me just the day before. You screwed me over! You'll buy me a ticket right now back to Mexico City. That's what you'll do!'

To my surprise, he didn't even hesitate but just agreed. 'OK,' he said. 'Let's go.' It may have been a wave of guilt on his part, or the relief of being finally able to get rid of me, but we walked out and he bought me a ticket for the same afternoon. It wasn't hard, there were so many dodgy travel agencies that we literally walked next door to get it.

In fact, I did have some money left, but I didn't tell him. In case of an emergency, I'd hidden it in my socks. I was in Mexico, after all, so I had been prepared — although certainly not for trouble like this. It was only two hundred dollars or so, but I figured it was enough to get me through a few days in Mexico City until I could arrange for some assistance. One last thing I asked from him: to give me some change for a phone call. My family hadn't heard a word from me since I arrived in Mexico. I found a phone booth, dialed, and as I heard it ringing in some long forgotten far away place, I was filled with a sense of warmth. Home. All of a sudden, it dawned on me what had really happened. While I'd held myself together during the worst of the hostile conditions, tears now covered my face. I had to gloss over bits of the story — just how much trouble I'd actually been in — yet, it was enough. Later, I heard that my mother's face literally went purple upon hearing my news.

While I remained in the vicinity of the hotel, I was half expecting my 'kidnappers' to reappear, but this was obviously a product of sleep-depraved delusional paranoia and, before I knew it, I was out of the city centre. I have no recollection of how I got to the airport, or how I boarded the flight back to the capital. All I remember is waking up as we touched down in Mexico City — the longest period of sleep I'd had in days. I could hardly stagger out of my seat and made my way out of the airport. I didn't even have a place to sleep for the night, but I didn't care; the worst was over and this was a minor detail now. There are complete, missing episodes after this. I must have taken a bus to downtown but how and to where, I can't remember. I found a cheap hotel somewhere near the Insurgentes in the city centre, and paid for a few days and, eventually, fell into a dreamless, bottomless sleep. I don't know for how long I slept but the comfort of finally feeling safe again knocked me out entirely.

The small hotel was a perfect sanctuary for a few days. I slept and slept and then I slept some more. I only left the room to pick up some minimal food from the local Oxxo, the convenience store nearby. I walked there like an old man, slowly and carefully, as my limbs and ribs still hurt from where I'd been kicked. And then I slumped back to the hotel for more recovery.

While revisiting the events now through writing, it would have been easy to describe what I saw along the border wall in Tijuana. The scene could be compared to Mad Max, that apocalyptic, futuristic movie, from director George Miller's nightmarish imagination, or perhaps, say, the free-for-all Burning Man Festival gone horribly wrong. Or, upon returning to the deserted streets of Tijuana, I must have looked like Michael Douglas in David Fincher's The Game, torn and utterly broken when he breaks out of a coffin in Mexico. But I felt it would trivialize the fear, the shock I went through, and what was at stake, to wax lyrical about the deprivation I witnessed. The reality of it was somewhat different from any movie or cultural event; much more stark and fatal. If you've ever been robbed or burgled, you're familiar with that sense of vulnerability that comes from being violated when your personal belongings are gone. It's like someone took a part of you. Now imagine it's you who'd been snatched rather than your possessions. I find it beyond words, really.

But, of course, it had all been my own fault. I was quick to recognize my culpability as the core of the trauma, and it was from this position that I needed to rebuild myself. This was the hardest factor to face. Bit by bit, as the days passed I started to process and digest the events. Images flashed up from time to time and triggered painful nervous sensations deep in my stomach but, overall, it was the sense of shame that ate away at me the most. Although it luckily never came to being shut up in that box I'd been threatened with, I shivered at the thought that there was a point when this had been a very real option, that I had actually agreed to it, despite the obvious indifference towards me displayed by the people who I had naively engaged to 'help' me. I don't like to contemplate further where I could have ended up.

Meanwhile, there were immediate issues that I had to face. I was running out of money and, although I was now safe, I wasn't quite out of the woods yet. I had nowhere to stay. I emailed a few friends about what happened and eventually I received immeasurable help from two friends. They were the ones who helped me get straight. Without them, my troubles would have continued. One of them was Andy Davis, my long-time friend from London. Remarkably, his girlfriend knew someone who lived in Mexico City, a musician, a violinist called Vladimir Bendixen. What a coincidence. I was put in touch with him and he was kind enough to offer me free accommodation in a lovely and, more importantly, safe, area of the city, Roma Norte. I was happy to take Vladimir's shelter, which turned out to be an empty, unfurnished apartment on the second floor, overlooking the intersection of two streets; Cordoba and Calle Queretaro. The place became the base for my recovery over the next couple of weeks. The other helping hand came from a childhood friend, Janos, who paid for my flight ticket back to Europe. It was the beginning of September and as all flights were booked, I had to wait until the end of the month to get home. The rest was up to me. I used the time to recuperate. When I started to feel my confidence returning and had got back on my feet, I started to venture out on small discovery trips, initially around the immediate vicinity, before widening my wanderings further and further. With this, my sense of self gradually returned. My first-ever camera, a Fujipix, had luckily survived the ordeal too, and had been left in the bag that was supposed to be sent on after me to the US. Having that camera to hand changed the way I experienced Mexico City; I did a lot of exploring by snapping pictures as I chanced upon various fascinating areas of the capital.

Cordoba was just a few blocks away from the enormous Avenida de los Insurgentes, the avenue that stretches through the capital with a length of nearly thirty kilometers, and it seemed to be a safe point of reference to stick to and move along. I began to venture farther afield than previously and soon my walks reached the heart of Mexico City. Zocalo, the main square in the city centre, was a good place to sample the more benign, touristic side of this otherwise dangerous beast of a city. But I received constant warnings about staying safe, and I always had to be careful not to walk through areas that were deemed unadvisable to encroach upon. The capital is infamous for its kidnappings, and dangerous areas are dotted across its map, but I made sure I stayed clear of these. Many people warned me to be careful, especially Vladimir, who told me a painful story about how he lost one of his antique violins in a street mugging. 'There aren't just areas in which you might be attacked, but some in which you will be attacked,' was one sobering piece of advice that stayed with me.

There was plenty of time to recover and I do believe it did me good that I didn't return to Europe immediately. This way I could process, heal and deal with everything on my own, remaining there in the country where it had all happened. If I'd left immediately, Mexico would have left an even deeper scar. I rested a lot and continued my walks around the city and, meanwhile along Queretaro, I befriended a young kid, Pablo, who was running an internet cafe just a block away from where I was staying. He must have been only sixteen, but had a good judgement that I was coming out of trouble, so he let me use the internet for free. We even stayed in touch afterwards for a few years.

Vladimir didn't only provide a place to stay but involved me in his social circles and asked me to join and photograph some of his performances. We drove out of the city on a trip to the mountain areas, and to the town of Santa Fe. With new, unexpected memories such as a seemingly insignificant drive out of town, or getting to know Mexico City on foot, I gradually, gradually, built myself up again. After a month in Mexico City, by the time I'd arranged my journey back to Europe, I was at ease with where I was, and more or less over the worst part of the trauma. On the last day, I said goodbye to Vladimir and thanked him for his help and, quite unexpectedly, I found it an emotional experience to leave behind the shelter on Cordoba and Queretaro. The place had been an enormous help to me, nurturing me as I ironed out my sanity and worked my way back to a normal life. But all said, I was quite happy to leave Mexico. When I checked in at the airport, I remember sliding down onto my seat in the waiting room and exhaling deeply. It was the first time I had felt a hundred percent secure in a long while. And later the next day, upon touching down in Paris, and then Vienna, I felt as if I could literally walk the rest of the way home through continental Europe. It seemed that easy. Something had altered in me for good.

Battle scars are battle scars. With distance re-contextualized and travel reinterpreted, kilometers measured in their hundreds or thousands seemed to diminish in length and became trivial as a result: my experiences at the Mexico-US border began to shift the way I perceived distance. Of course, I blamed myself for what happened but at the same time, beyond that one stupid decision, I had discovered that I possessed a rock-solid determination. What I didn't know then was that the ghastly outcome of my vain attempts to re-enter the US illegally has endowed me with fearlessness and a sense of invincibility when facing further challenges in life, with an enhanced sensitivity and a reliable moral compass in regard to foreign environments and people. It prepared me for the jet-setting lifestyle I was to embark upon later.

Whether I chose the next chapter of my life, when I was on the road constantly, unconsciously or whether it came as a direct result of Tijuana, I don't know, but it surely opened the door to endless off-road wanderings. Because of the incident, I became immune to distance, utterly unfazed by unexpected problems while traveling, completely indifferent to border crossings, to hostile immigrant officers, and generally blasé towards complications to my plans should they ever arise. It's not a daredevil approach I've emerged with; I wasn't about to jump off cliffs, out of airplanes or start consuming exotic insects. By having had my tolerance tested to the extreme, I have become balanced, more calm, perhaps slightly jaded and damaged too, but I have definitely risen a level. After being convinced that I wasn't going to make it out of Tijuana alive, everything has now been thrown into perspective. It was like I'd got somehow zapped, which neutralized the inherent worry in me: so what if the hotel missed my reservation in downtown Tokyo? Or in India, for that matter? What if I had to spend the night in a chilly corridor somewhere in Yunnan, near the Himalayas? Or, God forbid, sleep in the street for a night? What did it matter? Comfort became trivial. All in all, the episode dramatically changed the concept of travel for me.

That said, I did get to witness the machinery of fate close up, and experience first hand how it rolled out new options right in front of me. Less than a year after my misadventure in Mexico, I received an offer to move to Hong Kong. The position came with job security and, more importantly, sealed a direction in my life, which is is now based in Asia. And with it, all of a sudden, my previous penniless, day-to day-existence was washed away and within months everything fell into place for me, as if my stars were aligning and it was hard not to read between the lines and get the message. Just a year previously, I had been so determined to get back to New York at any price, but, really, what for? I would have had to restart the struggle of working in restaurants with no visa, and no clear future. So, ultimately, with Tijuana, fate knocked me off the westward dreams, kicked me back to square one to recalibrate life, while providing me with a never-before-experienced security and a new, fulfilling direction. I was given a second chance and this time I gripped it hard.

But it wasn't only distance that got reinterpreted. The present became something to value and, more importantly, to observe and absorb. Therefore, my camera turned into my ultimate tool, an extension of my arm to help me to freeze any moment in front of my eyes into pixels. After learning the value of today, I started to capture everything around me, places, people, situations; so many seemingly insignificant things started to become subjects to document.

You know that feeling when you're watching some old footage, perhaps from a hundred years ago, and everything looks so simple and innocent? And yet the people walking past the camera are all dead and gone, and even many of the seemingly permanent buildings surrounding them are no longer standing either. I have been transformed so that my present is how I see the world around me, how I walk around on a daily basis. I observe the present, conscious of the fact that I'm walking through a time that's already gone, surrounded by people who already belong to the past, and with all my power, through the medium of photography, I attempt to capture the moments as they roll by. Besides the pleasure I take in its documentation, photography elevates me above everyday troubles; it comes with a liberation that I can breathe in and in which I move around freely.

Photography has turned around how I view the cities that I visit and live in; whether it's the breathtaking opportunities to be captured on the streets of Hong Kong, or the opportunity to document the rapid change of modern day China, with Shanghai as its epicenter. I can see first-hand, in real time, one era shifting into another via its buildings, its people, personalities, musicians, and entrepreneurs. I have thrown myself into this task, with a sense of near abandon. It has been the truest task I have ever identified with; I am a photographer to the core.

I now treat cities as relationships, some of them long-term engagements, as I find myself spending years at a time in one place or another. For me, London, Shanghai and Kuala Lumpur have left their marks and have shaped me too, each representing a lengthy period of my life. Then there are brief affairs, when my sojourns in places such as New York or Bangkok are over within a matter of months or perhaps a year. And there have been a few one night stands too. Cities I have merely flirted with, staying for a few days before moving on. But within all of them, whatever the duration of my stay, there are the people I meet who are the codes to crack that reveal a deeper appreciation. The people, whether good or bad, are the stars that guide me. They are my own constellations within, and all I have to do is to find these dots and connect them. This is how you find your own map of the stars, your own story in a city. This book is my constellation.

A Lifetime of Images

An insatiable attraction towards images was deeply embedded in me from my childhood and followed me through my youth, I just didn't know what to do with it at first. In that sense, I could say I was a photographer before I actually became one. Being endlessly fascinated and driven by images all through my life, its significance only crystallized much, much later – neck-deep in photography somewhere in the urban jungle of 21st century Shanghai.

When I was around five years old, my mum found me in the middle of the room in a pile of photos and images I cut out from antique books. To her horror, they belonged to the landlord whom we rented our apartment from. I sort of "dis-imaged" them and got rid of the words, like you would bone a fish and have all the good, meaty stuff for yourself. Eventually we had to compensate him for the price of the valuable books, thus the seemingly insignificant ordeal turned out to be one expensive image-collecting for a five year old.

I grew up in Hungary during the last decade of communism, which was, generally speaking, a pretty stark, image-poor environment. In today's world, where social media constantly saturates our lives with endless visuals, one couldn't imagine such a puritan setting if one tried: magazines, comics and newspapers were very limited and rare, Mondays were strictly no-TV days – by order of the government of Hungary – and, even when we had TV programs running during the week, they were faded, second-rate, depressing re-runs from other countries, mixed with some black and white government-fed propaganda news programs on how well the economy was going.

There was *nothing* on. And yet, it was in this visually barren environment that my attraction towards images developed, armed with a fertile imagination.

I still very vividly remember a tiny, fragile newspaper kiosk in Ibolya Street, just off Egyetem High Road in my hometown Debrecen in the very early 1980s. The little store was sitting there alone for a few decades before it was eventually wiped off the face of the earth in a rush to clean up anything that reminded people of the old communist days.

This small shop used to be the centre of my universe when I was a child. It was everything to me. I remember sneaking out of the house, taking the exciting five-minute walk down there and going round and round the pint-sized, two square meter rusty steel and glass structure. I stared at the magazine covers endlessly, and wondered about the strangely exotic stories behind the enticing images.

Not TV or cartoons, this kiosk was my first glimpse of the outside world, and it opened up a whole new dimension to my small town existence. Some of the magazines were dated – they had been out there for some time and faded in the sun – while others were new and exciting with alluring, bright color photographs and illustrations.

They were burned into my retina forever. I can still see some of the covers if I close my eyes today. With each circuit of the small newsagent, I studied cover after cover until at one point it must have registered with me that images were my direction for the future. It didn't matter how – by drawing, photography or any kind of art form – I unknowingly set a focus for myself of ending up in the image business one way or another.

Compulsive image-collecting continued through my teens and concluded with a discovery that ultimately changed my scope and, frankly, my life for good. The local music library in my hometown had a subscription to the NME, the New Musical Express, the British music weekly, which covered pop and rock for over half a century, documenting the best of pop music from a London perspective.

The library had almost all the issues going back to 1969, which meant there was a tremendous amount of material to go through. While I followed the new issues arriving every week, I simultaneously went back to the old ones reaching back all the way to 1960s, and as a result, the whole history of British rock was gradually mapped out in front of me.

I visited the library almost every day, carefully studying every single page of my new lifeline and source of information. And this time it wasn't only about the images. Armed with a crumpled old English-Hungarian dictionary, I spent at least four hours there every single day and picked up my English reading by translating articles by writers such as Paul Morley, Johnny Cigarettes, Steven Wells or masters from the 1970s like Nick Kent. By the evenings my fingers and face were covered in ink as I made my way down to the street.

The NME featured pretty heavy and complex text, full of word-play, complex sentences with double meanings, some phrases that only music buffs were familiar with. But this wasn't a problem. On the contrary. I embraced the challenge as I wanted to know about my new favourites every week; The Cure, The Smiths, David Bowie, Manic Street Preachers, Suede – all unlocking distinct, individual dimensions in front of me, not only peek into the world of music but an insight into British society as a whole at the same time.

I was focusing so much on the subject that soon enough I picked up the rhythm, the flow of the articles. In fact, I think I picked up the rhythm before the meaning itself. Imagine reading in a foreign language constantly while not fully understanding it, at a young age. You soon pick up the sense of it. That's what I did and moved on to explore the vocabulary later. I initially walked into the library knowing only a few words in English, and about a year and a half later, I walked out with an arsenal of phrases.

And then there were the images. NME covers were statements. They were iconic, meaningful and symbolic. They started and ended entire musical movements, trends, while highlighting the artists behind them. They expressed style, landmarks, breakdowns, comebacks, death and reflected it back through mesmerising imagery with excellent and creative photographers such as Martyn Goodacre, Anthony Corbijn or my personal hero, Kevin Cummins.

Without being aware of it, I learned a visual language of magazines from the pages of the NME and planted the seeds of photography in myself; how to respect your subject as a photographer, how to emphasise them and bring forward their personality and let them do the work in your photographs.

I learned first-hand from those papers what the ingredients of an iconic magazine cover are, what a good DPS (double page spread) is, how to express emotions, and how to place a person in an environment that expresses them while making the elements work for each other, or how a great headline works against a striking photo.

Later, when I ended up working for magazines, supplying photography and shooting for over fifty magazine covers for various international publications, it all could be traced right back to my obsession with the NME, and magazines in general, which changed my life so drastically in 1994. At the age of eighteen, leaving school and family behind, I simply bought a coach ticket to London, left Hungary and never ever looked back. I lived in London for nine consecutive years and, ever since then, I've been living abroad.

My enthusiasm for images never ceased and there was no place better for it than the mid-1990s London to which I relocated. I was even more feverishly collecting magazines, papers, books and clippings, experiencing and indulging in the current trend, Britpop, playing music and hanging out with musicians and bands.

Now I no longer had to go to the music library to get my weekly fix; it was all around me, on the streets of Notting Hill and Camden Town where I spent my everydays. All I had to do was walk down to my newsagent and buy my inkies; the NME and the Melody Maker. Such a very simple manifestation of freedom mattered the world to me in a highly idealistic setting. And soon the pages turned into reality — I recall one memorable occasion marking that. There was a newsagent down in the Notting Hill tube station where the NME and Melody Maker first appeared every Tuesday, a few hours before hitting the rest of London. One day I ran down to get it and right in front of me I heard a Manchester accent saying: 'NME, please'. When the fellow turned around, I was facing none other than Ian Brown from The Stone Roses. A small electric shock jostled through me. I had come so far, on my own terms.

My rooms wherever I lived were stacked with magazines almost up to the ceiling; I just couldn't stop buying them. No matter how I lived at any given moment, poor or well, I always had a magazine in my hand. I fed myself with images relentlessly.

There were two major influences for me in the London years. I got one of my first jobs in Earls Court, where I was a night receptionist for a few years at a B&B. Here, I befriended an old man named Bill Hughes who had worked in the media all his life. He used to be a writer for a movie magazine called Entertainment Weekly and spent the 1960s and 1970s scribbling articles and interviewing film stars.

Life hadn't treated Bill well for his old age: he was broke, lonely, stuck in a B&B and waiting for checks to pay his bills from week to week. When I started to work in the hotel, we became friends instantly. He didn't speak to anyone else there apart from me; we were the two night owls of the hotel. When the guests went to sleep, we talked and talked until the early morning hours about films, music and books.

Talking to him night after night revealed that this old man was a publishing goldmine. Every night he brought down, invaluable memorabilia from his room to show me: one night, photos of him with Marlon Brando, then boxing gloves signed by Muhammad Ali, personal letters from movie stars, photos clippings, rare books. He had collected all these through his career. We were friends for years after and his influence on me was significant for my future as a photographer.

However, the process of picking up a camera had its origins in one single photo shoot, taken *of* me. My friend Andy Davis took me out one day for a boozy afternoon in the summer of 1997 to the streets of Camden to shoot an entire black and white roll of film of me with his old Pentax.

Andy was an amazing photographer, but more importantly he was the chief editor of Record Collector monthly magazine – and also gave me jobs and assignments, which initiated me once and for all into the world of magazines. One time we were sitting in the park opposite Ealing Broadway Station and he challenged me about my favourite band-of-the-moment, the Huddersfield-based Embrace. "I think they're shit, basically," he declared boldly, just to provoke me and to goad me into a rant on why I thought they were the most excellent band of the moment.

He listened patiently and then called me the next day from the office: 'Hey, you're meeting your new favorite band Embrace next weekend for an interview before their Glastonbury Performance supporting Bowie. I want a 2,000-word article out of it. I was really impressed at how you defended them.'

I was speechless over the phone. Then I got very nervous. But in the end it all went well. The story ended up as an eight-page spread and it was my first real magazine experience. It was glorious and intoxicating to see my article with 50,000 copies out on the streets of London and at the newsagents. The following week, the NME grabbed a few lines from my article and quoted it. It was a true victory and an incredible journey from the music library from my hometown.

From then on, I was the only foreign contributor at Record Collector, writing stories mostly on my favorites, including the early career of rapper Eminem and the famous Welsh band the Manic Street Preachers, while also working on book and album reviews. It was my first proper brush with magazine life, and it fit like a glove.

Living through the midst of the Britpop milieu, playing in different bands, hanging out and working in Camden for years, rubbing shoulders with the members of bands like Suede, Blur, Oasis on a nightly basis, or playing pool with Pete Doherty of The Libertines before he became famous, my life was transformed in a way I had never imagined. And through all that, like every other young music fan I was dreaming of becoming famous, an accidental pop star, always thinking that perhaps one day it would happen. So, naively, high on youthful vanity, just like any other musician kid, I imagined myself one day on the cover of the magazines. And while that dream was seeded, little did I suspect that, yes, one day I would fulfil this dream of being on the cover of magazines, but in a completely different way than I ever imagined.

If cities really are the key relationships in my life, and London was the first big, long term one, then I would call my encounter with New York an affair. It was a must, a continuation of my insatiable obsession with personally conquering enormous, dense metropolises, the one I had to experience with its cut-throat urban race to be the best. Its breathtaking streets and avenues and its ever-inspiring energy mesmerised me momentarily but ultimately it failed to be a real home.

While I was having relationships with cities, romance or the presence of real life girls had never infiltrated my predominantly self-centred youth and even if I had something going with someone, it never cut deep, instead of remaining secondary to my ambitions. However, something very important happened wedged between the brief period, a small breather between London and New York, and as always, like every major occurrence that has twisted and shaped my way throughout my humble story, it happened through magazines. This being perhaps the most life-changing of them all. I was living with my then-girlfriend in London when someone called to tell me that there was a Hungarian guy who didn't have anywhere to sleep for two nights before returning to Hungary and if I could help. As we had a spare room, I told him to come around and stay. But I did ask for a small favour in return. Our place was full of music magazines and papers that I had collected over the years, which became a heavier and heavier load with each move. So as he was from my hometown, I asked whether he could take some home with him. The bag I gave him was extremely heavy. I remember helping him get to the underground station but I also recall that pang of guilt I had at the sight of watching him carry the bulky bag down the stairs, into the gaping mouth of the London tube at dawn - a moment I did regret. But only for a while. As it turned out, the seemingly brief and meaningless encounter changed my life.

It took about a year but I did pick up the bag of music weeklies and magazines eventually. When I went to his house in my hometown in Hungary, I rang the bell and his sister opened the door. Living my decadent, bohemian life, the term 'love at first sight' never even entered my world but right at that moment, so unexpectedly, it struck me like thunder. I just stood there in the door, utterly helplessly, all of a sudden out of context of who I had been until then, and I remember the first thought that went through my head 'Ok, my relationship is over.'

I just couldn't get her out of my head and after she hinted to someone we both knew that she felt the same, our fate was sealed. Through a long-winded story that followed, which at first was trying and hard, she became my life-companion on the journey ahead, my dear wife and we're still in love and together after twenty years.

Ironically, while I was searching for my future in the West, one simple phone call from a childhood friend changed my course and unexpectedly derailed me into what had been the right direction all along—East. The next move changed everything entirely. My friend was setting up a business venture and needed someone he could trust, who had some experience living abroad, and more importantly was mad enough to make such a move on short notice.

'Hey, do you want to move to Hong Kong?' he asked.

Shocked, but already certain of the answer I should give, I replied: 'Let me call you back in an hour.'

My ten-year long discovery of China equalled the very quest of photography for me. That fascination with duality, which eventually crystalized in the constant capturing and re-capturing of the visually absurd beauty of Shanghai's new and old districts, Pudong and Puxi, staring at each other face to face over the Huangpu River, which fueled my photography for so many years, was there from the beginning when I first moved to China. Living by the Loh Wu border in southern China that separates Hong Kong and Shenzhen was my first inspiration of this kind, as the urban schizophrenic landscape splits into two completely distinct worlds and identities that seemingly even divide the climate. I often wondered whether the weather was aware that there was a border there, as on some days the division was so extreme and drastic. The Hong Kong side always seemed sunny and bright, while Shenzhen was grey and murky, covered in a thick layer of stained clouds as far as the eye could see. The answer to this was largely pollution, billowing from the horizon of endless factories spreading over the industrial zones of Guangdong province, vomiting aerial soil upwards, fading out the sun. It was in this diverse landscape that I first found inspiration for my lens, surrounded by scenery that just begged to be photographed. Those visual extremities, especially in the early days around 2006 when the country was slowly emerging from its cocoon with cranes, construction sites and giant Deng Xiaoping billboards towering over the swarming traffic below in Shenzhen, heralded a new way for a country rising to be a global superpower.

It was in this unlikely, stark milieu that I became inseparable from my camera. But the primary goal wasn't entirely to document the surreal environment. Originally, I was sent to this region to do quality control for a European electronics company, to inspect their products ranging from car stereos and small electronic parts all the way to Christmas lights before shipments left for Hungary. My job was to take photos of the products and email them to my home company to prevent the shipping of faulty goods, which had caused them significant financial loss over the years. Thus, on a daily basis I found myself working in Chinese nowhere towns, outside of Shenzhen and Guangzhou, in soulless factories going through boxes of goods, taking thousands of photos each day. The company supplied me with a good camera that helped to highlight the details of the products, in order to detect and filter the problems quickly.

The job gave me daily access to places that foreigners rarely saw and it gradually unveiled a China in front of me where the most remarkable scenes waited hidden under thick pollution in dull, sun-deprived spaces and made my days somewhat colorful. Christmas factories with fake-Santa Claus mannequins, fake-Christmas trees lying around by the hundreds, ornaments assembled by children and their parents sitting by the factory belt, hundreds of baseball bats laid out on a dirty yard before their shipment to the United States. Such unlikely sights inspired me to not only point my camera towards the products but to document what was going on around me.

I documented the life of factory workers along the endless factory belts, having their lunch, sitting in identical uniforms, moving in synchronicity along tables, eyeing me with playful curiosity, the only foreigner who entered their world; sweaty, tall and pale. My photos didn't yet have a sophistication to them, I wasn't even shooting in RAW format yet, in the digital negative that enables photographers to elevate their images to a professional level. But I was documenting nevertheless. The photos I was taking were the seeds of my photojournalist career later on. When I got home to Shenzhen in the evenings, I separated them from the product photos and I had a nice China collection starting to build up.

Meanwhile on the other side of the border, an entirely different kind of world had opened up. My weekly, sometimes daily commutes to Hong Kong were mainly business-related; to solve issues in person, to iron out email misunderstandings between my company and the local Hong Kong trading firms, or to attend fairs dedicated to electronic products. Hong Kong was the perfect escape, a terribly exciting, colorful world, and a breather from the grey Mainland Chinese nowhere towns. The meetings usually only took up a few hours so I stayed for the day, reaching further and further into the hot, urban jungle starting with areas like Tsim Sha Tsui and the depths of Hong Kong Island. I fell in love with the city instantly, it was a world like nothing else I've seen before; the perfect introduction to a life in Asia. It was here where I made the decision that I would never ever go back to the West to live.

Diving straight into the crowds in the mornings at the Loh Wu border as people were sleeping while waiting in line before a busy day ahead in the steaming hot metropolis was an experience itself. I remember that peculiar silence lingering in these corridors around 6 a.m., people leaning against the wall, eyes closed, frozen in that last moment of rest before charging skillfully at the border gates as soon as they opened into Hong Kong.

There was so much to explore in the city; in that culturally vibrant melting pot blending East and West, that exotic mixture of Asian and British colonial past, that claustrophobic yet mesmerizing photogenic urban density with its crammed skyscrapers, wedged over hills, its typhoons raging over the Victoria Harbour, throwing the Star Ferry around like a small toy ship on giant waves, or the tangle of Chinese characters lighting up the streets with neon signs in Tsim Sha Tsui. Even micro-urban scenes inspired me, like the characteristic red taxis waiting on a dark rainy day, the colorful trams trundling along the island, Christian cemeteries with skyscrapers rising over them, the grittiness of Chungking Mansions - images that burned both into me and simultaneously into my camera sensor and slowly forged a photographer's outlook onto the world.

But it was the move to Shanghai later that year when everything eventually fell into place and fully opened the Middle Kingdom to me in all its might. I will never forget my first night in the city on an early and chilly November day when the scent of the osmanthus flower filled the French Concession with its irresistible odor, a scent that I still associate with those early days and with Shanghai itself. It was really like arriving home, which I had never before or after felt with another city. I spent the next ten years there.

The move coincided with a parting of ways with the European company. They eventually pulled out of China, so with my wife, we decided to stay. As a result, I was left alone with my camera, jobless in the most explorable, photogenic city I had ever came across, with its incredible rapid transformations. There was nothing else to do but to shoot; the perfect setting, and it was up to me now what I did with it professionally.

Like many foreigners back then in those early days, I was working as an extra in films and TV shows. Movies like *The White Countess* starring Ralph Fiennes and Natasha Richardson were shot in the suburbs of Shanghai. There weren't many foreigners around back then so we were constantly needed, earning a few hundred U.S. dollars each day by merely dressing up in period costumes and walking around all day in movie sets of 1930s Shanghai. It was a magical time. Sometimes we were lucky and were involved in bigger productions.

Jackie Chan and Jet Li's *Forbidden Kingdom* movie was shot over the summer of 2007 and we were constantly employed for it, even meeting the film's star. I particularly remember one occasion when a bearded old man came out of a tour bus for snacks and someone threw him a can of Coke. How he caught it with his hand, with such a swift, sudden movement, like someone who had trained in martial arts all his life, left me gobsmacked. It was so unnatural. "What a weird old man," I thought. It turned out it was Jackie, walking around his set as Lu Yan, his character.

However, the Jackie Chan film wasn't important because of its global stars but because many of the friendships that formed on the set later blossomed into lifelong friendships. When I watch that film and see the few seconds of myself now, typically leaning against a wall reading the music magazine Q, it reminds me of the friendships created throughout that scorching hot summer in the streets of China's Hollywood, Hengdian, and how it shaped the following years in Shanghai.

The shoots were frequent and we were included in countless movies and TV shows on a regular basis. It was my first proper income in Shanghai. I also snuck my camera to the shoots and there was much to document. China built to the blueprint of major cities like London and Paris for movie productions working alongside each other simultaneously. In one street, there was a period drama unfolding, while in another, a movie about the Japanese occupation was being shot. Needless to say, these were smaller versions of cities, jammed into a few blocks, but still big enough to get lost in. It was bizarre to be walking in the shadows of Churchill statues, the Eiffel Tower or the Louvre, in China of all places, a few hundred kilometers out of Shanghai. But my favorite city set was 1930s Shanghai, which consisted of two or three major high streets. In one of the movies, we were riding in 1930s cars. Just the unlikeliness of these places inspired me and although cameras were forbidden on set (there were no smartphones then), I took a lot of photos.

It was on one of these shoots when I was informed that a small, local expat magazine called *Hint* wanted to publish two pages of my photography. It was a minor recognition but for me it meant the world, giving me a sign that my lonely walks around the city with my camera could be transformed into something bigger and recognizable. Slowly, local magazines took notice and I was approached by the editor of *That's Shanghai*, the city's leading expat magazine, JFK Miller, to be the house photographer, an offer that would eventually elevate my hobby into a profession, and after that, with relentless painstaking work to an international level. It was a milestone that gave me hope that I could make a living out of my hobby and it was the moment when my camera became an extension of my arm, my weapon for many years to come, spiraling me into incredible adventures.

THE SCENT OF OSMANTHUS

CACOPHONOUS ELECTRIC guitar bled from under the doors and into the corridors of the dingy subterranean complex that spread out like a bomb-shelter, splitting into different sized, sound-proofed rehearsal rooms. The air was stuffy, damp and hard to breathe. I'm not sure what the place was originally used for, or what it is these days, but around 2007 this hidden architectural gem, on — or rather *under* – Damuqiao Road in western Shanghai, was used as a base for the city's up-and-coming underground groups. It was where locally famous garage bands such as Banana Monkey, Duck Fight Goose and hybrid formations of Chinese and Western members like Boys Climbing Ropes, chiseled their repertoire into performable perfection.

That year, the Shanghai underground music scene began to flap its wings, slowly but surely buzzing into focus on the pages of the local media, and Damuqiao Road was the creative hub, the sweaty workshop behind it all. My regular business in this rumbling noise factory was to recruit musicians and to advertise the gigs. It was one of my daily routines to hit the rehearsal complex in the late afternoon, just as the musicians emerged from their sleepy cocoons to grab their instruments and make noise beyond the midnight hour. Usually, after Blu Tack-ing posters and ads all over the walls I'd sit down with a beer in the corridor to listen to the music filtering through, moving from door to door to find ever newer subjects of interest. If I liked something, I waited for a pause between the songs and knocked on the door.

I didn't actually need the job at the club. It was something that fell into my lap and that I just enjoyed doing. The venue I was recruiting musicians for, the Blues Room, was located on the corner of Nanjing Road and Tongren Road and this was where my enthusiasm for live music reached its peak. More importantly, this was the very place where my photography career began. The Blues Room was situated at an odd intersection. While Nanjing Road had been synonymous with Shanghai's main, glitzy shopping artery for over a century, Tongren Road evoked a knowing, dubious nod that acknowledged it as the dodgy end of downtown. The mere mention of the road carried negative connotations. It was one of those places that with the city's stated intention to 'clean up' for the upcoming World Expo 2010, was due to be swept off the Shanghai map sooner or later. In fact, 2008 was its last year as an entertainment street; its days were definitely numbered. The authorities hesitated for a further year because of the street's micro economy — it catered for foreigners on business trips; it was crammed with a battery of dodgy bars that offered cheap prostitutes, fake alcoholic drinks, the obligatory Filipino cover bands and *talking-girls* (a term used by Chinese girls whose English was good enough to chat up foreigners keen to spend on the overpriced drinks). The place was a Mecca of dicey entertainment for anyone who needed something rough and ready but still within the city centre.

The Blues Room was located at the other end of the road, a safe distance from all this, and although it was clearly the odd one out, it didn't mean that it was entirely free from controversy. Just a year before there had been a scandal in the American-style City Diner upstairs, when a dispute arose on New Year's Eve, in which customers and staff descended into full-on combat using fire extinguishers, chairs, glasses and anything moveable.

The incident nearly ruined the bar and the diner, and was well-chronicled in the media. When I took over management duties of the Blues Room, I still felt the smoldering aftermath of the brawl. It remained a sensitive subject. As the diner tried to recover from the media attention, the staff desperately tried to whitewash it with friendly-family lunch offers and kiddie meals. The owner of both venues was the same person—an ABC (American Born Chinese) rich kid who'd returned home after his childhood in Los Angeles, ready to throw his parents' money around. He sought me out for the manager's post because of my connections in the city, but I had the feeling that my presence was part of the whitewashing process; the Blues Room would begin a new chapter as a live music venue, run by a foreigner. Word had reached him that I was familiar with many of the kids, students and musicians around town, so he used me as a magnet to draw in a trendy new clientele—foreign and Chinese alike—to help remodel the joint. My official title was bar manager, but it was obvious that I didn't know a thing about managing bars. In reality, my job was to build up a weekly schedule of performances for the new direction—basically, to track down and book musicians.

My social scene was already full of musicians, but by taking exploratory visits to the sonic goldmine of Damuqiao Road, the rehearsal room dungeon, I intended to build up the Blues Room's repertoire from scratch, bringing in fresh blood on a regular basis. Many a great deal was born out of visits to the sweaty, grafitti-covered basements. The hiring was left to me entirely; the owner trusted my judgement, so I offered the musicians slots for the evenings, filling up the week with an eclectic program, offering jazz and blues, indie and rock music, sometimes even comedy acts. On my regular visits there, I'd sit in the corridors sipping a cold Tsingtao and this, unbeknownst to them, became the musicians' audition. A band that didn't impress me never even knew about it. I just moved on. I found several hidden treasures there, who ended up becoming regulars on the Blues Room's tiny stage.

While organizing their slots, however, I'd run into one issue. Almost none of the performers had useable photographs for the advertising posters. Therefore, I'd usher them upstairs to the tiny, dark pool-table room above the venue, where I'd snap some moody long-exposures. It was my first ever opportunity to explore and sharpen my photography skills; I could finally reach back into a toolkit I wasn't even aware I had, inadvertently picked up from the *NME* and other British music magazines a decade back, which became a photographic style that went down well in Shanghai. As things progressed, I began to come up with themes, new ways to depict the musicians, or else I just asked them how they wanted to be portrayed. If it wasn't the gloomy room upstairs, then I'd take them out on shoots against the backdrop of the ever-changing city—on construction sites dwarfed by the shimmering skyscrapers or on the lovely, shaded haven of the plane tree-fringed French Concession. Via these shoots, Shanghai slowly became my photographic playground.

My deal with the musicians worked both ways. They gained professional-looking photos that I granted free use of for themselves, while I began to build a portfolio of this up-and-coming scene. The bonus was that my photos were immediately plastered all over town, on posters and in local newspapers and magazines, and became instantly recognizable, further fueling my network, my reputation and my enthusiasm for this new line of work.

Down in Damuqiao Road, the source seemed to be inexhaustible. Once, as I was passing one of the doors, I stopped in momentary shock. "No, it cannot be," I thought. Inside, none other than Axl Rose, the singer of Guns N' Roses, was rehearsing the band's biggest hit, 'Sweet Child O' Mine'. That unmistakable raspy, high-pitched voice, stacked with stamina and anger, sounded so uncanny that I almost believed it was really him. After the final *'Where do we go?'*, the song ended and that empty, sound-proofed silence resumed inside, followed by a quiet Chinese chatter. I knocked on the door and entered. Obviously, I wasn't expecting Axl and band rehearsing their *Chinese Democracy* album for their upcoming tour, but the actual sight that greeted me was surprising in a different way entirely. A band of humble Chinese guys, dressed normally, almost office-like, were sitting on the amps blinking with their own surprise at the unusual sight of a Westerner barging through the door to listen to their practice.

Shanghai's local Axl Rose was a shy twenty-something insurance agent with glasses, a regular business guy who, during the day worked in an office and in the evenings slung a white guitar over his shoulder and let his inner rocker rip. The band played a few of their own songs for me and, right there, recognizing that they could attract both Chinese and foreign audiences, I offered them a regular Thursday evening spot at the Blues Room, for a fee of RMB 3,800 (US $550), plus complimentary drinks and a dinner. It was a generous offer, endorsed by the owner—and was certainly a good budget to work with. Thus, the band, named BlueTrain, became one of my first reliable, regular acts, and pulled in audiences at the wrong side of midnight with their astounding Guns N' Roses covers, wonderful John Mayer renditions and great, stylish Chinese songs that provided sing-alongs until the beer-buzzed early morning hours.

One of my favorite performers who became a stalwart at the venue was Jimy 'The Devil' Graham, an excellent African American blues guitarist and singer from New York. Or at least, that's what he told us. Jimy played every Wednesday night, and between tracks regaled us with anecdotes from his obscure past — tales from deep inside a bottle of Jack Daniel's. He often shamelessly repeated entire sets but no one seemed to mind. Jimy was our little slice of the Big Apple in Shanghai; guests loved sipping beer and whiskey as his mostly acoustic music filled the smoky room, his face hidden in the dark beneath his leather hat. Once business at the Blues Room began picking up, I booked a special night for him and called it *Jimy plays Hendrix*, in which our Jimy went electric, performing deafening renditions of 'Hey Joe' and 'Voodoo Chile' — losing himself in an onstage trance as he created wailing, demonic sounds on his guitar. The night was a success; he channelled Hendrix impeccably but, foolishly, I allowed him to play at full volume, resulting in such a loud show that people heading towards the Blues Room could hear his guitar above the roar of the traffic at the edge of Yan'an Road a few hundred meters away. Glasses and utensils shook on the tables and my hearing — and certainly that of everyone present — was temporarily impaired. That night surely killed off the dinner vibe, but went a long way towards enhancing the Blues Room's growing reputation as a live venue.

My other ace was JKQA, a Chinese Red Hot Chili Peppers covers band that guaranteed a full venue every time they hit the stage. As an acronym of their own names, JKQA was again, an ensemble consisting of quiet, humble young Chinese guys who, when performing, possessed such a electrifying energy that you not only forgot that they weren't the real life Chilis but that they were Chinese — they brought the funk of the Californian band alive to a remarkable extent. I booked them once a month and their shows were always sell-outs; people queued and crowds gathered on the street outside, craning their necks to try and get a glimpse of what the hell was going on inside. On these nights, the small venue turned into a proper moshpit, a music inferno with no place to sit or stand, just a mass of sweaty bodies jumping around the room—sometimes with added crowd-surfing too. On the night of their first performance, the owner came down and couldn't believe the venue's transformation. I remember his widened eyes taking in the crowd. The bar was almost overwhelmed with drink orders and the place was buzzing with the energy of a proper live joint; that night was a justification to him that, in me, he'd hired the right person and that my plan to move his business forward was working.

For quieter Sunday nights I started an Open Mic session that attracted a good crowd too—students, travelers, even foreign businessmen eagerly took to the stage with our in-house beaten-up guitars. Jazz was particularly popular, and I developed a special affection for gypsy-style jazz guitar music. This genre created a classic, if not timeless, atmosphere that magically transformed the Blues Room into an authentic music venue, giving it a classy touch. My choice for these evenings was San Fransisco native Doug Martin and his band. Doug could play like a genuine gypsy, with the accomplished 'wet-noodle-wrist' staccato technique that is so redolent of this music. I booked him for one evening each week, and stood watching in appreciation as his ensemble set the place ablaze with sparkling classics from the 1930s, including many by the legendary Django Reinhardt.

I didn't stop with local acts. Through my connections I also brought in French and American musicians from abroad. One of the biggest and most memorable names who graced the stage of the Blues Room was Lulo Reinhardt, great nephew of Django. Doug Martin introduced him to me, as they'd played together before in Europe. I was only too happy to arrange a small string of shows for Lulo in Shanghai. He wasn't just the hottest—and, of course, the coolest—act to have on our stage, but he was an unbelievable character, too. I invited him to come to China all the way from Germany, gave him four very well paid nights' work, supplied him with plenty of food… and yet items that didn't belong to him would mysteriously disappear during his residency. And, of course, it always came down to me to pay any recompense.

It wasn't enough that, upon arriving for his first night — when we finally met in person — he looked my wife up and down in a manner with which I wasn't entirely comfortable, but at the end of the show, I made the mistake of handing him the cash payment directly. The gig was advertised under his name, after all, but just as the money was leaving my hand, Doug Martin openly protested: "Nicky, don't!" But it was too late. Lulo, flashing a sly smile, placed the wad in his suit pocket and I believe that his band members never saw a penny of it. I was careful with him after that, and made sure I divided the money evenly.

But apart from these small issues, the Lulo Reinhardt ensemble had a very successful residency at the Blues Room, and played some unforgettable performances that stretched out over many a night into the Christmas period.

I also brought in a proper international star, albeit unintentionally. I used to hang out with a very kind young German guy named Sakias. We worked together on movie sets as extras and we got to be friends. About a year or so after I first met him, Sakias mentioned that his mother was in fact the singer Nena, whose huge early 1980s hit, '99 Luftballons', had been No. 1 in a dozen or so countries. Back then as a child in Hungary, I used to listen to Nena's albums, so it was quite a shock that she turned out to be the mum of one of my friends. Sakias told me that she was due to visit him in Shanghai that month so I invited the whole family to the Blues Room for dinner. Nena was obviously a little older than when I had last seen her on TV decades ago, and had a very strong, striking personality. She didn't get up on stage, but sat at her dinner table with us while, perhaps inevitably, that night's band dedicated a cover version of '99 Luftballons' to her. Years later, after he'd left Shanghai, Sakias also became relatively famous, following in his mother's footsteps with the brilliant, powerful 'Weisses Schiff', a song that gave me goosebumps, making me proud of the days when I used to hang out with this young innocent kid.

Being exposed to this colorful plethora of inspirational events and personalities on a daily basis, I couldn't stop taking photographs. There was so much to capture. Whether snapping away at performances as the musicians played, their instruments bathed in the gentle purple hues of the stage lights, or out during the day in the street on walkabout shoots with them, my photography was beginning to evolve and, unbeknownst to me at the time, was entering its cocoon phase.

Many photographers struggle to find their initial voice and often run into the mistake of just shooting randomly, failing to recognize their own direction, wasting tremendous amounts of time by tiptoeing about, flitting from subject to subject. Behind the essence of every art though, there's the focus an artist must find, something that really interests them, something that's worth concentrating on, to pull their work into a cohesive whole. I'm not talking about the millions of themes that, nowadays, people display on Instagram, exhausting every possible visual avenue by posting it to the public instantly, thus trivializing and cheapening their vision. Instead, I'm talking about a real artist harnessing and controlling their inner voice, directing it into a certain subject that becomes their forte. Without it, their work can become a murky soup of disconnected imagery. I aspired to find this certain spark from the very beginning, and I quickly found my voice chronicling the life of musicians through the lens. While exploring the subject obsessively, I was already unconsciously collecting material, building towards my first exhibition a few years later.

I enjoyed working with musicians immensely—they were from my world. Soon, I began to cast my net wider, beyond the Blues Room, targeting Shanghai's constantly widening musical landscape. Each musician brought a different quality, another human aspect, color to the visual language I was developing, and the subject drew an unbelievable assortment of talent towards me. I was like a butterfly collector—there were so much variety. Young musicians' personalities are often dipped in a healthy dose of vanity and to be able to capture and use this and marry it with expressive photography always produces great results. Portraiture lies in that certain silent dialogue between photographer and subject and it's my job, behind the lens, to tease out the personality underneath, with each click peeling back the layers.

This was 2008, and digital photography hadn't yet totally dominated the industry. There was still a sense of innocence to it all. That indifference, the overall yawn, that surfeit, that gorging on images brought on by the arrival of Instagram in the following decade, was still absent at this point. The musicians happily jumped at the chance of being photographed and couldn't wait to see the results—especially seeing themselves on the poster for the Blues Room.

At this point, I never charged for my shoots or photos. Occasionally, musicians offered me a small amount, but I never pushed it. As word of my work got around, musicians from other clubs asked me to take their portraits and even if I spent hours shooting with them, I didn't charge a penny. I knew they didn't have much to spare, and I considered it a fair deal anyway; my compensation was the shots I was collecting for my portfolio and, besides that, they used my photos for promotion, which only spread my work further around town, and this brought even more musicians my way. *Art first* was my motto. Considering money as secondary remained a pattern, and like the karmic rule that those things you let go will eventually come back to you, I was soon recompensed with an inexhaustible clientele.

There was yet another unexpected layer, though: my photographs took on a life of their own. Advertising the gigs with unprecedented poster campaigns across the city, my pictures soon became known and recognizable. Also, sending the posters to local magazines' listings pages brought me even further attention. My future employers and associates at *That's Shanghai* magazine were already taking notice.

It was a terribly exciting time to be in Shanghai and, for me, viewing the present as the past would come in handy again. Precisely sixty years had elapsed since the founding of the People's Republic of China, which had shut the lid on the vagrant and vivid Shanghai jazz scene that had thrived in the city since the 1930s, freezing it into a new, stark, colorless reality. But during the first years of the new millennium, I could feel the scene reawakening around me, as life began to bubble free to the surface again. A half-forgotten world of immigrants, jazz and blues musicians, actresses, actors, artists, restaurateurs, club owners, architects, newspapermen, and criminals all reappeared; rebuilding Shanghai via their mere presence and their collective dreams—which had been resurrected in all of us. We were *it*. We were the new generation of the lost, thriving in this ambivalent port city. It was like history repeating itself and it was incredibly inspirational working right there in the epicenter.

I instantly recognized that I must document this, another

fleeting Shanghai era, and threw myself into it with all my power. Foreign musicians trying their luck, bands forming then reshaping, talent coming and going, living in Shanghai, dying in Shanghai—it was also history in the making. I saw everyone around me as a unique, flesh-and-blood specimen of a certain moment that was there to be captured in photographs, and since then time had proved me right. I felt endlessly privileged that I could observe jazz singer Coco Zhao rising to his prime, that I could be there to chronicle local legends such as Alec Haavik, Lawrence Ku, the old raconteur jazz guitarist Eddy Goltz, Charlie Foldesh, Willow Neilson and Theo Croker, who—among many others—were the faces of Shanghai jazz; and when bands like Lions of Puxi, Weghur or Noukilla ruled the city, and that I could work with and be friends with them all. I obsessively documented their everydays and their performances, fully aware that the era wouldn't last forever and would indeed vanish with the next turn of the tide.

It was fascinating to observe how they made their living, the way they navigated the given conditions, migrating between clubs and events. They arrived from—among other countries— the US, UK, France and Mauritius, and I noticed an interesting criterion that shaped the foreign music landscape of Shanghai: the availability of visas. Around that time, only the prestigious JZ Club, the House of Blues and Jazz, and Melting Pot knew the proper government channels and had the right connections to get work permits issued, so visiting musicians gravitated there. Melting Pot on Taikang Road was the smaller venue, owned by the lovely Ruby Yao, a mother figure to all. Her aim was to create a family atmosphere that embraced newly arrived artists to the city, providing them with visas and often even a place to live.

Owned by Ren Yuqing, the still legendary JZ Club was undoubtedly the main institution for jazz, a must-stop for all musicians flocking to China's most exciting city. Back then, located under the plane-tree fringed haven of Fuxing Road, it was the center of the Shanghai jazz universe. A few blocks down on Wukang Road, JZ also operated its own music school, which was truly one of a kind.

Around this time Ren, teaming up with British organizer Mark Elliott, established the brilliant JZ Festival, another extension of the JZ brand, which skyrocketed the jazz scene of Shanghai to a new level. Later, this would grow to become one of the best Asian annual jazz festivals, showcasing a vibrant selection of international performers such as Joss Stone, John Scofield, Pat Metheny, Ron Carter, Kenny Garrett, Dianne Reeves and Dee Dee Bridgewater.

But it didn't stop there. Shanghai's music scene was flourishing with other brilliant venues in town such as Cotton Club, MAO Livehouse, Wooden Box, Heyday, The House of Jazz and Blues, and many more. The Blues Room, the place I was running, situated at the border of downtown and the French Concession, was a smaller venture but I would like to believe that its cozy and homey atmosphere humbly contributed to the local music scene; at one time or another almost all of the great musicians of Shanghai graced its tiny stage.

As word of my photography got around, more and more musicians began to ask to have their pictures taken, and I extended my network further than the Blues Room. I started to work regularly with JZ Club. I covered the JZ Festival annually, and I became the official photographer for the Melting Pot Club and, eventually, when audio giant Sennheiser opened its business in China, sponsoring and equipping major festivals and clubs, thus raising local standards, the German company commissioned me to work with them on a regular basis. This turned everything around; all of a sudden my work was everywhere.

Every growing business needs its own lucky charms and as my brand was developing I had my lucky-charm musicians, too. One evening when New York singer Carlton J. Smith played an amazing gig during his residency at The House of Jazz and Blues, just by the Bund, the iconic riverfront of Shanghai, I was in the audience. When he ran upstairs to his dressing room for a quick break between two sets, I followed him. As he collapsed into a chair, all sweaty in his always flashy, dramatic stage clothes, still panting, he looked at me in surprise and asked: "So, you think you can just follow me up to my dressing room like that?"

"Yeah, why not?" I replied, and got to the point. I offered him a gig at the Blues Room and from then on we started negotiating. Ultimately, the gig never materialized because his larger-than-life character was a bit too full-on for the tiny Blues Room, but during the following years Carlton and I became very close collaborators and are friends to this day. He took an instant shine to my photography and as he always appeared on stage in dramatic, ever-changing clothes, we started to collaborate through photography, producing posters and album covers on a regular basis. Him in a red suit against a black-and-white mountainous vista became a prime example of our work together. It's a photo he still uses on his tours around the world. Notably, the picture once covered Bali on billboards advertising his Indonesian tour. Carlton became one of my most important lucky-charm musicians. He always willingly and generously paid for the shoots but the bond was so strong, and still is, that I would take photos for him for free any time.

Another one of these lucky-charm musicians who undoubtedly defined the new millennium Shanghai jazz scene was the endlessly charismatic New York saxophonist Alec Haavik with his characteristic features and remarkable costumes. He was highly noticeable in his thick-framed glasses, his backcombed hair akin to Robert Smith from The Cure, and with his goatee beard and unbelievably mad clothes, he attracted constant attention. On stage, he was seemingly lost in his world, Frank Zappa-like, while remaining professional and highly enjoyable at the same time.

I started to work with Alec in early 2008 and he was an instant camera magnet; the lens absolutely adored him. By then he already had a massive fan base around town, and people approached him constantly for photos and autographs — which was a rare thing to see in Shanghai. Like Carlton, Alec had an extensive wardrobe filled with the weirdest clothes. However, our collaboration truly allowed his personality to inhabit another realm.

Always looking for something special, for a shoot I asked him once whether he would shave off his trademark hair and goatee. For the first time though, Alec said no. He reasoned that he would "look silly". So I asked him how could we spice up the shoot to take it one step further. In reply he exclaimed: "Nicky, I want to be a lizard." He explained his choice by saying that the lizard was his alter ego and it was his life's wish to "turn into one".

Exactly how I was to transform a two-meter tall saxophonist into a lizard, I didn't know for the time being, but the odd conundrum certainly triggered one of my maddest projects to date. After an initial debate about green costumes, which we decided were too predictable, we came up with the idea of body paint. We found an excellent Chinese artist named Kefei who agreed to do a full head-to-toe makeover for a whopping USD1,000. I became so obsessed with the project that I paid for most of it myself, with Alec pitching in the rest. We rented a hotel room for a day, and I sat there watching one artist painting another for seven hours. Up until this point, I didn't really appreciate his obsession with "becoming a lizard", but during the long painting process I watched the Alec I knew slowly disappear, as his whole personality changed.

By the time we both got into a taxi en route to my chosen location for the shoot, Alec had already become someone else. We headed for the 1933 Old Millfun, otherwise known as the Old Shanghai Slaughterhouse, in the north of the city — a huge, unusual looking concrete labyrinth which had been converted into an arts centre, a favorite snapping spot for professional and amateur photographers alike. I have to admit though that, in my excitement, I did not think through the shoot. Neither of us did. So when I appeared with this tall, bizarre-looking lizard-man, naked apart from his underwear, which was also painted green, it almost started a small riot. I had to abandon the lights I was carrying as onlookers, keen to grab their own photographs of this strange spectacle, began following us around the winding concrete maze in such numbers that soon enough the security guards joined in too, trying to shut us down for causing a public disturbance. The sight was nothing short of comic: me with cameras dangling around my neck, running alongside a lanky lizard creature, yelling in Chinese at the posse behind us to leave us alone — as the security guards descended upon us all, trying to break up the party.

Thanks to the adrenaline rush of the incident, I became addicted to such messy and problematic shoots, and mischievously relished the cat-and-mouse play with Chinese security guards that started here and would continue for years to come. From then on, I got a secret thrill if ever my photography just happened to halt the traffic in busy downtown areas, or even evoke public outrage.

As for Alec, he didn't wash off the green paint for days,

even performing at the JZ as the Lizard. He later told me that watching the last vestiges of his alter ego gurgle down the plug hole was one of the saddest moments in his life. A few years later, Alec got re-painted when we revisited the concept for a short film, *The Lizard's Journey*, which I shot in the intriguing misty mountains of Moganshan, just a few hundred kilometers out of Shanghai.

Another hilarious incident emerged from my work with Alec around 2009, one which certainly helped to enhance the Nicky Almasy brand around town. The incident occurred entirely unbeknownst to me, in the faraway city of Guiyang, and I only learned about it months later.

Alec was on one of his tours around China, and in one city the promoter asked him for a photo to use for the poster to advertise the event. Alec sent him one of my shots and insisted that I be credited. By the time Alec and his band of Shanghai-based jazz musicians arrived at the location, the posters, featuring Alec playing his sax, were everywhere—and in large print above his head was the name Nicky Almasy. The promoter had misunderstood Alec's instruction and had assumed that my name was Alec's. I was told that later that, at first, the band stood there in a state of disbelief before collapsing into fits of laughter, as the stage logo behind them screamed "Nicky Almasy" at the audience.

If people hadn't been aware of my name before then, it was now plastered all over town among the jazz fraternity. After that, it was common for musicians to approach me in clubs: "Oh, so you're the famous Nicky Almasy." It turned out to be an unexpectedly effective way of promotion and swept through the local jazz scene, supplying with me with jobs for the next couple of years.

Even back in the 1930s Shanghai was renowned as a magnet

for a range of unique characters and the noughties were a fitting sequel to that. With its enticing opportunities, the city in that era attracted a *laowai* (foreigner) population consisting of assorted inhabitants from all walks of life. This flotsam and jetsam thrown together in the same melting pot resulted in a happening city. Something was always going on, something was always cooking, its nightlife peopled with the most diverse characters, with venues such as the Blues Room attracting them like moths to the flame.

One night a handsome, well-dressed thirty-something guy stumbled through the entrance of the Blues Room and sat down at the bar, ordering a beer. During this predominantly nocturnal period of my life I spent most of my nights overlooking, managing the performances, taking care of the musicians until the early morning hours and I often engaged in late night conversations with the clientele. And Thomas was no exception. We got on well from the very beginning; he told me he was an interior architect, and had worked and lived in the city for a good couple of years now. Surprisingly, he was also of Hungarian origin on his mother's side, and although he had spent his childhood in Italy and Germany, he spoke almost perfect Hungarian.

Thomas was suddenly everywhere around me; I invited him to join me and my friends for dinner, for lunch, and he became a regular at the bar and slowly sneaked his way into my personal life. He was helpful, and things did get done; he promised to help find me a great table for my apartment and sure enough, at 9 a.m. one morning his guy appeared on our doorstep and delivered one. Soon he appeared bringing presents, often delivering unasked-for favors.

When he found out about the photo collection of musicians I was building, he became deeply interested in what I was doing and soon enough offered to help out with the shoots.

Occasionally he let me use the buildings and the houses he was working on as shooting locations. And I gladly accepted. Sometimes he even gave me keys to the places and often joined for the sessions, holding a reflector or helping out with minor stuff. As he got involved a bit more, he made suggestions about the shoots. Some I cared for, but most of them didn't fit in with what I was doing and I politely declined. I was fond of him and I liked having him around when I was working. Being well-connected and confident, his presence gave me a sense of security. He tactfully deflected the Chinese authorities away when one or two nosey guards interrupted us. Even just hanging out was great. He was a notable face at parties and various other gatherings, and he was the sort of person who could easily find sponsors for exhibitions—he could throw together a charity event in no time. Our acquaintance only developed further as the months went by.

But there were a few things I started to notice that struck me as strange about him. At first, I chose to ignore them out of politeness. For example, he could be extremely condescending to other people, terribly rude to waiters and service staff (a classic sign that discloses something rather suspicious about a person). He could stare at the person with contempt, but turn back to me with a friendly smile—he played it so carefully that it was hard to grasp these little moments but, ultimately, this is where I first started to notice those Jekyll-Hyde cracks in him.

Once, while we were hanging out and I wasn't paying particular attention, from the corner of my eye I caught him studying my face closely and carefully; an unusual act for such an intelligent man. In hindsight, I should have been wise to the pattern of his behavior; he'd left so many harassed victims in his wake, as he moved on from one sortie to another. I'm convinced now that in those moments, while he thought I wasn't looking, he was studying his latest prey: me.

Things were progressing way too fast; he wanted to be around me even more. Perhaps I was slow in recognizing this, and when I did and tried to rein it in, it already seemed impossible to put a brake on the situation. It was like vainly trying to stop a train speeding out of control, knowing full well that sooner or later it would crash horribly. The first sign that warned me that our relationship would end badly was when he developed a habit of calling me slightly too often. "Hey, where are you? What are you doing?" I remember hearing his friendly voice—which I still liked at that point—but I also remember thinking, "Thomas, what are you doing?" The phone calls then began to intensify—from a few times a day into an unbelievable, near-hourly occurrence.

Two things happened that resulted in Thomas' radical change of tactic that unleashed his true self. I received a job offer from *That's Shanghai,* to join them as a photographer and, coincidentally, at the same time my brother paid me a rare visit from Hungary. Suddenly, I didn't have time to hang out with Thomas. I did socialize with him as I did with others in general, but his sudden lack of exclusive access to my attention didn't seem to satisfy his needs, and with every absent day he grew more and more irascible.

I didn't realize how far his obsession with me had gone until the first abusive message landed on my phone. I thought it must have been a mistake, and that he'd intended to text someone else.

"Is that you? Did you mean to send that to me, Thomas?" I replied. There was no answer, just a tense silence from his side. Still operating under the impression that we were friends, I didn't think twice in pressing him.

As if possessed by some *Sith* spite, he unleashed an avalanche of abuse at me. It was if he had turned into a completely different person, ceasing to be the affable Thomas I'd come to know. I couldn't believe what was happening. All of a sudden, he began sending me as many as 50 emails and text messages a day. My phone was constantly buzzing as his long, half-Hungarian, half-English rants popped up one after the other with merciless rapidity. I didn't know that such long messages could be typed as quickly as he was spitting them out—pushing me to the limit of not even bothering to look at them any more. They were spiteful, bitter and jealous attacks, hurtful and poisonous to read. I watched helplessly as the situation began to spiral out of control.

Initially, one of the many conflicting issues about the whole matter was that no one in my circle believed me. It just didn't fit the description. Thomas presented such an immaculate social image of a kind, handsome, well-dressed guy, that no one could imagine that he was doing such a thing. But it looked like he reserved this dark side of his personality exclusively for his victims. It took me a while to convince others, but after showing them the messages they eventually understood what was happening.

One thing particularly worried me; he referred to my photographs as "our work", which he soon enough escalated to "my photos". Now, when you know you've taken a photograph but someone else claims they did instead, that's pretty much proof of their insanity. Thomas lived in an alternative reality, it seemed, and he genuinely did believe his own twisted version of the truth. As I continued to endure his unrelenting attacks, I realized that I was face-to-face with a psychopath.

Things got worse each day. Next, he demanded back the presents he'd given me. So I dumped them all outside the front of my house and told him, "Fine. Come and pick them up."

Then, he noticed that a small part was missing from a tripod he'd given me for my birthday. For the next three days he bombarded me with a sea of messages just about this missing piece of rubber.

The harassment went on for weeks until my eventual breaking point when he directed his attention towards my wife at her place of work, and began targeting her with messages. This pushed me over the edge, and I threatened him with blind anger: "You don't want to meet me in the street after this." He then back-tracked slightly and accused *me* of being aggressive. Things went so far that in the end I began to make arrangements for a lawyer to issue him with a restraining order.

At first, I didn't realize Thomas' insatiable thirst for a response. Anything I wrote back was like pouring more oil on the fire, fueling it further. Soon I figured out that by not replying and just ignoring him the number of messages decreased. About a week after I stopped all contact, the whole ordeal finally died down.

It took me a while to recover from the incident. It turned my life upside down for a while, as I was trying to concentrate on my new job at *That's Shanghai*. But Thomas did go away in the end. Months later, I walked into a bar and he was there. I walked past him without saying anything and sat down with a few people at another table. He got up in tears and left. I was only convinced further that something was seriously wrong with him when I heard later that he'd asked one of my friends, "What's Nicky's problem?"

Later, I found out that Thomas had ensnared many more victims. And there were more to come, too. Girls, boys, some were bullied, some were even blackmailed by him. All of them were left shaken by the encounter. In the end, despite all that happened, I decided that I felt sorry for him in a way, because he was obviously suffering from mental health issues and should have been diagnosed and treated.

For me on the other hand, the incident provided a great, if rocky start into photography with an abundance of valuable lessons about the ownership of images, and who to trust and who to avoid. It is a sad fact that it did make me a little more cautious about how close I should let people get to me or my work.

Meanwhile, over on Tongren Road, the reign of the Blues Room was drawing to a close. The spectacular World Expo 2010—a series of international fairs and expositions that heralded Shanghai's status as a world city—was just a few years in the future, and work to prepare the venues was beginning in earnest. Visitor sites were earmarked in both Pudong and Puxi but, more urgently, with the arrival of the Beijing Olympics in 2008, the government made a serious move to clean up Tongren Road. They did it in typical Chinese style—just one month's notice was given to the clubs, before the demolition machinery moved in on the complex that housed the Blues Room and so many other businesses. I was always amazed how, in Shanghai, these seemingly solid landmarks we'd all relied upon for so many years could be razed to the ground within a matter of days. It was something that never ceased to fascinate, horrify and inspire me, all at the same time. I can't remember who said it, but there is a quote about how, during wars, buildings, houses and streets could be ripped to pieces, becoming stark reminders of how they are merely temporary stage sets for our lives. Shanghai embodied that on a daily basis.

There was another factor that sealed the fate of Tongren Road though: an enormous Shangri-La Hotel was being built on the site, and there was no way such a luxurious hotel could be sited opposite a run of cheap bars. This was what eventually sealed the fate of what was now considered an eyesore.

The last few months, bleeding into 2009, were the last strokes of midnight for the Blues Room. The venue didn't have a proper performer's license, which could protect the musicians from the police and local security squads barging in and literally dragging musicians off the stage mid-performance—with many of them ending up getting deported. The threat of such raids was very real; it happened at too many venues around Shanghai, all due to preparations for the Beijing Olympics.

But, frankly, it really didn't matter any more. In their never-ending pursuit of profit, business owners and companies tend to introduce new sanctions that, ironically, slowly choke their own ventures, eventually squeezing out the quality and the soul. This predictable, sorry scenario always leads to a bitter end. I've seen it happen too many times. Indeed, the same fate was awaiting the Blues Room. Just when I had built up a solid clientele and mastered the cozy vibe that attracted so many, the owner began to undermine my progress by changing things little by little, seemingly on a whim. It all started to go horribly wrong when he stuck a pool table right in the middle of the venue, just below the stage, which instantly killed the live venue character, turning the place into a cheap, second-class bar. The musicians were petrified. In his desperation for more profit, the owner then squeezed the salaries, and ended up owing the staff—including me—for months and months, trapping everyone in a vicious circle—no one could afford to leave because of the money they were owed, forcing them to soldier on regardless. It was an unacceptable move from any employer under any circumstances. He didn't pay the electricity bill, either, and I'd often arrive at a dark, freezing cold venue in which the only available light came from candles.

Soon, the live performances were gone too, and the music

was reduced to a sorry playback from an iPod. The quality of the food dropped as well and because of such drastic changes, the clientele began drifting away. This dragged on for months until, one night, I got so pissed off that I just walked out of the venue mid-shift and left the godforsaken place for good. It was my answer to the non-payment game the owner was playing. Of course, he said *my* action was unprofessional and, predictably, used it as an excuse to never pay my back salary. But it was a symbolic gesture on my part—to abandon him and his sinking, self-crippling business before he abandoned me. I finally drew a line under our relationship when I sent him a message to "shove the $4,000 up your ass".

But even as the transformation of Tongren Road was finally complete and the new, glitzy Shangri-La towered over the tiny smoldering enclave thanks to its location at the other end of the road, the actual building that housed the Blues Room and CityDiner miraculously survived. But only the physical building. It's still there today, reincarnated as a place called Judy's. It stands as tangible evidence, signifying a site into which so many poured so much effort—and enjoyed such fantastic times. A great bygone era for those who still cared.

By the time I had totally wrestled myself free of the final Blues Room showdown and the bizarre ordeal with Thomas, I felt as if I had graduated, not just as a photographer, but in my life's journey. It certainly felt like something else was in the air. It was a new beginning for me—I was now working for *That's Shanghai* magazine, with a 50,000-copy print run.

Drawing inspiration from my years swimming the depths of Shanghai's music circles, I decided to form my own band, Monroe Stahr. We were actually quite good, but I made the fatal error of indulging my inner rock star and putting myself out as the ideal frontman, which I wasn't. As I wrote 90% of the songs, the rest of the band went along with this foolish idea and, to be fair, we did get relatively far, releasing an album and properly gigging around Shanghai. That said, while I felt my vocals worked on 'Summer Starts Here', the same couldn't be said for pretty much anything else, and the lead role should have gone to Nathan Denny, our guitarist. I should have been content to quietly play bass at the side of the stage and bask in the glory of having written most of the songs. If that had happened, I feel Monroe Stahr could have been a really good band.

The writing process and the creativity was exciting but, eventually, I got tired of playing late nights and after a disastrous gig at a benefit show in 2010 for the Dance For Haiti charity, after the devastating earthquake there, I decided to quit. In between the Blues Room and the band I'd found myself mostly living at night, drinking too much and gaining weight in the process. It was time to say goodbye to that lifestyle and usher into my life a radical new change.

As a footnote, Monroe Stahr was something I needed to do. Laying my youth entirely at the altar of music in some form or another, I felt it was time to participate right in the thick of it. I had to get it out of my system and while the band was the manifestation of this imperative, it also served as the epilogue to it all. This was my last genuine connection to music, but I am delighted to report that after my departure, the band continued on without me, surviving to this day as a truly special and successful covers band, The Gooda Boys, with the excellent Peruvian singer Paco Marcone on vocals.

However, one essential opportunity did come out of my time with the band. 'Summer Starts Here' somehow made its way to the *That's Shanghai* offices, which led to the editor-in-chief, JFK Miller, asking the band to headline their annual awards ceremony. I will always regard JFK as the person who 'discovered' me and lifted me out of amateurism. It turned out that he loved the song, and while we were exchanging emails about the band he discovered my photography site linked in my email signature.

Seeing potential in my ability to juxtapose music and imagery, JFK immediately offered me a position as the music editor of the magazine, responsible for eight pages of content, starting in January 2010. Needless to say, I jumped at the chance and got to work at once, making plans, coming up with sections and angles during the last months of 2009. My approach was to publish features and brutally honest reviews in the style of the *NME*, but within a few months of starting, I ran into a major problem. The Shanghai scene, I discovered, was far too small for such critical honesty. For huge, London-based papers with a national, if not international, readership such as the *NME*, this strategy obviously worked. But being so forthright and constructively straightforward in Shanghai meant exposing myself to endless conflicts with the musicians I was ostensibly trying to help — and in a worst-case scenario it could even lead to a beating. But, as ever, business concerns meant the magazine's structure was gradually shifting anyway, and there seemed to be a constant turnover in the editorial team. These changes slowly pushed me towards the position I always felt was made for me — *That's Shanghai*'s house photographer.

Things progressed quickly. When the woman in charge of food photography suddenly quit, JFK asked me to take over this section as well. Step by step my photographs began to appear throughout the entire magazine. However, my real chance came when he tasked me with a cover shoot for a feature entitled *Shanghai's Wealth Gap*. For this, the editorial team chose six people from different walks of life and juxtaposed their living standards — from the homeless to the super-rich — to highlight the contrasts of living in the city. The article included an interview with each of them, for which I had to shoot expressive portraits. I instantly recognized the turning point; I was given the chance to shoot my first-ever magazine cover.

We chose as cover star the one who best represented the average face of Shanghai: a girl working in a shoe shop, struggling daily to make ends meet. She was the real deal. We hired a local tattoo artist and at first JFK wanted to temporarily paint the Chinese 100 yuan note over her face. This was too complicated, we felt, and then tried the actual currency sign itself (a double-crossed 'Y' that's also used for Japan's yen), but we decided that this made her look like a cat. Eventually, we simplified the concept to the Chinese character 'qian', meaning money—even if the actual character was more complicated than the character of yuan.. The magic of the photo was that we didn't choose a model but a real person struggling with everyday problems. While this was evident in her features anyway, her irritation with the blinding light of my camera reflector only added to her somewhat defiant expression.

The new issue hit the shelves in the first days of September 2010 and changed everything for me. 'The Human Face of Money' ran the legend on the cover, the girl's face cropped in with the blood-red money character of painted over it. It was striking, expressive and beautiful; a perfect first cover.

Getting my first cover was a magical, almost sacred event. It triggered a glorious rush inside, as suddenly my photography was everywhere. At the same time, there was something eerie about it, in which the particular moment that I'd chosen and clicked to freeze into a permanent image was now multiplied and staring back at me—and everybody else—everywhere I went. When it happened, I tried not to exaggerate it; it was just a photo after all. However, I felt the achievement was one that had the ability to turn my career around, and whenever I had a magazine cover appearing at the beginning of the month, it never ceased to be a cause for quiet celebration. Fast forward to the present day, and I'm delighted to have shot more than 50 covers over the years for several different international magazines—I've got used to it to a certain degree. But I still have to come to terms with the bizarre sensation I get if ever I spot someone in an airplane seat next to me studying a cover I've shot, as my shyness ensures I keep my mouth shut. So, that September in 2010 I felt that I was the lucky one, and that it had happened to me finally. An image of mine was now smeared all over Shanghai—in restaurants, cafes, bars, schools, even doctor's waiting rooms.

Nothing had changed, and yet everything had changed. Prior to *That's Shanghai*, I was running around town with my camera, feverishly capturing everything in my path, mostly for my own purposes. The difference now was that I was getting paid to do the same. However, the step up brought one significant change, which to me was worth more than money—access. In short, working for a major magazine effectively handed me the key to the city. Suddenly, all the doors miraculously opened. It really did feel as if Shanghai belonged to me in a photographic sense.

Working under JFK Miller and his deputy, Ned Kelly, was endlessly inspiring. They knew how to rally me into action, coming up with ideas for photo essays, steering me towards what I did best, what would become my defining work, constantly teasing the best out of me. Sometimes they pushed me into unbelievable scenarios.

Once, we had a story in which we were covering how one piece of trash makes it through the whole city, eventually ending up in landfill. We needed the final shots and we chose the biggest landfill on the outskirts of Shanghai for a shooting location. As we hadn't managed to get the permits to enter the site on time, and the magazine's deadline was approaching, we decided to take matters into our own hands. But the idea of smuggling me and my camera into a regulated site obviously hadn't been thought through properly.

As we approached the location by car, we could smell the stench for miles. Imagine the reek of accumulated rubbish from a city with a population of 25 million. We flagged down a truck bringing in yet another load, and the driver was only too happy to accept my RMB100 note (about $15) and I hid under the seat, right by the steering wheel.

Once inside the compound, he dropped me off at the side of one of the 'roads'. I found myself in a small town of towering trash; the piles were high as apartment blocks. The stench wasn't just in my nose any more, it punched me right in the stomach. Needless to say, I got caught within minutes. I was a very unlikely sight: a tall, white guy with a camera, walking around an enclosed area in which only Chinese people worked. I was escorted to the main building for a routine interrogation, but soon dropped back outside the gates without further action against me, but also without a single photograph on my memory card.

Meanwhile, I'd learned the meaning of the adage 'you're only good as your last issue', which provided me with a sober overview of my own work amidst the often merciless but constructive criticism that JFK and Ned Kelly dished out to keep me in line. I recall once when I was sent out just hours before closing an issue to take a photo that could illustrate a piece on the restrictions on the use of the Shanghainese dialect in local schools. I knew exactly what to do. It was about 4 p.m. so, as fast as I could, I ran to a nearby school, just as the children were leaving to go home. I approached a group, and singled out the loudest boy of the bunch and asked him to cover his mouth, as if someone told him to shut up. He had no idea why I was asking him to do this and I didn't tell him, lest he suspect that within a few hours he'd find himself in print on the pages of a foreign magazine.

As a team, passion and a strong work ethic cemented us into a hardened unit in an exotic environment, in which we constantly had to come up with new ideas. A constellation of nationalities comprised our great editorial team—English, American, Australian and Hungarian. Being sent out to capture striking photo essays each morning, I was always on the move, rummaging through the old crumbling and swiftly disappearing neighborhoods that spread out north of Beijing Road and behind the Yu Gardens that still unexpectedly thrived during their last years of existence, before they too were reduced to piles of rubble, swept away as if they'd never existed.

Exploring these areas was like descending into a photographic goldmine. The editors always provided me with a Shanghainese companion, which was a tremendous help, as *laowais*—foreigners—weren't always welcome in the underbelly of the city. Whether shooting old, traditional kitchens in derelict houses with peeling walls and burn marks like little hand-painted forests sneaking up to their ceilings, or chaotic salons of traditional hairdressers, or just capturing striking local life existing within the microcosm created by Shanghai's unique East-meets-West *Shikumen* housing architecture, we were out each day. Occasionally, we were chased away but, even if I finished the day with only ten excellent photographs, it was all worth every effort. I even made a photo essay out of the fascinatingly messy electric wires hanging from poles like industrial noodles just before they were cleaned up for the World Expo 2010, that major event which elevated Shanghai to one of the most important cities in the world.

Publishing these pictorials, however, was often difficult. The Chinese tend to strive towards the shiny and the new; they like squeaky-clean images that project ideas of modernity to the outside world—even as foreigners such as myself sought out the traditional beauty of the historical gems tucked away in the shameful shadows of the ever-spreading skyscrapers. For many Chinese, such out-dated areas were something to hide away and ultimately destroy. Utterly preoccupied with the breakneck speed of its developments, China failed to realize that Shanghai was increasingly losing its identity and that they were demolishing their own heritage. It's like someone who undergoes so much plastic surgery that they end up losing their original features. This too was an ugly facelift. Leading up to 2018, the authorities managed to completely bulldoze some beautiful neighborhoods further north of Xintiandi, and the areas surrounding of the extensive Yu Gardens. Among many more, they also—outrageously—flattened the enormous, historic neighborhood of Laoximen, with its incredible winding streets that had housed Shanghainese communities for generations in the former walled city that had been there for 500 years. There was a lot of public debate about this, but public debate counts for little in China.

True, these houses were in bad condition, but instead of embracing their historic architecture and updating their interiors with modern renovations, the Shanghai municipality mercilessly replaced them with sterile skyscrapers and shopping malls. The hapless victims of this broad-stroke destruction, the residents of these neighborhoods, were offered compensation of 200,000 yuan and a new flat—but miles away on the outskirts of Shanghai, dislocating them from the familiar environment in which they'd spent a lifetime.

Riding through these districts on my electric scooter on a daily basis, I could see that destruction was scheduled everywhere — the Chinese character *chai* (拆), meaning 'demolition', was sloppily spray-painted on the houses. In a few weeks, it would all be gone. To deter residents from resisting their forced relocation, the authorities smashed holes in the external walls to render the condemned houses uninhabitable. I came across heartbreaking scenes. I remember one old couple who'd been evicted from the house they'd lived in all their lives, camped on two chairs in the middle of the road, surrounded by all their earthly belongings. It was all they could do to protest. They sat there for a few days until the authorities got around to removing them.

I specifically targeted these doomed, already marked blocks and, even after they'd been bulldozed, I went back to shoot the remains, sometimes capturing people's possessions abandoned among the rubble. I was usually the only person around apart from, perhaps, a few desperate locals scavenging the debris for anything recyclable. Sometimes I had a stroke of grim luck, as I managed to catch a few houses disappearing in billows of their own dust as they crumbled to the ground before my eyes.

I went back several times to document this sorry situation. I witnessed up close entire blocks disappearing overnight. Houses ripped in half, with decorations, posters and pictures still clinging to their exposed walls, rooms gaping towards the open sky as if they'd been carpet bombed; all of this was a photographer's dream, even as it spelled out a living nightmare for the former residents.

Not surprisingly, such photo essays of mine often received the thumbs-down from the censors at *That's Shanghai*. I remember the staff holding its collective breath as our print deadline loomed, anxious until the last minute that the thought police would reject our articles, and it was always an unexpected surprise if one survived through to publication.

It wasn't all doom and gloom, however, as this was just one angle to the fast-moving, rapidly changing city. Shanghai is the city of the future, and it fascinated us with its relentless thrust. The diversity of my subjects spoke for itself; in the morning I could be shooting migrant workers from Anhui Province, crammed into container homes that were boiling hot in the sun, while in the afternoon I was snapping photos of the filthy-rich in their luxury apartments with breathtaking vistas over the city in Pudong. The palette constantly widened, and I often couldn't believe the subjects I was commissioned to record: the oldest couple in Shanghai, a man who kept grasshoppers as pets, witch-doctors, wheelchair fencers, girls who intentionally had their shin bones broken, the gaps between them then stretched in dodgy plastic surgery procedures that promised to make them taller, toy makers, tailors, pest controllers, limousine drivers, taxi drivers, metro drivers, models, shop owners, restaurateurs, bakers, chefs, businessmen—I could go on and on. Plus, through our regular interiors feature I was invited into some of the most striking and diverse homes in Shanghai.

The parent company of *That's Shanghai* is called Urbanatomy. And that's exactly what we did. Through our articles and pictorials we dissected the city into tiny pieces, before combing through the shreds, peeling back the city's dense, multi-layered urban tissue. This abundance of subject matter lasted for five years. In that time, I can safely say I shot Shanghai from all possible angles.

Fortunately, my new employers were happy for me to freelance in tandem with my magazine work and so, with my name constantly in print, I saw my clientele triple. Finally, all the free photo services I had volunteered in my early photographic career began to pay off.

Just as I was finding my feet at the magazine, my work with musicians also came to fruition. A British pianist I'd met called Mark Pummell, who owned BD Studios in the city's art district on Taikang Road (locally known as *Tianzifang*), said he was fond of my work and offered to host an exhibition.

We called it *In the Midnight Hour*. We had a small opening and many musicians attended and we celebrated our work together. The exhibition ran for three months and the pairing couldn't have been more ideal; the studio was constantly used by musicians, and it was a busy hub. While print sales were moderate, I was delighted that my photos gained such great local exposure.

Much later, Andy Warhol's personal photographer, Christopher Makos—with whom I worked twice via *That's Shanghai*—gave me some advice when I met him in New York. He said: "Print, print, print! So, when the electricity goes out, you're still a photographer." Christopher further noted that you have to get your photos seen over and over again—shove them in people's faces so that they become known. It was brilliant advice, and I still wish I'd heeded it but printing the Shanghai musicians collection for the exhibition certainly gave me momentum and acceptance as a photographer.

Despite its rough edges, during the Noughties Shanghai was an absolutely charming place to live. Before the 2010 Expo, the city was still an untouched haven thriving with an abundance of opportunities. You could arrive with nothing and end up landing the most amazing jobs. Investing my time and efforts into photography, the city gave me a natural, powerful sense of belonging. I absolutely loved Shanghai. It was my home for ten years, and it was the city that made my name.

Furthermore, I was endlessly mesmerized by its dichotomy, how the two faces of Shanghai, the modern and the old, Pudong and Puxi stared at each other as if looking into a distorted mirror, over the Huangpu River. It was such a drastic, stunning visual contrast: the lowly, disappearing neighborhoods pitched against the backdrop of the mighty skyscrapers looming over them; it was a subject I couldn't possibly *not* have photographed. I felt this draw, this magnetic inspiration, every single day. The diversity was present in everything. Shanghai has always benefited from a mix of Chinese and foreign influences, a city so rich in a fusion that manifests in everything: art, food, music, architecture and, ultimately, people.

I lived in the residential jungle of Puxi. This is where I worked and slept, and I seldom cared what was happening on the other side of the river. But as the skyline of Pudong gradually rose towards the heavens, my focus shifted to something entirely different to the jazz clubs and the crumbling neighborhoods, something that elevated me to another level in photography, eventually leading to published books and further recognition.

One of my favorite things about Shanghai, which I still miss to this day, occurs every autumn, just as the heat of summer begins to cool down — the irresistible scent of the osmanthus flower fills the air, especially around the former French Concession. It always signified a new change for me, a wonderful drop in temperature after the hot humid months, its soothing fresh breeze coming to my rescue. The contiguous foliage of the characteristic plane trees forms a shelter around the area, a sanctuary within which I created a home for myself and my wife, and I confess that I still feel nostalgic and somewhat homesick for my early years in Shanghai whenever I look back. It cuts deep when I remember it. I don't think I have ever been happier than when I was living there. I recall first arriving in the city in the autumn of 2006, just as the scent of the osmanthus flower greeted us with its perfumed welcome. It was all so new, and yet I instantly felt as if I had arrived home. Later, after it did indeed become our home, such feelings only intensified. Without doubt, Shanghai was the most significant thing that ever happened to me. From the moment I arrived I felt as if I was there for a reason, and felt that it was my calling, my duty, to document the changes the city was undergoing, and I felt that I stepped up to that role, fulfilling it with respect and humility.

The Invisible Architect—
The Untold Story of the Shanghai Tower

It was always the greatest of excitement: waiting for him on those cold winter mornings at the crossroads of Mengzi and Madang Road, just outside his office. This tower of a man, the embodiment of modern architecture, the tragedy, the invisible architect behind the glass and steel behemoth money-monster that he himself had created. He appeared under the archway in his long coat, flagged down a taxi and we were on our way again to the other side of Huangpu River for yet another site visit to his 128-storey masterpiece.

A journalist once likened my five-year collaboration with architect Marshall Strabala to the one between the Swiss-French architect Le Corbusier and his favorite Hungarian photographer Lucien Herve. As much as I admire Le Corbusier's work, I've never studied that partnership closely, but I could tell that Strabala's and mine was based on mutual trust, respect, with a lack of ego and selfishness, only focusing on what we loved: our work. It was a collaboration which turned into a friendship.

And perhaps that was the reason that it lasted through and beyond an unspeakable storm of difficulties, betrayals, seemingly never-ending lawsuits, thus giving me an opportunity to be around a workaholic during the time of his deepest professional troubles. It gave me a chance not only to document his work through the lens, but to witness his personal struggle behind it all, the tremendous pressure that could only come from being the man behind the second tallest building in the world, the

Shanghai Tower.

On one of those pleasant April days of 2010, when Shanghai's bone-chilling cold finally retreated and gave way to mild spring days, I was in the back seat of a taxi on the way to a shoot for *That's Shanghai* magazine. I wound down the window, enjoying the gentle breeze sweeping through the car. It seemed like any ordinary day; running from one photo shoot to another, collecting visuals for our next issue. Suddenly, there was a message on my phone. It was from JFK Miller, my editor.

"Nicky, ask your driver to turn around and come back to Mengzi Lu. I'm interviewing someone important and I need you to shoot a few portraits of him." I did just that and a few minutes later I found myself in a stylish, spacious, bright office located in a modern warehouse complex, stacked with architectural models and printed renderings on its shelves. There were floor plans rolled out on enormous desks with busy staff leaning over and studying them carefully. The office turned out to be Marshall Strabala's, the chief architect of the Shanghai Tower, the world's second tallest structure at the time. By then I was used to all kinds of shoots; it came with the job to walk into the most unexpected scenarios that needed to be chronicled, but all of a sudden I felt this was different: in fact, this must have been the first time I ever felt nervous doing a photo shoot.

There were a few reasons why this moment took me by surprise and why I was almost star-struck when I entered and JFK introduced us. A few years prior to this, around 2008 when Pudong's other landmark skyscraper the SWFC or 'Bottle Opener' reached its final construction stage, I was living out my final musician fantasies somewhere in Puxi, on the other side of the river. I was managing the bar and at nights I played in a band, so I slept through most of the days. I was already documenting the rapid changes sweeping through the city with photographs for myself; however, capturing the construction of SWFC, the second of the three major skyscrapers defining Pudong's skyline, completely flew by me. The building not only represented the city's ambition to be the country's financial centre centre, it also marked a new era for China. With all its 100 floors of concrete, metal, steel and glass, they put it up extremely fast, within three years and, suddenly, it was just... there, shimmering over the river in all its might.

From the very first day of moving to Shanghai I was completely mesmerized by the city's rapid changes, minor or major, and its incredible ability to reinvent and reshape itself as an enormous, complex, urban entity, seemingly overnight.

The failure to shoot the construction of SWFC was an ongoing regret that hung over me that year; I was angry at myself that I'd let something else distract me. So when I saw the incredible renderings of the Shanghai Tower, an even higher, stunning 128-storey super-tall building that looked like a slightly crumpled, cylindrical piece of paper, I jumped at the chance to document it from day one.

Shanghai Tower was the last installment of the three major skyscrapers, the Three Brothers in modern Shanghai's financial district, Lujiazui. The first one, completed in 1999, was the Jinmao Tower. With its stainless steel pagoda design, it referenced China's historic architecture. Nine years later, the completion of the SWFC by a Japanese developer, Mori Building Co., represented China's present. The third one was conceived as a more transparent, open idea, with a dynamic form which brought along the design of Shanghai Tower; a double-skin twisted glass building with no facade, looking in all directions instead of one—thus representing China's future. The three-buildings project had been initiated much earlier, in the 1980s by leader Deng Xiaoping, to make Pudong into China's number one financial centre and so, in a way, these three towers not only placed the crown on the area's development but cemented China's position as a financial superpower.

True, I didn't have any access to the site but I never saw this as a problem. In fact, what I loved about my new pet project was that there weren't any real obstacles in my way; yes, there was a fence, but the building quickly grew over it and I could go there any time I wanted to shoot it from outside. Further difficulties, such as searching for possible vantage points or sneaking into buildings within close proximity, seemed to be good fun, an adventure spreading out over the next couple of years. I was extremely excited about it, especially knowing that this was all up to me. By then, I had already mastered my trick of making fake loud phone calls while walking past security to secretly access higher levels. In China, every building has a bored *bao'an* (guard) at its entrance and gate, but they are usually lazy, and so if you, a foreigner, make a loud phone call while walking past them, they figure you're having trouble finding someone and, avoiding the language barrier issue, they generally don't stand in your way and let you get on with your business. This trick got me onto many Shanghai rooftops over the years and helped extend my portfolio of the city.

Meanwhile, something else happened that enabled me to shoot the tower's developments even more extensively. The ground-breaking had already taken place by 2009, when I was lucky enough to be offered a teaching job right next to it, on the 19th floor of the BEA Finance Tower, overlooking the entire construction site. This changed everything.

I did like teaching English at the company. It was a good opportunity, and brought in welcome extra income. But getting a great vantage point on the Shanghai Tower, or rather the hole in the ground that it was back then, from week to week, gave me an additional kick of excitement—another reason to get out of bed so early on Monday mornings. Even an unfortunate accident that happened to me on the very first day I started teaching didn't put me off. With the BEA office tower itself having only been recently completed, the owners had yet to put a sign on one of the newly-installed glass walls within the office in which I was teaching—and on a terribly unfortunate morning I walked right into it. Suddenly, in the squeaky clean, brand new office, there was blood everywhere—spraying out of my nose, covering my lips, my white shirt and the floor. It wasn't only painful but it was extremely awkward. The students—a dozen businessmen in suits—stared at me from the other side of the glass wall as I was struggling to regain my balance. If the situation hadn't felt so genuinely terrifying, with all the blood making a mess, I would have probably collapsed laughing at the comic absurdity of it all. Imagine walking into an invisible wall at full speed. Suddenly, I felt this enormous blow and from the unexpected impact I almost lost consciousness. As a result, I broke a tooth and blood oozed from my nose uncontrollably. I quickly managed to get to one of the bathrooms where the cleaning ladies helped me stop the bleeding. Even the bone between my eyes had cracked. It was very dramatic and they thought I'd never return to my new place of work.

At the hospital the doctor suggested an operation, but I refused. If this had happened in the US or anywhere else, I could have sued the company and easily won—surely, I wouldn't have needed a teaching job for a few years. For several days afterwards, the company was concerned that I'd take them to court because, after all, it had been their responsibility to put up a sign. But that was never my intention. Yes, I was pretty shaken up by it for a while, and I sustained a concussion and felt dizzy, but I just had my tooth fixed and came back the following Monday. So instead of a dispute, a special bond formed between me and the company right from the start, and I kept the job for a few years after that. And, of course, I also kept my great vantage point from which I continued to photograph the Shanghai Tower.

So that day, when I suddenly found myself in Marshall Strabala's office, I was completely taken aback. I had enormous respect for the man; after all, he was the mastermind behind my new secret photography subject. In later years, after we became friends, I noticed the same nervousness in people whenever I introduced him to them and I totally understood where it came from. The man was behind such monumental projects as London's Canary Wharf and the world's tallest building, the Burj Khalifa in Dubai, so he was, in every possible way, larger than life. Just over fifty years old, heavy-set but not overweight, he was always elegantly dressed with slicked-back hair, and he radiated an assurance and a down-to-earth sense of gravitas. With Marshall, you felt that you were in the presence of someone grand, someone important.

Despite my own nervousness, the shoot was brief and to the point. JFK introduced us, I took the photos — they weren't bad — he concluded the interview and we left Marshall's office. For now, that seemed to be the end of it. However, this unexpected encounter stuck in my mind and it inspired me to weave my plans and ideas further around it. "Now that we're in touch through the magazine," I thought to myself, "what if I ask him if I could take photos of him while he's working on the Tower? What if I ask him if I can get photography access to the site?" The possibilities seemed endless, and made my secret project all the more exciting. On the other hand, deep inside I had to face the reality of it, too: these were just fantasies I was creating for myself. Surely, he wouldn't care or even be interested. JFK's article came out the next month and was titled 'The Master

Builder', and for now that was the end of it. I didn't see Marshall for a few months after that.

But JFK did. He met up with him and his wife, Joan, in Singapore for dinner, and my name came up again. "Hey, do you remember that photographer, Nicky, who shot your portrait back in Shanghai?" JFK asked him. "He's documenting the construction of your building all by himself. Maybe you two should get together and talk about this in the future?" Marshall agreed and, to my great surprise, JFK gave me his email address.

I didn't hesitate. I sent Marshall an email straight away, pitching the idea of running a pictorial on him (or a 'photo essay' as *That's Shanghai* called it) in the magazine. I suggested shooting photos showing him working on the site, taking measurements of the building, talking to the workers. The plan behind the pictorial was real but, in all honesty, it was more of an excuse to get onto the site. By this time, this had became my obsession. I would have given anything to get in.

The Shanghai Tower was not much of a spectacle around 2010 and 2011, little more than a bare concrete stub sticking out of Pudong's muddy ground, surrounded by trucks, rubble and piles of building materials. Most people didn't even take notice, only those who were actually in the know were aware of the scale of what was being built there. No one really paid attention to the fact that the second tallest building in the world was slowly rising out of the earth. Apart from a few invisible enthusiasts around town, I don't think anyone was excited about the development as much as I was. Even though Marshall hadn't answered — and, yes, I was a bit crestfallen about that — I continued my photography trips to the nearby streets, and didn't give up on documenting the building works from the outside. By now, I had convinced myself that I was probably too insignificant a photographer for this project. "This will be a 128-storey skyscraper,' I kept telling myself. "Get real. Why would anyone want you for this?" And I drew some comfort that I'd managed to get as far as photographing Marshall for the feature. That was already a worthy addition to my modest collection during the early stages of the construction. But the more the weeks passed by, the less hope I had for doing the pictorial.

These days, I know how unpredictable Marshall is with emails, and with online activity in general, especially when it comes to contacting people, but back then I had no idea. His reply landed in my mailbox about a month later with characteristic spontaneity: "Nicky, so sorry for the late response. I was traveling. Yes, absolutely! Let's have dinner together tomorrow!" I'd already given up on the whole idea, so this reply took me by surprise and I was over the moon when I received it.

Back then, Marshall was frequenting a restaurant called Jacky's, just outside his office, and this is where he invited me the following evening. I can still recall traveling there in the rain on my beaten-up scooter, thinking along the way: "What on earth can I say to an architect who builds super-tall buildings? Will we have anything in common to talk about? This might get very awkward indeed." And the closer I got to Jacky's, the more my excitement turned into apprehension. As I entered the restaurant, I got the first glimpse of a sight that I became so accustomed to over the next few years—he was sitting with a bottle of red wine in front of him, drawing and scribbling away on a piece of paper. Marshall was completely obsessed with architecture; he lived and breathed it, hence his habit of drawing everything he was talking about. He couldn't talk without a pen in his hand. He simultaneously drew and talked, doodling little sketches of any subject that came up, and they usually materialized on restaurant napkins. When he saw me, he looked up over his glasses and motioned me to sit down. He asked me to choose something from the menu and we started talking.

I already knew about Marshall's troubles with Gensler, the global architectural firm that had brought him on board to design the Shanghai Tower. For legal reasons, their disagreement had been played down in JFK's article, but for Marshall, it was very much a major issue in those months, and for years to come. According to him, the two sides had butted heads from day one—as soon as work had begun on the Shanghai Tower, their relationship erupted into major disagreements, which led to his split with the company, culminating in legal battles between the two parties. In fact, when I met him, Marshall was entering the deepest troubles of his architect career. The background was an extremely intricate web of legal disputes between him and the firm.

The story began way before even the ground-breaking in November 2008. It had all started two years earlier, when Gensler entered the bid for the third super-tall skyscraper in Pudong, Shanghai. They poached Marshall from SOM, aka Skidmore, Owings & Merrill, another global architectural firm, for whom he'd been working since the 1980s. SOM was responsible for the Burj Khalifa, the tallest structure on the planet. That building's architect, Adrian Smith—Marshall's ex-boss and more importantly, his mentor—had already designed buildings in China; he was the man behind the Zifeng Tower in Nanjing, and was also the architect of the first of Pudong's three major skyscrapers, the Jinmao Tower. When Gensler brought Marshall on board, they basically capitalized on his portfolio, on his expertise on super-tall buildings. They hired him exclusively to win the bid for the third installment of the skyscraper trio of the Three Brothers in Pudong, the Shanghai Tower. Marshall was based in Chicago at the time, but as soon as discussions about the designs began, they had him on a flight to Shanghai. Marshall hadn't been keen on moving to China but as Gensler eventually won the bid and the construction started, he had little choice but to relocate to Shanghai.

At first Marshall thought that the partnership with Gensler would be a good fit. "Because buildings are about the use of the inside, I thought their expertise on the interiors would benefit the exteriors," he told me in an interview later. "But it really didn't work out that way. I was hoping for interaction, but there wasn't any. They just said: 'When you're done with the design of the building, let us come in.' The idea about building super-tall buildings is very foreign to an interior decoration company. An interior design takes place under six months. It's very quick, very repetitive. Whereas a super-tall building takes eight years. So it's a different kind of mentality, and what I found was that a lot of the things I thought were important that go into these iconic buildings were just not part of Gensler's culture."

A dispute broke out, and it was just a matter of time before the two sides felt they were no longer able to work together. But by then Marshall's design was in place — and it belonged to Gensler. According to Marshall, the real trouble started when the firm assigned architects for him who didn't know much about super-tall buildings either, and there were constant confrontations as he stuck to his own tried-and-tested methods. The disagreements eventually led to Marshall leaving the firm in 2010. More precisely, he was fired; he said, one day he arrived at the office to find that the locks had been changed.

Despite the dispute with the American architectural firm, the Chinese client, the Shanghai Tower itself, insisted that Marshall stay on, owing to the fact that he was the only one who knew the building's design inside out.

"I had a contract with Gensler as the chief architect during the competition," he told me. "It was a logical step for me to stay on and finish the building. They were involved to some extent, but there was a lot of technical work that needed to be done on the exterior wall and Gensler wasn't a good technical architect." He continued: "The client (Shanghai Tower) soon realized they were out of their league. But, in a very heinous step from them, decided to sue me. They used my name, my portfolio and my past experience to win the project. Then, when I delivered the job and while I was still working for the client, they tried to marginalize me and said 'Strabala wasn't involved'. But the truth was that I was involved from day one and I was involved until the project was finished."

As the construction progressed the client itself requested that Marshall be present all the time, as he was the only one who was familiar with the design. He never actually had a problem with Gensler's name being credited for the building; after all, the design of the Shanghai Tower did belong to them. He was fighting back because they took all credit for his work while at the same time trying to bury his name.

Regarding my involvement, I don't think a global architectural firm would have bothered to talk to a lone freelance photographer like me regarding shooting the construction process. Such companies automatically hire the biggest and most expensive names in the business. But since Marshall was out on his own, frankly it hadn't even occurred to him to hire a photographer to document the site. Well... that was my window of opportunity.

That evening at the restaurant I showed him some of the photos I'd been taking of the works-in-progress, and he became very interested. My obsession must have shone through, as he studied my pictures carefully, taking notes, pointing things out, marking them, making suggestions on certain angles for future reference. I could see that he liked what I was doing. We talked until midnight. By the end of the evening I'd realized that he was a very down-to-earth guy and that I needn't have worried about communicating with him. We had a few drinks and, there and then, we agreed to put together a photography book on the different stages of the tower's construction. More precisely, his work on it.

The collaboration started slowly. Marshall arranged for permission so that I could enter the site, which took a few weeks. The first time we went there together he took me around Pudong and pointed out locations from where I could take hero shots later on—photographs that show the face of a building and reveal its identity. Walking around in the sweltering summer heat, this was the day when I took the photo of him with the skeleton of the building as the background (a photo that many websites still use illegally without crediting me). We didn't go on site that day, instead we ended up having lunch together and discussing further what we wanted to do with our project.

A few more weeks went by before the day finally arrived when we entered the site. Typically, I got the call from him one evening that we were going in the next morning. It was almost always like that over the following months and years, I hardly ever received any warning. I don't know whether it was a test regarding my dedication or if he was just simply forgetful, but this was always pretty much the routine, calling me the night before. Needless to say, I dropped everything and made myself available. We met at the south entrance, which back then was just a worker's lodge, and he handed me my site name tag and a safety helmet with his new company, 2Define Architecture, printed on it, and there I was—finally on the site of the Shanghai Tower.

The building was still pretty much a skeleton back then, with a mere forty or fifty floors rising over Pudong. Shanghai Tower's unique architectural feature was that it had a double skin structure that worked like a thermostat, maintaining the temperature between the inner and the outer surfaces. The curtain-walls — which enclose the space within a building but don't actually support the roof — were already in place and so were some of the inner-skin windows, but only a few had been installed. We went in with two other young Chinese architects who were working for Marshall at that time. In our helmets we must have looked like three spacemen stumbling across the surface of Mars as we cut through the enormous piles of rubble, hardly visible in the thick dust surrounding the base. We made our way to the upper floors. I didn't show it, but I must have been slightly shaking from the excitement: finally, I was inside the perimeter fence, and the shots I was taking were exactly how I had imagined them. I could hardly believe that it was actually happening. We mostly confined ourselves to a few floors and these would become the focus of our visits during the next couple months.

On that same day we did manage to venture up to the top, and climb out to one of the red cranes stretching out a few hundred meters from the structure over the abyss. Compared to what it would be upon completion, the building still wasn't that tall at this stage, but it was nevertheless a terrifying height. In the coming years when people found out I was working on the project, they often asked: "So you don't have a fear of heights then, right?" But the truth was that I did, and I still do. However, I was so fascinated with the project that I had to put my fears aside, as much as I could. And this was the first time I put myself to the test. Between the crane and the building there was a one-meter wide — and few hundred meters deep — gap that I had to leap over. Beneath my feet, the surrounding 20-story residential buildings seemed like tiny boxes scattered over the terrain, and cars looked like minuscule ants scurrying around. One meter is not that much, but when you have nothing in between and only a deep chasm beneath you, it becomes a big distance. I made the jump after taking a photo of my feet over the gap and from that day, it was obvious that I had to buckle up and quickly overcome one of my greatest fears if I wanted to be involved in the project.

Height wasn't the only danger; the site was full of hazardous metal pieces, scraps, nails, rusty wires sticking out from the most unexpected places, and anywhere you stepped potential jeopardy lurked. There were holes in the ground with steel spikes at the bottom that could impale you if you took the wrong step and fell. People were working overhead, and they could drop tools, or pieces of the structure, which could be fatal if one of them hit you on the head, or any part of the body for that matter. Not to mention the amount of dust that surrounded us whenever we went. As we walked around, another unexpected sight was human faeces everywhere. There were certain selected floors that had toilets, so the workers, not willing to take the lift over twenty floors to find them, decided to sit down and do their business anywhere that nature called.

Meanwhile there was something else I had to get used to with my tower visits: Marshall talking tirelessly about the building. Although I found it interesting and absorbed most of the information and sometimes he went into such fine technical details that his words fell hard on my dilettante ears. I still enjoyed listening to him, and tried to take in everything he had to say, finally working closely on my dream project. He knew every detail, measurement, material, every single screw on site. He knew the structure inside out; after all, to begin with he'd first built it in his head.

Everyone on site knew Marshall, from the workers, through the operational departments and upper management, right up to the owners of the building, the Shanghai Tower Construction and Development Company. Everyone relied solely on his expertise.

Marshall was hands on. He was in charge, having regular meetings, and they didn't make any decisions without him. In one of the interviews I conducted with him later, he explained that it was crucial for the sake of the building to put the dispute aside: "The most important thing was doing a good job for the project, not what's right for Gensler and not what's right for me. The job had to be finished, full stop."

It might be a shocking revelation but I never got paid for the Shanghai Tower project. Not a penny. Many people I knew speculated about this around me throughout the years, because it was such a big project. For most of the time I accompanied Marshall as his personal photographer, and whenever someone heard about my involvement, they assumed I was raking in a huge amount of cash every month. And in one sense, yes, I was getting richer: but actually, I was getting richer in another sense; with treasured photographs and invaluable experience. The involvement elevated my name to another level in Shanghai circles. Eventually, in February 2018 when I last saw him, Marshall did hand me US $3500 in a big stack of notes. I remember us standing by the ATM near Tianzifang after a boozy dinner and I had trouble shoving the money into my pockets; it was so much cash. But that was separate—that was for my final, five-day stint on the tower after everything had been completed, when I finally got to shoot the finished building.

Not getting paid was a calculated decision on my part, something I would never regret. I pretty much did the same as I had done with the Shanghai jazz musicians before. I didn't want Marshall's first impression of me to be a money-grabbing chancer; one who'd suddenly come out of nowhere and was pressuring him for payment. I had other sources of income, and was incredibly happy just being around him and the building and, besides that, I knew it would lead somewhere. Besides, over the years, he constantly spoiled me with expensive dinners and by generously lending me his three-bedroom apartment to use when he was out of town.

That evening in the restaurant when I first met Marshall properly, we didn't mention money, but as far as I was concerned, it was a win-win situation for both of us: I got my guaranteed access to the construction site and he got a constant supply of photographs documenting his most ambitious project. It was a verbal agreement. I looked at it more as favors we were doing for each other. A few people around me years later learned about this and judged Marshall to have been exploiting me. Especially as everyone associates a skyscraper of this magnitude with millions of dollars. But I'm asking, what good would it had done if our arrangement had included money? If you look around, in the end money always ruins everything: friendships, relationships, partnerships. It was me who wanted access in the first place, so how would it have looked if on the first evening I had said: "OK, how much?" I don't think I would have even got that far if I'd tainted the situation with money. Our work, our friendship would have never materialized, never gotten anywhere. I recognized this instantly. I invested my time and work in the tower (which I enjoyed) and I knew it would benefit me in other ways. So, instead of getting caught up on this, I just ventured full swing into the next chapter of my life.

And I did calculate correctly. Things began progressing around me as a direct result of my involvement. Our visits became regular and whenever Marshall went to the site, I was with him, even documenting his meetings with executives and officials behind the huge, multi-million-dollar operation. Although I was working for the magazine at the same time, I was quite flexible with my time and I could switch things around whenever I got the call.

Even the workers on site recognized me now. Marshall asked me to shoot from certain angles, take detailed shots of materials, of certain floors, while I took my more artistic shots of the building and him—we were rapidly building up a huge database of photos. My hard drives were filling up with the tremendous amount of material; hundreds and hundreds of gigabytes of videos, photos and voice recordings were collected, and there was more coming each month. Funnily enough, while the pictorial on Marshall that I once planned for the magazine never materialized, I ended up with a collection that far exceeded all my initial humble expectations.

On one occasion, when Marshall threw a big party in his office for architectural people, he printed many of my photos to exhibit that night. It was a glorious occasion for me. I was congratulated on my work and my association with Marshall. Coincidentally, in that year of 2012 I won the Best Architecture Photography award in the US for ENR, the Engineering News-Record, the prestigious weekly magazine, which is a bible for architects. My photo of the three towers, with the yet skinless, glassless Shanghai Tower in the middle, entitled 'The Three Brothers' was even used for the award ceremony in New York.

Around that time things were rapidly changing in the world of digital photography and Canon released their EOS 5D Mark II camera with an excellent video feature and so, besides still photographs, I began to record video material of our visits. This is when I started my 'construction update' series featuring Marshall talking about the current developments on the tower. It was all my editor, JFK's, idea. He suggested that while Marshall was struggling with the legal battles that were attempting to silence him, we should do something using social media to get his voice heard. Back then social media still hadn't reached its all-pervasive position that it has today, but the idea worked. I went over to Marshall's place near Taikang Road, and set up my equipment in his living room. We brought some architectural models from his office as a prop—the Burj Khalifa and the Shanghai Tower among them—and we started recording.

Marshall worked well with the video format; he was focused, engaging, his flow was smooth and he was good with words. There were hardly any edits or retakes. After all, I only asked him to do what he loved most in all its simplicity: drawing while talking about architecture. Only this time in front of a camera.

Simultaneously, print media publications began to feature him, and credited him for the Shanghai Tower, and this exposure helped his cause. He was winning in the magazines and online platforms while losing pretty much everywhere else. Even the *New York Times* planned an article on him as part of a series that analysed the plight of architects with the same troublesome issue—falling out with their architecture firm and fighting for their integrity. There was a lot of back-and-forth with them, but in the end the piece never materialized.

Meanwhile, my exposure in the city was growing and people started to associate me with the Tower and architectural photography in general. I began getting assignments from another firm, B&H Architecture, and Marshall recommended my services left and right.

The reactions among different nationalities when I mentioned that I was working on the Tower were telling; foreigners were blown away upon hearing it and looked at my photos with amazement. Many people wanted to come with me on my shoots, but I knew it was impossible. The enthusiasm went so far that the owner of a famous Shanghai nightclub asked me once: "Nicky, please take me in somehow. I'd be your assistant. I'll carry your equipment!"

While it excited foreigners greatly and they wanted to know

every little detail about what was going on inside that incredible half-completed structure rising over the city, reshaping the skyline, I'd found it funny how the Chinese, who value something only if it's new and shiny, usually reacted. As the building didn't look anything like it does today, most of the time they regarded it with either total indifference but more often it was a shock. "What are you doing on that filthy construction site with the workers? It must be so dirty!" They couldn't fathom foreigners' excitement.

Once I was on the Bund, Shanghai's waterfront area, attending an event in a building where the windows overlooked the Pudong skyline, shimmering in the evening sky. At one point, a Chinese girl asked me what I did, and I told her that I was a photographer working on the site of the new construction and—as the tower wasn't that well known yet—I pointed to the other side of the river at the half-finished naked structure, almost expecting to be met with a nod of approval. Her reaction was concise but priceless, and summed up the reaction of many Chinese: "In that?" she asked me with horror and contempt in her voice. In later years, such reactions shifted somewhat as the work progressed and began to reach its conclusion. The locals became interested when the building was almost finished, because being involved meant a connection with the government.

The online exposure we generated with Marshall did help, even if his own situation only continued to deteriorate. While the Gensler lawsuit dragged on, another dispute broke out, this time within his own, new China-based firm, 2Define Architecture. I'm still not sure what triggered the major disagreement between him and his business partner, Wang (not his real name), but it erupted into an epic conflict. The fights which followed were as nasty as they can get. In their homeland, the Chinese would never take a foreigner's side, especially not openly, and soon enough the other architects, joined in and went after Marshall, too.

Wang did everything he could to damage Marshall and his reputation. Things escalated quickly; there were major clashes regarding the office they shared, arguments over intellectual property and their company's projects. Wang really did his best to hurt Marshall, and being Chinese, he was on home ground and winning with it. One thing I learned during my 10 years in China is that in any conflict, minor or major, from a small traffic accident to a full legal case like this, you'll definitely lose against a Chinese national in their own country. They tend to side with each other no matter whether they're right or wrong, and a deep patriotism fuels their actions. If you're an outsider, you're lost. Pulling in favors from some of his government contacts, Wang even managed to freeze Marshall's Chinese bank account, leaving him financially paralyzed.

Around this time, I began to worry about my own safety too; I realized that Wang could do basically anything. I was deeply involved, working very closely with Marshall as his personal photographer and my name was often associated with him. Besides, Wang knew me well; we often went on site together and I met him in the office regularly. All in all, as another foreigner, I was too much in the picture, a potential target, and therefore I too felt exposed.

Amidst the disputes, Wang began calling me, trying to turn me against Marshall. I was always polite, and didn't take sides. I tried to stay on the fence and remain diplomatic, while not betraying Marshall. "This is your dispute, Wang," I told him, distancing myself. "And, to be honest, I don't even know what it's about in the first place." This was true in a sense. But it was a dangerous situation because I knew Wang would destroy anything to hurt Marshall and he would come after me if I angered him. We foreigners felt fragile, like sitting ducks, in China, especially against someone such as Wang, with his strong government contacts as support. If he managed to freeze Marshall's Chinese bank accounts—I reasoned with myself—he could crush a freelance photographer like me without any effort.

Marshall and his wife Joan were constantly harassed, and the late-night phone calls never stopped. They were worried that Wang might even pay someone to physically hurt them. But although he maintained his campaign against the Strabalas for a long time, for some reason he never made a move on me.

Things got even more vicious after Marshall removed all his hard drives and architectural models from his office. There must have been a property arrangement between them (the office was registered in Wang's name, but I don't know this for sure) because Wang chose this opportunity to sue Marshall for 'breaking in', claiming that he had the evidence was CCTV. He sent the footage to everyone he knew, including me. Marshall then fought back and hit a nerve: he sued all three of them on American soil, where the latter two had planned their futures and were about to open their own architectural businesses.

The battle dragged on for years. Wang was so adamant that nothing stopped him for the longest time. I heard about it all too often from Marshall and his wife, and it took two-and-a-half years for the situation to improve. And yet it wasn't until half a decade later that Wang eventually formally stood down; he realized he couldn't win and settled out of court, paying Marshall US $500,000 not to take the case to trial. Furthermore, Wang's lawyer insisted that he send out retraction emails to me and a few others, in which he admitted making "negative comments about Marshall Strabala", and which ended: "Please be advised that we withdraw those statements ants and regret involving you in our dispute."

Meanwhile, being in the middle of this storm I couldn't

help but reflect upon the past. I stopped and looked back for a moment. In a situation when everything was at stake, with serious risks involved, I had to wonder at how far I'd come, from just snapping photos of the Shanghai Tower site from the outside just a few years previously. Here I was, not only documenting the construction and winning the best architecture photo for 2012 in an international competition, but also friends with Marshall. I was amazed at how far photography had turned things around. But there was one particular turn on the horizon, a surprising outcome I'd never expected.

There's a motto on ENR's award ceremony poster written above my Three Brothers photo: "Behind every building is a person you should meet." I had begun with a simple plan to document the Shanghai Tower and ended up chronicling the struggle of the man behind it all. Most shocking to me was how things turned out in the end, and how Marshall ended up benefiting from my photos. In the beginning, I was convinced that I'd be the only one to get something out of it by requesting access. But during the legal battles, when his opponents tried to prove he wasn't even involved in the construction, my photographs and videos stood as indisputable evidence of his ongoing presence on the site. I watched in amazement as my photos popped up throughout his interviews on American morning shows and channels such as CNN. Countless architectural websites and magazines used my photos when referencing him. Suddenly, my work was on ENR, and I was on the cover of a Korean architecture magazine, *Space*, and my involvement with the *Financial Times* was in the pipeline, too. Most of the websites never bothered to credit me and there are dozens that still use my photos without my name. To this day, I find myself forever contacting sites, warning them to acknowledge the photographer.

The most memorable day of the whole five-year ordeal, the

one that perhaps summed up everything, occurred on August 13th, 2013—the day of the topping-out ceremony. Actually, it wasn't even a real topping-out ceremony, as the tower topped out a few months later. In truth, Shanghai Tower needed a pretext to celebrate the achievement, and chose reaching the height of 632 meters.

Nevertheless, the tower came alive that day—I'd never seen so much life around or in it before. Although the building was a multi-million-dollar project from the outset, life on the construction site itself on any average day was surprisingly humble, a very Chinese, minimalistic working environment. There were only the few hundred workers scattered around the building, the operational management and the closed group of a few dozen leaders, the chain-smoking clique of Chinese government executives who appeared for important meetings then cleared off as soon as they were over. The day of the topping-out ceremony was completely different. It was the typical example of China showing itself to the world; with all its bravado and peacock-like fanfare, with buckets of money thrown at it in an effort to impress.

The entire, all-day ceremony was built around a steel beam that was about to be lifted to the top and secured into place in front of the cameras. In the morning TV crews arrived. There was live coverage, and media outlets were given organized tours and access to the very top; press conferences were taking part on the premises and a helicopter circled around the building for hours on end. They even brought cannons on site to blast out barrages of colorful confetti the moment the beam was being lifted from the ground. I was next to those, you can even see me snapping photos in a white shirt on YouTube with the rest of the media as the cannons go off.

But for me it was nothing new. In fact, I found the celebrations much less appealing than my day-to-day access to the site. By then, I knew the building inside out. All the otherwise messy, and therefore photogenic, builders' clutter had been cleaned up for the public's benefit. There were no wires hanging from the *Alien*-like light fittings on the curtain-walls; there were no random construction materials lying around, even most of the rubble had been tidied up.

The zones in which we had worked previously were now completely sealed off; everything had been made sterile, anything unsightly had been covered up, and anything that might have been a health-and-safety risk had been removed. One-third of the glass windows were now in place, and the lower floors were no longer much of a spectacle for the photographer's eye. It was a scorching hot day and a tremendous amount of ice had been brought in to serve as makeshift air conditioning for a temporary conference room, in which the few hundred guests, mostly insiders, and the speakers, had gathered.

On this occasion, I wasn't there to take pictures as Marshall's personal photographer—I was on an assignment for London's venerable *Financial Times*, which had teamed me up with its designated writer; this is how I gained full access to the event. It was my first and last time on site without Marshall. I can't exactly recall how the paper approached me for the project, but it demonstrated how far my reputation had spread. It was certainly another step up the ladder, but I was in such a hurry during those years that I hardly acknowledged its significance in the hustle and bustle that constantly surrounded me.

"Nicky Almasy, *Financial Times*" is how I introduced myself at the press-register and, instead of marveling at its strangeness and how unlikely it must have sounded, my mind was preoccupied with Marshall, who was conspicuous by his absence. "Does he even know about this at all?" I wondered.

I texted him soon after I arrived at the ceremony: "Are you here somewhere? Where can I find you?" — it seemed the most obvious thing in the world that he was here somewhere. How could the chief architect of the Shanghai Tower not be invited?

"Nicky, what do you mean? Where?" came the answer.

As it turned out, Marshall hadn't even been invited by the organisers, because Gensler was on site and they didn't want the two men to clash that day. The first time Marshall heard of the ceremony was when I informed him about it that morning.

I shot the press conference and it was one of the most significant, eye-opening experiences of my life; just a perfect and a frightening showcase of how people can distort truth. It was glaringly obvious that there was one person missing from the table, Marshall Strabala, the chief architect of the Shanghai Tower.

A very upset Marshall Strabala arrived at the site later in the day, accompanied by his team. He tried to conceal it but I could see how pissed-off he was. After the event concluded, the two of us took a taxi and retired to a restaurant near his house. I'd known Marshall for three years now, and I'd never seen him so upset and, quite frankly, broken. "Those fuckers!" he hissed, staring into space with a troubled look on his face. He polished off a bottle of red wine quicker than I could finish a pint of beer.

Meanwhile, I introduced the *Financial Times* journalist, Lara (not her real name) to Marshall and she requested a full tour of the Tower site. The arrangements were painstaking, but eventually we set a date for the following month that worked for all of us. But when we arrived at the Tower on the designated morning, Lara foolishly handed out her *Financial Times* ID card to an official. The Chinese management — always suspicious of the foreign media — refused us entry and cancelled the visit on the spot. We were, however politely, thrown out for the day.

During the topping-out ceremony everything had been open for everyone. But that day was over. This wasn't a blatant rejection. Instead, it was handled in the usual Chinese way, all hush-hush; they sensed something was going on and informed us that, for some reason, the site was dangerous that day and ushered us out as quickly as they could. All because of one ID card.

We had to reschedule and returned at a later date. This time we made sure that Lara didn't attract undue attention. This time we got in. Marshall spent the day taking her around the site, from the basement to the top of the now 128-storey building. It was the proper architect tour treatment that took half a day, and it was appropriately rich in details for her article. Later, Marshall treated us to lunch where the interview continued.

A month later, when the piece appeared in the Financial Times — more precisely, in the FT Weekend section — it didn't even mention Marshall's name! He had been completely omitted from the story. Although the article was a milestone for me, and included a whole page of my photographs, properly credited in the Financial Times, it was a total disaster for Marshall. When I picked up a copy in a supermarket on Anfu Road that sold foreign newspapers, I was consumed by conflicting feelings. To be published in the *Financial Times* should have been a glorious moment for me, but instead it was mixed with bitterness and disgust about Marshall having been left out entirely. Lara apologised to me in an email, but I didn't have the heart to even reply. It was all too late.

To completely dismiss someone so central to your story, someone who'd been essential in you gaining access and had afforded you valuable time for such an important feature — especially a key person such as the project's architect — is rightfully considered a sin in magazine and newspaper circles. The decent thing would have been for Lara to have backed out of the feature altogether.

My meetings with Marshall continued during the two remaining years before the project's completion. Many things changed around us, both professionally and personally. Marshall became more balanced, especially after the most significant breakthrough: Gensler suddenly dropped the case against him. This reset everything. At last, the matter looked settled. But then Marshall did something I never expected: as soon as the case was closed, he immediately counter-sued Gensler for damaging his reputation, for defamation of character. It was a reasonable action, and he was right to do it. He had to respond to all the grief they had caused him over the years, and I admired his tenacity.

As life went on, there was a personal continuity to it all: meanwhile, through all the troubles we became close friends. Our wives got to know each other and we regularly got together for dinners. Sometimes it was strange to see how times had changed. Although we met through the tower and it always remained the core of our past, now there were get-togethers and entire dinners when the Shanghai Tower wasn't even mentioned. We were just friends who often called each other when we had some time to spare. We used to frequent Lotus Land, an Indian restaurant on Taikang Road, which became our favourite. Whenever we went there with our wives, Marshall and I secretly went ahead first and had a few drinks before they arrived. That place made a small fortune from us, as Marshall loved his red wine tremendously, sometimes having two or even three bottles, and I didn't spare the beer, either. Many good memories tie me to this place and whenever I'm in Shanghai, and if he's in town, we have dinner there.

Marshall kept his ad hoc, last-minute approach regarding our visits. One day I was sitting in my office right at the other end of the city in Hongqiao when my phone rang. "Nicky, there's a typhoon coming and I'm going up to the top of the building. Do you want to come?" Just a few minutes earlier I had been just marveling at how many things I had to do that day; a sea of emails to answer, meetings and errands to run. But I could never miss out on the tower. Especially not in a typhoon. So I took a deep breath, stood up from my desk, grabbed my camera and told my assistant that I'd be back by midday. As soon as I was out the door, leaving a busy day behind I hopped on my scooter and sped all the way to Marshall's apartment and from there we took a taxi to the site.

The morning the typhoon reached Shanghai, the top of the building was still open; ferocious winds assaulted its metal and concrete structure. As we stood there in the milky white fog on the 120th floor we could hardly keep our balance. We were blown around by the high winds and everything that wasn't nailed down flapped about or rolled around. The sound of the howling wind and the groaning of the steel girders made for one incredible noise. It was like being at sea in a raging storm, except in the middle of a city. We could feel the tremendous force challenging every last particle of the building as it blasted us with forces topping 100 kilometers per hour. Moments like this made me realize what it takes to design a building of such magnitude; how much risk is involved. When JFK asked Marshall about this in his early interview, The Master Builder, Marshall replied: "The biggest fear is you don't want to get it wrong, because no one wants a 130-storey mistake on their record."

By the beginning of 2014, windows had been fitted to cover almost half of the building, but shooting on the still-incomplete upper floors was still exciting. A day before Chinese New Year, we went on site on a cold but clear February day and once again headed straight to the top. By then the red cranes were reaching over Pudong to the building's full height, over 632 meters and

128 storeys. The Shanghai World Financial Centre with its mere 100 floors was dwarfed against this new twisting giant that reminded me of a steel and glass snake spiraling up toward the sky, changing colour and tones with the weather conditions. Marshall asked me to take a photo of him with the Jinmao Tower in the background. It was symbolic; he wanted to send it to Adrian Smith, his former boss and mentor at architecture firm SOM, proving that he'd beaten Smith's building, beating him by 30 floors.

That day Marshall wanted to inspect the TMD, the 'tuned mass damper' located around the 100th floor. This is a huge moving weight, like a giant pendulum, that serves to balance tall, especially super-tall buildings. It's a device that acts as a stabilizing force, and offsets any structural vibrations on the upper levels which, especially in the wind, can lead to feelings of discomfort and disorientation for anyone inside.

This is when and where I shot the photo of Marshall with his iPad in hand against the city's winter backdrop—the photo that's now exhibited in the Shanghai Tower gift shop. As we stood there I looked at the damp red metal arms of the cranes reaching over the city while the cold wind strafed the higher floors. It was typical Shanghai winter scene: bone-chillingly cold, wet and damp; a little foggy too, but still we caught a beautiful sunset overlooking Puxi.

Two days later, my phone was alive with messages: "Did you see? Did you see?" people asked. "Did I see what?" I soon learned that two Ukrainian guys had broken into the Shanghai Tower and had climbed out on to one of the cranes in the early hours; they posted a terrifying video on YouTube the next day. They broke in at night, cleverly using the reduced security due to the Chinese New Year, and had spent the small hours on site, waiting to catch a beautiful, freezing dawn on film. I'm not sure if they had already been hiding in the building when we were there, but it was pretty close to our visit—especially that evening, when Marshall and I became stuck on one of the upper floors due to a problem with the workers' elevator.

Such climbs are reckless and stupid and should never be encouraged, but I had to grudgingly respect these guys. Actually I thought it was an amazing act, and their footage looked not only beautifully dangerous but stunning as well. Not surprisingly, they got millions of views and, during those few days, even my tower video increased by thousands of views because all of a sudden, everyone was interested in the Shanghai Tower.

Unbeknownst to the Ukrainians, they brought something to the Shanghai Tower that the Chinese government never managed to: momentum. As it slowly drifted towards its already-late completion in 2015, I wasn't the only one who felt that despite being the second tallest building on the planet, it somehow didn't get the exposure it deserved. People marveled at it throughout 2013 and 2014, as it so strikingly appeared and became the prominent feature of the Pudong skyline but, by 2015, the endless administrative works just dragged along for so long that most people lost interest.

There were so many promises of openings which were later cancelled that no outsider knew what was going on any more. Being part of the project from very early on, I always gave it special attention. I can safely say that there were only two occasions when the Tower was in real, proper focus: on the day of the topping out ceremony and when the Ukrainians broke in. Full stop. Which is rather disappointing when it comes to a project costing 14.8 billion yuan (US $2.4 billion). By the time it had become a new permanent feature on the skyline any public excitement about it had waned into complacency.

Things turned even more sour when tragedy struck. On

New Year's Eve, 2014, I was filming from the top of my favorite vantage point on the Tower, from Indigo Hotel's Char Bar on the 29th floor. I had used the bar for years, as I considered it was one of the best positions in Shanghai from which to take photographs. It looked straight out over the river, framing the buildings that lined up on the horizon in a perfect geometric angle. This was from where I shot most of my photos and videos—even my award-winning photo of the 'Three Brothers' back in 2012.

On New Year's Eve, I got up there relatively early, around 8pm. The mercilessly cold December wind was blowing very strongly, and I remember it was even hard to pin down my tripod. My ears hurt from the powerful gusts continuously pulling through the open space.

Below me, on the Bund, enormous crowds had gathered to celebrate and the spectacle laid on for the evening involved brand new light installations on the Shanghai Tower. Thousands of people turned up to witness it. I looked down in amazement from the top of Indigo Hotel. The lights began flickering on the exterior of the building from the early evening, as they began testing the set-up for midnight. I couldn't help it; the colorful little shocks reminded me of Frankenstein's monster; so much trouble, grief and lies had adhered to this building over the years, and tonight it finally came alive as thousands of pairs of eyes were fixed on it.

At exactly midnight, as soon as the light show started, a stampede broke out in the gathered crowds. No one knew exactly what triggered it, but 50 people died instantly—it was the biggest disaster ever to befall the Bund. A rumor suggested that someone had thrown fake 100RMB notes out of the M18 nightclub, which was located at the corner of Zhongshan and Nanjing roads, on one of the upper floors. It was reported that the crowd started to move suddenly as people struggled to catch the notes as they fluttered in the air, and people nearest one of the major staircases lost their balance and stumbled to the ground, as hundreds of people could do nothing but trample on top of them in order to save themselves. There's a terrifying video on YouTube where you can see the panic and helplessness of those stuck in the middle. The result was devastating; according to witnesses there were girls whose mangled bodies were completely crushed, forming the shape of the stairs.

Over the next few months, silence and darkness fell upon the Bund. The lights on the Shanghai Tower, and all the landmark buildings on the Pudong side of the river, were dimmed. The official reaction was typical, something I had reluctantly become used to whenever something like this happened in China. Authorities, feeling guilty about their own shortcomings regarding the lack of security, went silent about it and swept the whole story under the carpet. Apart from the newspapers the very next day, no one mentioned the tragedy again; it was erased, just like everything else unpleasant. Even the exact number of victims was covered up — it could have been well over fifty. And the temporary vigil set up by the families was soon removed too. It was almost banned to talk about it, which just further deepened the magnitude and the tragedy of the disaster.

We never really had a chance to talk about the deadly stampede, but one thing I know for sure was that Marshall hated the new lights on the tower. "You know when someone arrives at an event in flashy, colorful clothes when it obviously requires an elegant suit?" is how he answered me when I quizzed him about it one day.

Prior to this, I had been present to film the meeting when Shanghai Tower officials asked him to come in and discuss the exterior light installations. The heads of operations gathered together again, chain-smoking in a dim neon-lit temporary meeting room in the basement. The long table in the centre was decorated with yellow safety helmets arranged in a line with a plate of fruit in the middle. I remember thinking: how can they be making decisions on a skyscraper's aesthetics when they can't even decorate a table properly? No one does tacky quite as masterfully as mainland China.

I know it's a strange thing to say, but personally I always found the Shanghai Tower more exciting while it was under construction. This surely came from my photographer's perspective. While it was being built, everything about it was extremely photogenic—the giant sparks from the welding cascading over its metal skeleton at night, the glass coat that spread around it and covered it in a giant puzzle-like embrace. I found such sights endlessly inspiring. To see the tower rise, growing from week to week, month to month, electrified my days throughout the first half of the 2010s. I was almost in love with the building. I remember my wife joking one day when we walked past it: "You look at it like you've bloody built it!"

I think my obsession with the tower was rooted in the love I felt for my profession, and in finally finding the ideal subject. On top of that came the access I was granted. This made it exclusive and intimate, all in one: something so alive, so magnificent, so shifting, so problematic and so tragic, with one man's story behind it all. It was everything I'd hoped for in terms of a subject for my photography, and I admit freely that it all became very personal to me over the years.

It was beautiful to see it all coming together, and to see how the tower rose to its full height. But at the same time, as the project edged towards completion it became less and less challenging. The outer skin's glass coat soon covered the upper floors and where once the wind swept through, and the once-dizzying heights that set the photogenic backdrop for the messy construction, now turned into organized observation decks, closed floors with identical offices occupying the space.

The construction reached its completion at the end of 2015, but the official opening was still further delayed.

The year that Gensler unexpectedly dropped their court case against Marshall marked the end of an era, and finally brought his professional struggles to a satisfactory conclusion. All of a sudden, a heavy weight was lifted from his shoulders. Things were finally looking good for Marshall. Straight away, he opened his new, fully-owned architectural firm Strabala Plus—and his office now occupies almost the entire 34th floor in the Shanghai Tower. The view from it is spectacular, overlooking Pudong and the vast open space between the double glass skins. Apart from the stunning architectural models of the tower itself, the Burj Khalifa among many others, and the space's clean stylish decor, one of the things I love about the office is Marshall's tiny resting cabin. It's a cosy little space hidden by the window, not more than two meters wide, that's out of everyone's sight. It's basically just a comfortable armchair and a small desk. It's a place where he can rest take a nap or just gaze out over the city. And the last time I saw it, there was only one book in there: *Hudec* by Nicky Almasy.

After the battles we'd been through together and our friendship that had developed over the years, Marshall said that whenever I was in town I could work from his office, and that I could come and go as I please. It's an amazing feeling to be there. All these years, it was so natural for me to stick by Marshall. I never questioned his integrity and he has repaid me with his generosity ever since, in any way he can, wherever he can. Not to mention that he never lets me pay for dinners or drinks that often cost hundreds of dollars a time, or that he also lends me his apartment. Or that when he flew me in from Kuala Lumpur in early 2018 to shoot the completion and we had to cancel for technical reasons, he still paid my US $3500 fee in full.

Every time I visit Shanghai, the first thing I do is head straight to the Shanghai Tower, and Marshall and I often go down to the basement to have lunch together. Last time, we visited the gift shop on the ground floor. My photos can be seen in different forms, on notebooks and postcards. But not yet in book form.

The book we planned the first time we met in the restaurant is still in the pipeline. In 2015, Marshall handed me 80GB of Shanghai Tower material that he said I could use alongside my photos. It was a sensational hoard. The files included original drawings, design sketches, floor plans, all details of the tower, videos on earthquake shake-table tests—just a goldmine. However, for years the process of actually producing the book was paralyzed by various publishers' fears that Gensler might sue them. Publishing our work turned out to be a very tricky and troublesome business indeed. While Marshall gave me full access to the construction site and the photos belonged to me, it was still, rightfully, Gensler's building. So no matter how many publishers were keen on it, their first question was, "But is this OK with Gensler?" I often asked myself the same question. However, there was no way of knowing. Finally, to put an end to the ongoing doubts and unanswerable questions, and to stave off yet more rejections from publishers, I went to Gensler's office in Shanghai.

Straightforwardly, I explained the story and asked them what to do, who to approach. Surprisingly, no one was able to answer my question. No one even knew the whole story. The penny dropped there and then: only the US office, and Arthur Gensler himself, were familiar with Marshall's involvement and, as the entire dispute had taken place back in 2010, it was barely remembered in Shanghai.

We came close to publishing the book a few times. The prestigious, architecture-focused Images Publishing was one of the most serious companies that approached us. Their consulting partner, Paul Latham, was extremely keen on putting it out, and we met him on several occasions when he flew in to see us in Shanghai. Marshall came to the meetings, and very generously said that since they were my photos so he didn't want a penny from the profits. He also offered to buy 1,000 copies in advance. However, Latham presented me with a very unfavorable offer; I would only start to make money on it once it had sold its 5,000th copy. I wanted to agree to the deal, as I'm always convinced that major publications will reap a benefit down the line, but my manager at the time, a German lady, said we should keep on searching. After her involvement was over, I returned to Images Publishing and said, "Let's do it." But then, they too came back with the worry about Gensler. A dead end again. I had a few months' back-and-forth with one of their consultants, Joe Boschetti, who worked under Paul Latham, but this turned out to be another waste of time. After months and months of email exchanges, he wrote to inform me:

> "Unfortunately, without Gensler's involvement, we
> would be hesitant to proceed. We would need Gensler
> to provide an endorsement for the book, possibly
> plans and drawings, and to confirm details such as
> specifications and historical information."

I sensed a glimmer of hope when he added, "But, Nicky, we do really want to publish the book. I have written to another person in Gensler and will phone their office in the morning."

Boschetti tried to contact them again several times, but in the end he had to admit that all his efforts had run into a further dead end.

At the same time, somehow deep down I knew that the completion of the Shanghai Tower would coincide with me leaving Shanghai after a decade. There was something in the air, a sense of continuity to it all. I still find this odd, because there was no direct connection between the two; the tower had nothing to do with my decision to leave the city at all. But perhaps it had marked the time, the end of an era when the excitement had ran out for me. Suddenly, Shanghai was like a book with no pages left for me to read.

After ten years of living there, my wife and I eventually left Shanghai in early 2016 and moved to Bangkok. I turned my back on the tower thoroughly and with purpose, like a chapter ending, as I looked forward to the next one. I archived all the files on hard disks and never looked at them again. Of course, we stayed in touch with Marshall; at least that much wasn't affected.

As you let go, echoes from before have a habit of coming back to you, and with the Shanghai Tower this happened in a totally unexpected way. Just as I thought that all my architectural photography work had been to no avail, two things happened. First, I won the best architectural photograph of the year for the second time in an international competition. This time it was at the World Architectural Festival's Arcade Awards, in the exterior category. On one of my last visits to the tower's now-completed site, I looked up and snapped a photo of the top floors disappearing into the descending mist. The contrast between the sharp glass edges of the outer skin and the thick, milk-white haze worked so well that it caught the eyes of the judges, and my photo was chosen as the winner. As a result, the image was exhibited in London. I saw that as a small victory crowning my years in Shanghai, but nothing prepared me for the second one.

The same year, I was asked by the General Consulate of

Hungary in Shanghai to shoot all of László Hudec's buildings in the city. This Hungarian architect was a legend of his time, and an international architectural icon for the future, with his Art Deco aesthetic, and the numerous examples of his expressionist architecture defined Shanghai during the 1930s, and has continued to do so ever since. That invite led to my publishing my first official book, *Hudec*.

I'd always had a good relationship with the consulate. We did smaller projects together; they always asked me to shoot the national holiday celebrations, for instance, and it made sense that we should document Hudec's legacy together. They flew me back into Shanghai for the project twice. It was refreshing and also quite odd to return to the city after I'd moved away. The consulate provided everything except the accommodation.

As my wife and I had given up our apartment, I didn't have a place to stay, so for a few days I crashed with a friend. But such a big project required a certain level of concentration, and I found that working from someone else's place, tip-toeing around with all my bulky camera equipment in the mornings and again late at night, just didn't work. I knew I needed another solution. I was considering booking a hotel room but I didn't want to spend that much money as the shoots were due to take several weeks. As it turned out, Marshall was in town and, as usual, we met for a drink and dinner at Lotus Land. He told me he had to fly to Chicago the next morning for a month, so I took my chance and asked him if I could stay at his place while I shot the Hudec project. He happily said yes and handed me the keys the next morning.

To have a three-bedroom apartment overlooking Shanghai from the 30th floor all to myself was the cherry on the cake, and it provided me with a superb base from which to begin my new, incredible project. I also found it rather symbolic. Evidently, my days were dipped deep in architecture. Waking up every morning surrounded by Marshall's architectural models and framed renderings on the walls was inspiring — a great kickstart to go out and shoot historical buildings all day. Hilariously, for some reason Marshall was storing models of the Burj Khalifa and the Shanghai Tower in one of his unused showers, and I couldn't help but snap photos of this surreal installation. It was autumn, slightly cold outside — something that was missing from my new life in Bangkok — and I enjoyed every moment of it, especially the consulate car picking me up every morning and bringing me back. Late at night to go over the files.

The book was released the following year and became a real success; both the Chinese and the foreign media loved it and, perhaps unsurprisingly, it was also a hit back in Hungary. My photography had always been published in magazines, and so to see my name on the cover of a book cemented the achievement for me; it was a real milestone. In a way, it was compensation for the Shanghai Tower project that never happened but, for me, this came with even more value. The fact that as a Hungarian, my first book was about one of Hungary's most celebrated artists added to its significance, and it felt as if my career had come full circle.

The Hudec book made me relaxed over the publication difficulties regarding the Shanghai Tower. It was followed by the publication of my second architectural book, *Gonda*, and I was delighted when my photos got the biggest recognition I could possibly hope for — they were printed on one of Hungary's national stamps.

These achievements put my life into perspective and helped me understand how one event can lead beautifully into another, as long as you can exercise patience. In terms of photography, my book publications felt as I'd finally driven off the unmade, bumpy road to success, and now the terrain began to smooth out beneath me. Your first book release should never be underestimated, if that doesn't sound too glib. Naturally, it changed my life.

I visit my former home Shanghai once in a while, and on every occasion it's always a little like time travel. The Shanghai Tower became a super-tall monument of an incredible ride. Every time I gaze up at it, an avalanche of emotions cascades down its shimmery surface, floor by floor, and the memories flood back. I simply can't detach this gargantuan structure from the five years I spent inside it as it began to take shape, and I am unable to take it for what it is, just a skyscraper. I see the different stages, the excitement, the betrayals, the struggles and also the immense inspiration that fuelled me for years. It makes me proud that I was part of it, and that I could contribute to its exposure even in a visual, minor, anonymous way.

But what remains undimmed within me, which I'll never forget and what really matters, are those wonderful dinners for the four of us, Marshall, me and our wives, sitting at Lotus Land — those great evenings, all the conversation and the laughter under its warm, orangey homely hues.

Vampires over Cambodia

In a downtown Bangkok pub, beneath one of the exits of the skytrain's Phrom Phong station, I was waiting for someone. I had a pint in front of me. From the inside, the Robin Hood looked like any other pub; I might as well have been sitting in Soho, London. The clientele was mostly British guys sitting around talking, some of them immersed in their sports pages, others fixated on the football match filling the screen in flickering green hues. Some were just staring out into the traffic rolling by outside, contemplating where they were in life and wondering how, of all places, they ended up in this exotic, wild and scorching hot city of sin, Bangkok. I love observing the British in pubs, especially ones located in major Asian cities. A little piece of Albion torn out of context thousands of miles away from home and yet, pretty much the same goes on inside, wherever in the world you are. Here, talking business, opportunities, life in Asia; some with tiny Thai girls' arms folded around them signifying that they're already settled here. It was an average night in the Robin Hood. There was no sign of tension in the air; we're still a few months away from Brexit and the resignation of David Cameron. The Thai King, Bhumibol Adulyadej, was still alive, and Donald Trump isn't yet the President of the United States. It was May 2016.

Tom came in. He was a handsome guy whose slightly sunken eyes looked around the room with an irresistible smile he can never wipe off and, as if he knew me already, he made his way towards my table, sitting down opposite. I was still a newbie to Bangkok. I'd only been here a few months, so my former editor and friend Ned Kelly from Shanghai hooked us up with the usual "you guys should definitely meet" recommendation. And, for whatever reason people say that, I gladly succumbed, unaware that the encounter would provide a gateway to my first break in Bangkok.

Tom is from Oxford and works as a doctor, or more precisely as a scientist, for MORU, the Mahidol Oxford University Research Unit, a patient-centered organization that focuses on research and treatment of tropical diseases In Africa and Southeast Asia, predominantly in Cambodia and Thailand. Tom radiated kindness and intelligence from the first moment I saw him. It soon became apparent he was extremely well-read and this instantly formed a bromance bond between us. Soon enough, we were bar-hopping, sinking deeper into the neon-lit night around the downtown districts of Nana and Asoke, and riding high on beer-buzzed conversations about our favorite English writers such as George Orwell, Martin Amis and Christopher Hitchens.

Our conversation eventually drifted back to our professions. Tom told me that with MORU he did a lot of field work on malaria research with the locals in rural Cambodia, and I told him that was a photographer and videographer—and that I was looking for freelance work in Bangkok.

"Look," Tom said, out of the blue. "Actually, we need someone like you in Cambodia. We're filming the progress of our field work with these shitty little cameras, and we're struggling to edit the material together. Besides that, no one has time for it. Why don't you come with us and document our work professionally? We could pay you, and it would be a great experience for you as well."

And before I knew it, the deal was sealed. It was the most British way of getting a job in Asia: just walk into a pub and change your life over a pint.

People often throw offers around after a few drinks and, in my experience, few of these ever materialize into genuine work, but Tom was in touch the very next day, already suggesting dates for the assignment. He said he'd discussed it with MORU and everyone had agreed—they were all happy for me to come on board. Events unfolded rapidly and within days I was invited to the MORU headquarters in the Tropical Disease Hospital near Victory Monument in Bangkok. I met the team and within a week or two, arrangements had been made for my journey to western Cambodia. It was as simple as that; a car picked me up from my house and, along with a Malaysian doctor, we were on our way to MORU's base camp, on the other side of the border.

If you follow Bangkok's gigantic avenue, the Sukhumvit, northwards, it runs straight into Cambodia's Pailin Province. The border itself is about a four-hour drive from downtown Bangkok. When we arrived, Tom was waiting for us at the crossing and I watched him with awe as he, flashing his ever disarming smile at one of the guards, casually walked across the border between Thailand and Cambodia without even having his passport on him. Completely at ease with the local conditions, he helped us with our papers and visas and soon, we were ready to move on. But not before one of the immigration guards scolded him, albeit with no real weight in his voice, for acting with such nonchalance: "We know you guys, you're doctors working in the province. But please don't do this. It's a border, after all! You can't just cross like this."

Tom just smiled, and nodded politely as we made our way to the small convoy parked nearby.

Once you leave Thailand, the scene and the conditions drastically change as you drive through Pailin and then Battambang provinces; the highways are replaced by dusty country roads, the lanes get obscured by the sand sweeping over them, and as you progress they get bumpier and bumpier. And that's if they're dry; during the rainy season, accessibility gets washed away altogether, leaving mud that makes the region of remote villages practically impenetrable. Our Jeep was in a convoy and we headed straight into the rural areas, driving for another three hours before reaching a tiny village called Vealroleum, our base for the weeks to come.

MORU has had a presence in the area for nearly a decade. They conduct malaria research and treatment in twenty villages within a hundred kilometer radius. Their operation is centered around Pailin Hospital near the Thai border, which facilitates most of the serious malaria cases. The organization focuses its efforts on controlling the spread or emergence of multi-drug-resistant *P. falciparum* malaria, gradually working towards its total elimination. Within the summer months of 2016, MORU launched a new project, the one I was there to document, establishing a village malaria worker program in the area to provide early, free diagnosis, and also to offer treatment to the locals if the disease is diagnosed. In western Cambodia, malaria infections occur mostly in rural areas among people working in the forests, which prompted MORU to set up its research centre as close as possible to where the infections take place: right in the heart of the rural hinterlands.

MORU chose a very effective way to raise awareness about malaria among the locals, where education and infrastructure is in otherwise poor shape. As traditional Cambodian drama is popular with rural communities and attracts large audiences, the workers established a small festival, which traveled from village to village to educate locals about malaria, to shed light on the severity of its threat, to appeal to people who might otherwise never receive any kind of health education. Working together with the local Battambang health authorities, MORU organized a series of drama and music workshops and performances in twenty villages, in order to mobilize communities in the fight to eliminate malaria. All efforts concentrated on the cause—a parasite transferred to the human body from infected mosquitos. MORU also hired community leaders to help locals prepare for the dramatic performances with extensive rehearsals, while other local artists were hired to write songs that could be sung at the performances. The project was called Drama Against Malaria.

In part, my job was to document MORU's operation in the area with photographs and videos, collecting material for a few weeks, following them around as they set up temporary camps, taking blood samples from the villagers and sending them away for analysis. The task was to shoot images and video footage that told the story of how the organization interacts with people and patients and also to cover some of the operations in the malaria hospital at the MORU centre in Pailin. I was also required to film and photograph the festival performances as they progressed, moving from village to village. As well as amassing a photo collection of MORU's endeavors, I was required to edit a six or seven-minute video that summarized the operation.

Although, ultimately, I was heading into a highly dangerous malaria zone, I knew I was in good hands with the handful of doctors around me 24/7, armed as they were with an arsenal of medicines, prepared for anything from injuries through to stomach problems all the way to snake bites. It would be a lie if I said I was never worried, but there was an air of safety that surrounded the MORU team, which perhaps stemmed from the knowledge that they were good people doing good deeds. Their business was health, so it provided me with a constant sense of security. But it was far from bulletproof, in terms of all the potential dangers that rural Cambodia offered.

First of all, there was malaria itself. We were right at the epicenter of a high-incidence region in which infections broke out on a daily basis, deep in the forested areas. But I was lucky in that regard; perhaps because of my blood type, mosquitos don't bite me, but I couldn't rely on such biological good fortune entirely. Although we were sleeping under mosquito nets — our daily work, from early morning to sundown, was out in the fields, so we could never be careful enough.

Then there were the venomous snakes, which seemed to be all around us. Being European and never really encountering one of these huge reptiles before, it was easy to slip into a state of blissful ignorance, and therefore carelessness. Until you see one, that is. On the second day after we arrived, the locals found a large poisonous cobra slithering through the backyard of the house, right next to us. We heard a commotion, sudden shouts coming from outside. As we ran into the street, three youngsters were brandishing the meter-and-a-half reptile with excitement; its head already bashed in, glistening in a misshapen mess of blood, but the black menacing eyes staring emptily and its black tongue still sticking out — sobering reminders that indeed the danger was real and all about. The kids were used to cobras, however, and had a laugh with the unfortunate animal, throwing it around before eventually cooking it for dinner. It was the first time I had ever witnessed anything like this, and observing the snake close up, with its alien, dragonesque features on the one hand, and yet the beautiful patterns of its scaly skin on the other, I found the scenario unexpectedly difficult to take in that evening. The toilet, basically a wooden shack over a hole in the ground, was located fifteen meters from our house, so venturing out in the middle of the night to do your business always filled me with trepidation — first you had to unpack yourself from the mosquito net, then navigate through the darkened house, before taking the risky journey outside and back again.

Some things caught me off-guard. For example, when I encountered my first scorpion, a white one, inches away from my finger while moving some boxes from one of the rooms to assist the team, my entire sense of security evaporated at once. And when, the next day, another scorpion bit one of our colleagues, and I watched his arm swell up like a balloon, I added another clear and present danger to the list. I realized that a scorpion bite could happen anywhere—being much smaller than most snakes, they can creep into shoes or bedding without you realizing it. My second scorpion appeared in the kitchen on one of the wooden pillars while I was waiting for lunch. Our chef-on-duty treated it with no particular interest while cooking. He approached it and with one quick movement casually and expertly, without saying anything, he simply cut off its tail, separating it from its torso, leaving it to fall to the ground.

And then there were the landmines. There are up to six million landmines—still active—buried in the ground in Cambodia, and most of them are in Battambang province. They are a legacy of three decades of civil war and were laid by, among others, the Khmer Rouge under their leader Pol Pot, who ruled Cambodia with terrible ruthlessness from 1975 to 1979. The mines have taken a severe toll on Cambodians; the country has some 40,000 amputees, the most in the world. Whichever village we were working in, we regularly encountered children, adults, even pets with missing limbs or eyes. It was very common, and we had to be extremely vigilant and always tread carefully as the roads were laced with them. There was no wandering around in the fields; we could only walk on designated paths or the oft-travelled roads. This could make my photo shoots difficult, as I like to find unusual angles for my shots. The team regularly warned me, in what became a running joke: "Nicky, please stay on the paths.

Don't be the second famous Hungarian photographer who dies from a landmine, *please!*" They were referring to Robert Capa, the celebrated Hungarian war photographer who died in 1954 after stepping on a landmine in Vietnam when he left his Jeep to take a picture.

I used a drone for aerial photography for the first time in Cambodia. We appropriately named it 'The Mosquito' and I had to be careful with that as well. If, for example, it accidentally landed in a field, *any field,* off the road or a beaten path—even if I saw where it went—it would be impossible to retrieve. The omnipresent signs warning of landmines, with their skull-and-crossbones on a red background, dotted the roads wherever we went. I learned quickly that in Southeast Asia there was no walking through fields, or out in nature at all, due to the threat of snakes, and the landmines only added to the peril. For years, even when back in Europe, I wouldn't walk across a field or any green area, even a lawn, out of my instinct for self-preservation.

Driving deep into the rural areas, we came across a building with a sign hanging over its facade that surprised me—'Pitt & Jolie Foundation'. The small building belonged to Brad Pitt and Angeline Jolie, when they were 'into' Cambodia's problems; they even adopted a child from here before they seemed to lose interest in the region altogether. The small building, now half-abandoned, was a fitting testimony to the fleeting interest in genuine world problems from Hollywood stars—often for publicity alone, I suspect—and how such A-list elites would eventually turn their backs on remote places like Battambang. There was a guard in front of the building who, for a decent bribe, took me inside. But his position was nominal, as the house's sponsors hadn't been seen around for years now.

We were sleeping under mosquito nets but that didn't stop various bugs and insects from crawling under them overnight, and I often wondered how or where they'd entered my limited and fragile safety zone, and what actually prevented a scorpion from entering, too. In the mornings I literally swept out the bugs from underneath me. They came in all assortments; and when I pushed them off the sheet I'd hear their hard chitin shells hit the wooden floor as they fell from the bed by the dozens.

Daytime, and the continual tropical heat took its brutal toll. The constant exhaustion was something that, ultimately, I just had to learn to ignore. We were without air conditioning for weeks; this had been something I had expected at the beginning of the trip, as I imagined that the sweltering alternative would drive me crazy. But I soon learned that the quicker I dispensed with the desire for comfort, the easier the days became. Our electricity was supplied by a generator that was regularly switched off, resulting in problematic charging of my photographic equipment. There was only one spot where internet access was available in the area, and even then the signal was very weak. This was from the top of a hill, and because it was only approachable by car or motorbike, few bothered to access it—maybe once a week or in an emergency. On the few occasions that we drove up there, I remember the strange scene in which we all sat in silence on the roadside next to our vehicles, catching up with relatives, answering emails or browsing through the news we'd missed during the previous week.

The conditions at the house in which we were staying had a charming simplicity about them. We'd been invited into a family home, and our hosts accommodated us and cooked for us when we weren't out on field work, treating us with respect and with a degree of curious interest. One colleague, a thin, extremely tall blond Dutchman, looked a little like a giraffe and whenever he walked among the locals he became a focus of amusement, especially among the children, who treated him rather like a circus animal. They'd poke his long legs, before running away laughing. One of the doctors found herself sharing the partition wall next to her bed with a cow on the other side, and its mooing echoed through her dreams loudly through the night. In all, our stay was mostly pleasant and filled with homely coziness—but that's not to say there weren't small annoyances to be endured in such isolated village life.

The most unexpected and utterly ridiculous issue, one that I could never have imagined might cause me problems, was the roosters. We were staying in the heart of the village and usually went to bed late, after midnight. There were ten of us sleeping in one room, while the rest made do with hammocks on the balcony. It was hard enough to get to sleep anyway, thanks to the inevitable snoring that resonated out of so many slumbering mouths, but these unexpected nuisances trumped that. These little, seemingly insignificant, curses of village life peppered our early morning consciousness in the most unforgettable matter. When the roosters awoke, you could forget about sleeping. They started their cockcrow as early as 4 a.m., and they didn't stop until 7 a.m. or 8 a.m. With nothing else to do in my enforced insomnia, I listened to them carefully and figured out that they were messaging each other between the neighboring villages. The first one was usually ours. He did his part which stirred one in the next village. That one answered, and woke up another in an even more distant village. It was the ultimate chain reaction nightmare to lose sleep over. Within minutes seemingly the whole countryside was crowing the dawn. I vividly recall being utterly frustrated when I heard the first one, twisting and turning, knowing that any chance of getting back to sleep was impossible. As one of the team members cried out bitterly from beneath his pillow at a rooster one morning: "Jesus Christ! What have you got to say that you didn't say yesterday? What's so bloody important?" It seemed such a ridiculous way to lose precious sleep and waste energy. Indeed, motorbikes and cockerels—welcome to the sounds of Southeast Asia.

Our team needed its rest; we needed to conserve as much energy as we could muster. We set out each morning early and would spend the day in the scorching heat until long after nightfall. Before noon, we attended rehearsals to watch and document as the children and adults prepared to perform for their evening festival shows. I shot a lot of material each day: interviews, B-rolls of supplementary material, drone footage, then more interviews with drama instructors and community leaders. Sometimes we packed up and drove to another camp where MORU, with the aid of local doctors, were taking blood samples from the villagers. And then we drove back again to where the dramas were due to take place. The stages would be set up in the late afternoon, which I shot as a time-lapse sequence, followed by a short rest before the performances began, usually around 8 p.m.

The shows were a combination of small performances strung together; some brought traditional Khmer songs to sing, some brought renditions of Cambodian hits, some prepared short sketches, but all were related and tied back to the main topic: malaria. Some of the performances were adorably clumsy, but that made it all so charming and irresistible to watch. There were real surprises; kids in mosquito costumes danced, sang and performed amusing skits. There was a recurring story staged in every village, performed by half-a-dozen kids, about two farmers working in the fields, one of whom got drunk and forgot to put up his mosquito net when he went to sleep. At night, three mosquitoes—or kids dressed as mosquitos—whizzed by. They stopped at the first farmer, tried to poke through the net but couldn't get in, then they "flew" over the one who was too drunk to care and they bit him. The play ended with him waking up, shivering from fever and when they called a doctor—played by another child actor—he diagnosed malaria. While they read out the important reasons to protect themselves from the disease, his "wife" scolded him. The children were very much in touch with their newly-discovered thespian sides; the skit offered laugh-out-loud moments while being, of course, deadly serious at the same time.

The small plays were as entertaining as they were educational and some of the kids demonstrated a stunning ability to act. I vividly recall one of the boys, aged around ten, who had an outstanding and irresistible stage presence. Off stage, during the day when he was around, he was a cute, regular-looking peasant boy who worked in the fields and walked around in bare feet, but when he was in the limelight you couldn't take your eyes off him. He shone like a star. He was one of those talents that would have had a bright acting career if given the chance in a theatre somewhere else on a proper stage. All the performances carried a slightly childish naivety but there were some innocently naughty scenes too. One was played by adults, where two sexy mosquito ladies were seducing a local man who, again, drunk from the rice wine, forgot to put up his mosquito net. When he fell under their spell, he caught malaria. The audiences were responsive, they laughed, singing along to the songs they knew or craning their necks to see the plays as they unfolded on stage. They enjoyed it very much and it seemed like something that lifted them out of their everyday routine, something that made them forget Cambodia's heart-wrenching recent history.

It was impossible not to recall the events that had led to our presence in this country in the first place—just a few decades before Cambodia had been ripped apart by a civil war that saw scenes of unspeakable terror, torture and genocide. This was a country where anyone unfortunate enough to wear glasses was killed on sight because they were considered 'more clever' than everyone else—a grisly anti-intellectual tactic inherited from earlier Communist and repressive regimes to stamp out dissent and political discourse. The ethnic cleansing by the Khmer Rouge took horrendous turns, leaving mass graves and a deadly underlay of land mines all around the region.

Working in Cambodia for just a few weeks, I noticed an underlying fear in everyone. The legacy of the years of terror was grimly apparent in people's lack of self-confidence—which had been brutally hammered into the ground. The atrocities had left deep scars in the village folk who were still petrified of uniforms and outward displays of authority. The fear was especially noticeable in men's eyes; they seemed to lack that certain spark of defiance, that determined, invincible will to protect their family from danger. I saw this natural element lacking, shattered to pieces and replaced by doubt and despair. And this meant that, as a foreigner in this country, if you happened to be away from the safety in numbers provided by your team, and ran into a menacing figure of authority, you were alone. No one was prepared to step in to help you.

I attended a village wedding with a local associate and, during the day, we were unlucky enough to encounter a policeman who was disgustingly drunk. He was obviously an angry man, too, and in his intoxicated rage lauded his state-sanctioned power over the terrified locals, who sheepishly, and wisely, gave him a wide berth, although this served only to clear a path for him that led directly to us. No one dared raise their eyes from the ground or, God forbid, raise their voice to him as he charged at us, with his machine gun slung around his neck, obviously intent on picking a fight. He had sunglasses on so that you couldn't see his eyes, and he reeked of the stale smell of local rice wine, and of that elementary evil that oozes from the authority figures of a rotten regime. He was simply uncontrollable, remonstrating loudly for no apparent reason, and only my associate's local language skills and experience of how to handle such individuals saved us from getting into some serious trouble.

Some military men didn't need a drink to be rude; it came naturally to them. At one point, all the white guys and women of our team were photographed in the most crude manner; a uniformed man in deep dark shades walked around them taking pictures of them from all angles, as if they'd just arrived from outer space. It was an obvious power game from the local authorities and we laughed it off, but it was evidence that the remnants of the ruthless Khmer Rouge were still present, bubbling under the surface. Sometimes, though, we came across one or two soldiers who were friendly and, after watching over the site as the villages performed their drama, they were happy to sit and share a drink with us. I recall one moment when I was having a beer with two soldiers and as I glanced down at the wooden table in front of us, I witnessed the eerie contrast of my camera with its long telephoto lens lying next to a machine gun.

The Drama Against Malaria shows were a breath of fresh air for me; it was rejuvenating being isolated from the modern world for a while. Compared to the developed West in which everything ends up on social media as soon as it happens, here nobody clung to a mobile phone, no one even took pictures on one, no one posted where they were or what they were doing; they were just living the moment, enjoying themselves by taking part in the activities. I could see the simple, unspoiled joy in their faces as they experienced what a drama festival really was for the first time. Some were entirely engaged, losing themselves in the plays, while some were simply just staring into the colored lights flickering over the crowd and on the stage. It was not something they were used to.

There were some unexpected troubles, however. The stage reflectors and the surrounding lights attracted all manner of flying insects from the nearby forests. On the first night, after the sun had set, we found ourselves in the middle of an insect storm, literally swallowing and spitting bugs. There were thousands of them swirling around in swarming whirlpools. It was very dramatic; on stage the performers had trouble singing as the insects flew into their open mouths, nearly bringing the event to a standstill. Only the children and I seemed to enjoy the invasion; the kids were jumping around to catch them before stamping on them; while for me it meant a visual treat, a fitting addition to the footage portraying the extremes of rural Cambodia.

Not every night was spoiled by insects, and the performances marched on with enormous excitement. But there was one other killjoy—worse than the insects—and this was the presence of local politicians. Some, using the events for their own aggrandizement, launched into lengthy, mind-numbing speeches one after the other and, worse still, their endless torrents of word-diarrhea were scheduled at the beginning of the program, which pushed the actual shows back an hour, putting a damper on audience enthusiasm. The locals listened with all due respect but we, the few foreigners present, couldn't help looking at each other, fuming inside as the suits droned on and on, sullying the evening. "Politicians are politicians anywhere," I thought to myself refusing to film any of it.

When we returned to the house in Vealroleum each evening our hard work was rewarded with the doctors cooking dinner and laying on generous crates of the local Leo beer. After the meal, small parties formed, with people dancing and singing. The setting was somewhat surreal: one CD played constantly, the hilariously titled *Dengue Fever*, which was full of Khmer hits—

and we all danced to it, surrounded by countless unexploded Khmer landmines hidden from sight. Around midnight when the party died down, the doctors played cards on the poorly lit balcony and, if they were lucky and tipsy enough, they were able to fall asleep before the roosters took over the early morning airwaves.

One of the funniest and yet quite dangerous stories came from a night like this. Sitting around, Tom jokingly revealed that I was from the original land of the vampires, Transylvania. This was just an amusing exaggeration—I am not a vampire—but the Cambodian doctors listened with eyes wide open. They had heard of vampires but couldn't quite fathom what they were exactly, other than predators who bit their victims on the neck and feasted on their warm blood. Recounting the legend with his typically British tongue-in-cheek humor to the fore, Tom had no idea how his story was about to be misinterpreted. To most of the doctors it was indeed a joke, but it did scare some of our more naive companions who'd never even been out of Cambodia in their lives. They took it seriously. Tom sent shivers down their spines with tales of vampires flying across freezing cold foreign lands to drink people's blood while they were sleeping. In his beer-buzzed enthusiasm he built up the stories with ever more detail, until an enormous gust of wind suddenly hit the village—such blasts had ripped the canopy from the front of our house before—and he concluded his scare story with the line: "That's Nicky, coming back from one of his vampire trips."

We'd all forgotten about it by the morning. For us, it was just an amusing joke designed to entertain us while we were playing cards. But I noticed that one of our companions, Mr. Hung, couldn't take his eyes off me. Everywhere we went, he was looking at me suspiciously, and in utter seriousness. It didn't stop on the second day so I asked Tom what it was all about.

"Hey, do you know what's up with Mr. Hung? He keeps staring at me in a funny way."

We eventually confronted Mr. Hung, and it turned out that he thought Tom's story was true. Tom was flabbergasted, and it dawned on him how his tales were being interpreted and the impact it could have within the community.

"Don't be silly, Mr Hung," he reasoned. "If the villagers hear this, Nicky could be in real trouble. You remember the snake from the other day that they killed? Nicky could end up like this with his head bashed in! If people start to believe that he is a real vampire it could cause us serious problems! We're dealing with blood here, taking samples from the villagers, sending them away to Bangkok for testing—and it has taken us a long time to gain their trust. This could jeopardise our entire operation!"

Mr. Hung stepped back, seemingly getting Tom's point. "Okay, okay," he said. "I understand, I won't tell the truth!"

Tom went pale. "It's not the fucking truth, Mr. Hung! It was a joke!"

It then took another twenty minutes to explain vampire myths from Hungary, and how it was simply wrong to take such tales seriously. To our relief, Mr. Hung finally seemed to get it. However, just when the case seemed to be closed, he added a final: "Okay, I understand." But then, after a momentary silence, his imagination sparked up again and he asked: "But is it true, though?"

Whether Mr. Hung truly did change his mind or still believed Tom's story deep down, we never knew, but luckily he never did repeat his suspicions about my supposed vampire origins to anyone else in the village, and so the episode eventually came to an end. But I did lose my sense of security during those few days; it was so unexpected and random. Afterwards, I wondered about the gullibility of the locals, and what kind of trouble could be triggered from such seemingly innocent Western humor. I also realized that I was surrounded by an entirely different set of people than I had been used to all my life, and that there was a genuine possibility of falling foul of their beliefs and indeed ending up like that snake bloodying the sand of the tiny village square.

We moved our base from Battambang to the northeastern Stung Treng Province, which was a good seven-hour drive from Cambodia's tourist paradise, Siem Reap, and eight hours from Battambang Province, our previous location. MORU's research centre was set up in the northern side of the country, near the border with Laos. It was my third major deployment with MORU and this time, again, we descended into an abyss of the unwell, malaria-infested rural territories encompassing ten villages along the Sekong River. The settlements themselves were obscured in the hinterlands and we could only reach them by motorcycle, as our cars couldn't wrestle with the deep sand filling the roads. The tiny paths we took were fringed by burnt-out forests on both sides with the smell of still-hot embers smoldering, lingering in the air. This was a common sight in Stung Treng and the charred black areas radiated out over kilometers and kilometers. This was the locals' idea of fertilization; they burned down the forests, thus reducing nature back to zero in order to make the land fertile again.

The villages were mainly populated by Lao and other minority groups. MORU's approach, again, was to create awareness about malaria and infant vaccination via its festivals of dramatic performances, with the intention that the ideas would resonate through the population. The theatre group MORU recruited went from one village to another conducting workshops, using traditional ethnic art and stage shows as tools of engagement.

They invited locals to share their traditional costumes, arts and dance and organized games, singing competitions, malaria quizzes and a comedy sketch about the disease, performed by the children.

This time our base was a local clinic, the Siem Pang Health Centre, on the banks of the Sekong River. The old wooden structure, basically an abandoned hospital that MORU had taken over, had long corridors branching into separate examination rooms and wards set up for malaria treatment. My accommodation here was actually a repurposed sick-ward that could host up to five patients, but as the clinic was not yet fully functional, I was afforded the luxury of having my own, spacious room. I looked around, and it was bare save for a few medical accessories scattered around. A strand of ivy hung in the corner, attached to the bed with a wooden stick.

The night we arrived at the MORU headquarters in Stung Treng, I watched in silence as two of our helpers stretched a mosquito net expertly across the high ceiling, enfolding my bed in the middle. A certain kind of expertise was required to climb under the net, and by the time I'd tucked in the edges to prevent any insect ingress, the screen of my just-opened laptop was already decorated with a collection of tiny exotic creatures. I only discovered later that the net itself was poisonous, as a pest repellant had been applied to its surface—as soon as the bugs came into contact with it, they would die. As I relaxed beneath my canopy, a beautiful creature, a huge green praying mantis, landed on it and observed what I was doing from the outside while I took the opportunity to study its amazing body structure from behind the barrier between us. I let it be and soon fell asleep. In the morning I found it frozen into a stone-like statue, its living green color having faded into the deep brown of death. As I moved it, it fell to the ground like a lifeless piece of a broken branch.

Malaria infections were even more devastating in Stung Treng—the disease was as prevalent here as the common cold was among any Western population. Working outside all day, and into the night too, we were putting ourselves in the direct line of danger. As a precaution, I opted to take an antibiotic called Doxycycline, one of the recommended medicines for exposure to contagious tropical diseases. It provided relatively reliable protection; even if I did become infected by the parasite, the drug prevented it from spreading inside my body. There were no notable side effects and I so took it religiously, continuing the course for a further four weeks after the trip had ended in order to ensure that I was safe.

By this time, I was well-accepted part of as the MORU team and discovered that the Cambodian doctors had adopted a nickname for me, Dr. Photo. The drill was the same as in Battambang: in the boiling heat of the early morning, we visited villages on the other side of the river. We rode our motorbikes to the ferry, loaded it up with our equipment, and crossed to the other side, continuing our way deep into the dusty rural hinterlands. On the other side of the river our daily base was a school. The days were like working on a movie shoot, with a lot of waiting around while they built the stage for the festival performances, and then watching the village folk rehearsing. When we asked the children to be creative on a blackboard in one of the classrooms their drawings depicted mosquitos or mosquitos biting people, flying over the Sekong river. It was heartbreaking to see, and rather telling that their reality revolved around this issue; I was proud to participate in a project intended to eliminate malaria in these distant provinces.

I used this preparatory time well, documenting the rehearsals. I also asked one of the helpers to take me out to the burnt forests so that I could launch my drone to get some aerial shots. To make the best use possible of my free time, I also came up with my own project. As I was photographing so many children in the villages, I decided to put together a photo-essay called *Kids Of Rural Cambodia*. I planned it as a long-term project that would reach into my maturing years. The idea was to shoot a collection of beautiful portraits in the classrooms and fields, with the intention that, if I was still alive in thirty years' time, I'd come back to take their photos again as adults, and in the book their young faces would be juxtaposed against their older selves on opposite pages.

I loved working in Cambodia. By then I was happy with my position within MORU and I was familiar with their working processes. I blended in with the team, which was like a family, really. Tom wasn't with us this time, but I met new friends and colleagues and we worked together very well. I'd wake up early in the mornings to the sound of cow bells, as cattle walked right beneath my window. I'd sit outside the health centre with my coffee and observe the locals as they busied themselves with their daily routines, on tractors and motorbikes, smiling at me as they passed by.

As the hospital was located on one side of the river and the villages we were visiting on the other, we had to make two crossings over the water, one in the morning, one in the afternoon. The commute was a daily routine for us; after the motorcycles were loaded up its deck, the fragile vessel's tiny wooden ramp was raised and it set out across the river. The ferry wasn't much of a proper boat. Basically, it was just a wooden deck with a motor attached to it, with a few poles in the corners over which a canopy had been stretched to provide shelter from the sun and the rain. On the very last night, we finished quite late and took the last ferry back to return to the hospital. I'm not sure how the boat operators missed it, but I'd already noticed something was wrong, when too many people rushed to the boat and — in a hurry to avoid being stuck on the other side overnight — motorbike after motorbike rode up on the frail wooden platform. The ferry got so overcrowded that it began to list, the hull submerging even more than usual below the water line. I sat on the edge of the boat as they were loading it up, and I remember looking over the vista, fringed by palm trees with stars shining over the dark river. The scene was scarily beautiful.

Almost predictably, moments after moving away from the river bank, the ferry became uncontrollable. It began drifting in circles and dropped much further into the water than safety would recommend. Within seconds, I could feel the panic unfolding; people began to shout from the river bank as the hurried movements of the ferry operators were illuminated by the moonlight. In that section of the Sekong, the currents are peculiar and fragmented; in sections the water is deep, and then a line of rocks stick up from the river bed like barriers, before the deep section returns and continues all the way to where it flows into the much mightier Mekong River.

Now we were drifting dangerously closer to one of the rocks and soon enough — as the shouts became louder on the boat — we collided with it. The deep, scratching noise from beneath the hull sounded sinister as the dark water flowed around, its level rising too close for comfort. There was a lot of commotion, on both the ferry and the river bank. From the boat, the operators jumped onto the protruding rocks in an effort to free the ferry. But it was too late, we were stuck right in the middle of the river. The weight of the people and the motorbikes wedged the ferry right onto the uneven rocky surface. I heard the engine's intensifying, straining noise as it struggled to keep the vessel in balance. The operators were trying to distance the boat from the rocks, but the speed of the current kept forcing it back onto them. In the flicker of torch light beams, I then saw the dark water flow up over the top of the rocks with such great force that it filled me with fear. I couldn't believe what was happening on my last night here! All my equipment was on the boat—two cameras, five lenses and the drone. If it capsizes, I thought, even if I manage to swim ashore, I'll lose it all. The bank was so close and yet so far away with the fast-flowing water seemingly an unsurmountable barrier in between. The ferry struggled helplessly for minutes that seemed endless. Then with a loud cracking sound, the operators managed to push it off the rocks. With further shouting and much commotion, they managed to wrestle it free and navigate it towards a small dock nearby.

As I was preparing to leave the next day, I reckoned that the experience was a sobering, parting gift from Cambodia, underlining the dangers the country has on constant offer. But I was wrong—the parting gift came a little later, and was a much more rewarding affair. By the time we'd got back to the hospital, dinner had been prepared and a crate of beer had been opened for us. It happened to be my birthday and the team surprised me with a cake decorated with 'Happy Birthday Dr. Photo'. I was touched. An unexpected birthday party was a much more fitting end to my memorable time in Cambodia.

Our work with the MORU projects had immense effects over the following years. The organization played my videos in many countries, from England to Africa—wherever they had an office—and they proved to be an extremely effective tool for MORU. They discovered that instead of attempting to get their message across with unengaging charts and statistics about their operations, my short films brought it all to life. Through the faces of the children and scenes from the dramatic festivals, it all became more real. The very challenging problem of malaria in Southeast Asia became more tangible, and our efforts were rewarded by a constant outpouring of positive responses from interested parties.

For my part, upon returning to Bangkok, I found I had a readymade group of friends from MORU, the organization being a melting pot of local and international doctors. They not only continued to supply me with work on meaningful projects that brought in a good income, they also gave me a sense of belonging. Every time I visited the MORU office, wedged within Mahidol University and the Hospital for Tropical Diseases, it was as if I was coming back home, with a social network already in place, and I continued to join the team for great dinners and wonderful nights out. More importantly, having now worked in rural Cambodia, unbeknownst to me, I had already completed my initiation into the region. Thanks to MORU's malaria project and having already lived in Bangkok, I had found my feet in Southeast Asia, my place of residence for the foreseeable future. And all from a drink in a pub.

The Hungarian Prince

It was a little over midnight and the dust-swept streets were almost completely deserted as my tuk-tuk turned the corner of a sinister-looking alleyway just off Paharganj Market. The enormous crowds that walk this chaotic retail labyrinth during the day had now been sucked out by fatigue and had retreated to their rickety dwellings for the night. Only a few packs of dogs prowled around, scavenging the remains of the day. There was litter and waste everywhere and only the wind seemed to be doing any work of cleaning up. Not very thoroughly, though. With rugged thrusts it gathered up the garbage along the side of the street, before dropping it carelessly around doorways and in front of the closed shutters of shops.

It's a rare moment when New Delhi, the capital of India, is this quiet, and my tuk-tuk seemed to be the only distraction that disturbed the peace as it sped loudly through the main bazaar. We stopped in front of a small hostel and I walked up to the entrance. The driver stayed behind, nervously pacing around his vehicle. Being from a lower caste, he wasn't allowed to enter the premises so, as I continued my way in, he recoiled abruptly. I turned back and only saw the whites of his eyes in the dark, darting left to right anxiously, waiting for his promised tip. He knew very well that I could walk up to the room and he wouldn't be able to do much about it. Instead, I turned back and handed him a fistful of crumpled rupees. Without saying thanks, he jumped into his battered vehicle and noisily disappeared at the end of the tiny lane for another airport run.

My room was on the top floor, overlooking the moonlit rooftops of Delhi's low rises. As I scanned the sleeping urban vista spreading out below me, a quick reflex, that urge familiar only to photographers, suddenly rushed over me; for a few seconds I convinced myself to go down and take photos of the sleeping Indian capital. But at the last second, something held me back and I collapsed feebly onto the bed.

I wasn't in the best of shape. A stubborn fever had been sapping my energy for a good couple of days. My chest rattled like a broken coffee machine and I could swear that there was liquid sloshing around my lungs that was impossible to cough up.

Worse, I'd lost my sense of smell and taste, and every time I thought of it, a growing panic washed over me: how long will this last? Will it ever come back? It didn't matter what I ate, the food rolled around as tasteless mushy matter in my mouth, and it must have been the first time that I was convinced that water actually has a *flavor*. It must do, because I missed it as the liquid slipped down blankly, flat over my numb taste buds. In that desperate state, only the irony brought a faint smile to my face; here I was, in a country with an endless range of intense odors both pleasant and unpleasant with scents of spices oozing out of every corner, and I wasn't able to experience any of it.

I glanced at the other bed in the room, still untouched. I usually travel alone. It's the same scenario everywhere: another country, another city, a different hotel room and their ever-changing interiors in the most unimaginative varieties.

This time, however, was different. I was expecting company; my friend and long-time traveling companion, Miklós Both, was arriving the following evening. We had decided to meet here in

Delhi before hitting the road together, moving down southwards from the capital.

We always travelled like this, wherever we were; marrying the cheapest form of transport with humble accommodation in order to get as close to the essence of our destinations as we could. Expensive places tend to isolate you and we knew this; so we traded the fancy hotels for inexpensive downtown hostels and shabby inns where there's always a good draft of human traffic and useful information sweeping through. All you have to do is sit down with a beer near the reception and before you know it, you're already talking to someone. Unknown routes, cheap offers and great advice flies around like useful molecules among veteran travellers, digital nomads, self-appointed wandering hermits—all you have to do is catch them.

This wasn't the first time we had travelled together. In fact, our very acquaintance had formed on the road, and hardcore travel has sealed it into a friendship over the years. Fittingly, the first time we met was in a hostel in China and we clicked instantly. Well, admittedly, it didn't go *that* smoothly. Not at first. Miklós was only thirty years old when I first met him but he already had a great body of work to his name. He was a well-known, critically-acclaimed musician, composer, performer, singer and guitarist for the Hungarian folk-rock ensemble Napra, and he had numerous awards under his belt. Before he turned thirty, he had been honored with the Hungarian Gold Cross of Merit for his music and had won the Best World Music Album of the Year in 2008. So, you could say, he was pretty famous. Although his international folklorist career was still in its embryonic form when we began traveling together, it was already cemented in Europe, later elevating him to a status of a modern version of "Béla Bartók armed with an electric guitar"—a phrase journalists liked to use when describing him.

However, Miklós' fame was totally unknown to me when our paths first crossed. To my tightly-sealed Shanghai world, where I was living at the time, his was an entirely different universe. Back then, my life was peopled by magazine editors, architects, jazz musicians, writers, adventurers and the like, landlocked within the walls of the Middle Kingdom's only truly foreign city, Shanghai. Besides, my Hungarian past was a distant and utterly distorted memory that I rarely reflected upon. The cultural scene of Budapest or even Hungary in general couldn't have been further from my mind, and I was completely unaware of who Miklós was, or why he was important.

At first, I didn't even care, to be quite honest. I was in Beijing to see a friend of mine, Krisztián Szücs. I had been living in China for a couple of years at that point, when in late 2011, I received an email from Krisztián out of the blue, announcing that he was planning to travel across the country with two friends. And he invited me to join them. The trip was scheduled to last an entire month — from early November to the first days of December. It began in Beijing, stretching southwards, taking in cities such as Dali, Lijiang, Guilin and Kunming in Yunnan province, China's southwestern region, before reaching its final destination, Hong Kong. Once Krisztián had joined them, and because I happened to be nearby in Shanghai, he suggested that I come along too.

My first encounter with Miklós was formal; I would say even a bit hostile. He struck me as a serious guy with an arsenal of talent and an entire intellectual empire hidden behind his safely-guarded fences. He was a larger-than-life figure, someone you don't forget, even after meeting him once. He embodied one of those rare human constellations in which talent, intelligence and intellect team up with great physical looks. He possessed a seemingly insatiable hunger for culture and interaction with people. He was, in fact, addicted to it and he channelled the adrenalin this generated back into his art, through ten-minute folk symphonies, sung with a paradoxically sensual voice and ornamented by highly-contagious guitar licks.

His presence was hard to ignore when he entered the room: his handsome face, his piercing gaze, his slick smile, his confident posture, and his always immaculately groomed swept-back dark hair. This was a fierce combination indeed, a real hard candy for the opposite sex.

It wasn't easy to pinpoint Miklós. He had a timeless quality about him that gave an impression of someone visiting from a bygone era, while remaining edgily modern. Years later, the Tibetan singer, Yang Ji Ma, who possessed an otherworldly witch-like ability to glimpse the unseen, nailed it by simply saying to me, nodding towards Miklós: "Don't you see it? He's a prince." And there it was. All you had to do was to glance at him and it all made sense.

I only found out later that upon our first encounter in Beijing, Miklós initially hadn't been too keen on my joining their trip, and I didn't blame him for it at all. Here he was, in the company of close friends, letting go, far away from Hungary where everyone knew him, where he had to keep up a profile. Besides, the trip had been mostly his idea in the first place—so why would he want some unknown Hungarian guy invading his privacy when he was finally finding some time to relax? I heard later that I owed my invitation to Krisztián, who'd remained adamant and insisted that I would fit into the group.

Miklós' initial but short-term hostility wasn't helped by the fact that I had begun a phase in my life when I was filming everything around me. To him, this came across as even more invasive. Later on, when I got to know him well, I understood how meticulous he was about his public image, and so it made even more sense. All of a sudden, I was infiltrating his close circle of friends, and I came armed with a video camera, recording everything on this supposedly private trip. One evening in Beijing, we even had a minor run-in, when he asked me to switch off my handycam. He wasn't actually hostile, but he was straightforward; he was far from rude, but I could feel that my presence, and especially my camera, made him nervous.

I'm not exactly sure what inspired his change of heart, but the situation improved pretty quickly. I guess the moment must have come when he realized that my camera wasn't there to invade his space, so he relaxed in a matter of days, even becoming playful in front of the lens. I think he must have understood that I had no idea who he was and that his fame wasn't important to me. Maybe this even appealed to him, or perhaps it was something else, but he soon accepted me, and from then on, a pleasant initial acquaintanceship evolved between us.

Travel wasn't the only common interest we shared. His sensitivity to aesthetics reached beyond music, and he had an uncanny knack for visuals, too. Miklós was an excellent photographer and, as it later turned out, a great documentary filmmaker too. From the start, he understood that my approach to photography was similar to his—that ravenous hunger to collect visual specimens from every corner of the world. So, once the initial difficulties between us were out of the way, we began talking. Lenses and opinions were exchanged and I think we both recognized the possibility of a future collaboration. And that's when things got exciting.

Prior to joining the trip, I'd had a whole day to kill in Delhi, but thanks to my fever, I felt too weak to leave Paharganj's immediate environs, and I only left the hostel when necessary. Instead of venturing on another photographic trip of urban discovery as I usually did, I took small, tentative walks around the dusty market before retreating back to my room in order to rest. This was atypical for me. As soon as I arrived at any destination, I couldn't wait to leave the hotel and dive straight into the ever-unpredictable grid of the metropolitan abyss. This time, however, with my energy depleted by the fever, the area of Paharganj felt especially challenging. Whereas I usually shrugged off with amusement the beggars and aggressive salesmen who patrol the streets of Indian cities and follow foreigners around, they now greatly tested my patience. This and the scorching heat chased me back to the hostel to lay low, at least until Miklós arrived. To minimize the need to venture back out I brought back snacks to the room, and I didn't even need to choose well. My lack of appetite and inability to taste anything pretty much reduced the problem of eating to its basic physical impetus; it could be anything as long as it filled my empty stomach.

I received Miklós' text late in the evening during my second day in Delhi; he said he had landed and was on his way to the hostel. And sure enough, not long afterwards I heard him climbing the stairs. His robust, contagious energy soon burst through the thin wooden door, bringing the world with him.

"*Zhege difang*" said one of us, and we both burst out laughing uncontrollably. The expression was our substitute for saying "Hi", when meeting in the unlikeliest places. It simply meant "this place..." in Mandarin, but for us it took on a whole other meaning, another dimension that described the absurdities of our chaotic traveling lives.

Forgetting his exhaustion from an extraordinary journey—he'd taken a day trip from Delhi to Brussels and back to attend a cultural conference—and my frail condition, we soon found ourselves in a dingy neon-lit bar off the bazaar, sipping ice-cold Kingfisher beer. His band, Napra, had just completed a tour of India, and the other members had flown back to Hungary, but Miklós planned to stay and explore the country. Meeting in Delhi was a fitting continuation to our travels. There was a lot to catch up on and as we hadn't seen each other for months, we spent the evening chatting away and getting drunk as lords before retiring to the hostel to get some rest.

With a trip to Varanasi planned, the next morning, as my condition hadn't improved, I decided to check into the nearby Ganga Ram hospital, which was a good 20-minute rickshaw ride from the Paharganj Market. It seemed the sensible thing to do, bearing in mind the traveling ahead.

After diagnosing me with bronchial infection, the elderly doctor sent me straight down to the emergency room in the basement for half a day of in-patient treatment. I lay on one of the beds and watched through a veil of delirium as the hospital staff rushed around me. They cleared my lungs with an oxygen mask and put me on a course of ivy, a traditional herbal remedy for respiratory conditions. The experience was an oddly rejuvenating little break from the merciless rush of the city and I was really hoping that I'd get better quickly. Soon enough, I was discharged and released back on to the tumultuous streets of the capital.

I hailed a rickshaw on the vast dust-swept Panchkuian Marg, picked up my medication and headed straight to the nearby Hungarian and Cultural Centre to meet Miklós. The centre, also known as Balassi Institute, is Hungary's representative cultural presence in India, a small enclave that consists of a two-storey building facing a spacious garden, and an unexpected refuge.

As the institute had been involved in organizing Miklós' tour with Napra, they had provided him with a room, but he characteristically declined it, eschewing its comforts in favor of the chaos of Paharganj. Although we spent a relatively small amount of time at the institute, mostly using it as a safe place to keep our luggage and camera gear, his presence was a telling juxtaposition with the surroundings. Watching him walking around the corridors against backdrops of framed pictures that read 'Famous Hungarians Abroad', I couldn't help but notice the implications.

It was one of those reasons why I loved photographing him and documenting his work. There was an underlying relevance and timelessness about him; whether he was sitting in a cafe fumbling around on his computer, or on stage bringing an entire arena under his spell.

Years later, he had a TV show focusing on finding talented gypsy musicians in the poverty-struck hovels of Hungary and elevating them into successful recording artists, but even here, in India, he couldn't resist the urge to search for talent during his travels.

I can't exactly recall how Miklós met the classical Indian dancer T. Reddi Lakshmi, but by the time I got to Delhi the two of them were already planning a collaboration. He asked me to help to shoot a video of a piece she was performing, and this time the Hungarian Institute came in very handy; he choose its garden as a location and we set the shoot a day before we left for Varanasi.

Lakshmi performed a piece by the poet Sri Swati Thirunal, which was about Lord Krishna's divine play, staged in three separate parts. Lakshmi was a relatively new dancer back then, just about to embark on a professional career, but the potential was already apparent in her act, and I could see why her performance captured Miklós' attention.

We settled down at the far end of the garden in front of a Shiva statue and shot the dance in a whirlpool of hungry mosquitos and choking humidity. Lakshmi wore beautiful Indian attire that took hours to put on and with the applied make up she looked mesmerizingly beautiful; moving gracefully and illuminated by the portable lights held by a few kids Miklós had hired from the street.

After we wrapped up the shoot, Miklós and I went back to Paharganj and, armed with our cameras, we ventured into the night, down the small lanes and alleyways that ran across the backstreets of the market to do some hardcore photography of Delhi nightlife. Not caring which way or how deep we went, we took in whatever we could. We walked into local shops, eateries and hairdressers, hung out with local kids, talked to vendors of small restaurants and even crashed a wedding by stealing the best moments of kids jumping around and fighting on the dance floor.

Miklós took one of his exquisite photos that evening in a pitch black alleyway. There was something so candid about the moment, as invasive as photography can get. I was a few metres ahead of him in an entirely dark section when I passed this figure next to me. When I looked back I saw two or three blinding flash shots that illuminated the otherwise completely dark lane, revealing the unlikely scene of Miklós towering over an old man looking up at him. There was something so eerie about the scene, it burned in my retina forever, redefining the meaning of the word *shooting*.

Although Miklós' presence had brought back some of my energy and the adrenaline of the evening kept me going, I still got tired very quickly. My fever was high again when we retreated to the room, so I packed quickly before falling into a dreamless sleep, ready in spirit for the trip to Varanasi but perhaps not in body.

When the train finally rolled out of New Delhi's tumultuous railway station and began its journey through the rough outer fringes of the capital, we settled down for a 14-hour trip to reach Varanasi, the holy city of India. As the cheapest in-land transportation in the country, the legendary Indian Railways never fails to leave a long-lasting impression on anyone who has ever graced its battered seats and rickety corridors.

I watched Old India passing by as we rattled alongside slums, through nowhere towns, over rusty metal bridges, with the only occasional brief stop at half-deserted stations. When you take Indian Railways, it's like an old film running outside the window, flashing unpredictable images one after the other in rapid succession. If you look closely, even the train's window-mount is shaped like an old film frame, curving slightly around the edges, perfectly enclosing what must be the most photogenic country in the world. And the movie runs for no one in particular; it doesn't have a story line, a beginning or an end. It's no Bollywood, not even Hollywood, but something mightier and magically captivating: it's life itself.

How absurd is it that they charge next to nothing for a journey like this? It's to keep India's blood flowing via affordable tickets, I guess. It only costs the equivalent of a few dollars for a half-day ride and in exchange these extraordinary scenes and images burned into me and occasionally into my camera sensor.

But you can never fully escape the chaos outside. There's no such thing as an uneventful Indian train trip as ours demonstrated. As we sat back in our compartment, discord sneaked in disguised as two middle-aged men, possibly from a high caste. They took their seats with a great hustle and bustle, and then took in their surroundings with contempt, as if they didn't belong there. They were friendly to Miklós and me, though, and soon we were engaging in the usual travel-chatter—"Where are you from? Where are you headed?"—while at the same time they displayed utterly hostility to their fellow countrymen seated nearby. The mere presence of these two gentlemen wreaked social havoc in our compartment into the night, and rolled into one chaotic episode of incivility that, at one point, included them threatening to throw some evidently lower caste people off the train, merely for our entertainment.

I remember snippets of the evening. Miklós accidentally spilled his curry over me, covering my trousers and trainers in dhal with one single creative splash in the brightest hues of turmeric yellow. Without being able to enjoy the aroma, it looked like the most perfect gastronomically-infused abstract artwork. Our companions then gestured for a cleaner. A bald old man appeared and obediently swept up the rice from the floor while the trouble-makers threatened to throw him off the train, too. In the unfolding chaos, Miklós nudged my elbow and whispered to me, "Look, he's a shaman." I glanced down and, sure enough, the cleaner had six fingers on each hand, skillfully wrapped around the broom.

The situation eventually calmed down. The two agitators drank shots from Miklós' stash of palinka—strong Hungarian fruit brandy—and, in return, they snored through the night like wild boars. "Tomorrow, we'll show you the real Varanasi," they kept repeating over the rattle of the train in the dark, but when we arrived the next morning, they jumped down onto the tracks and took a death-defying short cut to the platform, disappearing from our lives once and for all.

Upon arriving in the city, we checked into a relatively cosy hostel near Dasaswamedh Ghat. The place had a beautiful top-floor balcony overlooking the River Ganges, as it calmly curved towards the deep orange horizon. The hostel had a pleasant patio area with tables and chairs, which offered a welcome haven after the long night of travel. Varanasi spread out enticingly below us, but I had doubts how much walking I could endure. I told Miklós to go off on his own for the day, as I knew how much was out there waiting to be discovered and I didn't want my sickness to hold him back. I was just glad that, at last, we had reached our accommodation so that I could rest for a while.

My fever hadn't backed down one bit; around my eyes the skin had swollen into oedematous bags. My sense of taste and smell were still absent. At one point, swimming in my own sweat and delirium in the dark room, I mistook the palinka that contained forty percent alcohol for water. I only found out when I switched on the light and saw the two identical bottles in my hand. I realized with astonishment that I hadn't even felt its kick, let alone its fruity taste.

Whenever I felt a little better, I ventured outside alone. I took small walks reaching into the old town while trying to stay close to the hostel. It's one thing being sick in India and another in Varanasi. Under normal circumstances, the city would have been the most amazing photographic adventure but now, in my condition, I found it a hostile environment. Apart from the scorching heat and the crowds swarming though its narrow streets, shocking spectacles dotted the roads wherever I went. Walking along, my eyes were drawn to both people and animals with unspeakable deformations, skin diseases and external tumors of every possible form, curling up in doorways. Sickness and death is on daily display around Varanasi, it's part of the landscape. Through the crowds in the cramped lanes, dead bodies were being constantly carried down to the pyres set up along the riverbank.

Varanasi has been inhabited for 5,000 years, which makes it one of the oldest cities in the world. It's where the temporal and spiritual overlap; it is considered the earthly gateway to nirvana. According to Hindu beliefs, dying in Varanasi and getting cremated along the banks of the Ganges river that runs alongside the city breaks the cycle of rebirth and leads to salvation. Thus, it's a major centre for pilgrimage; people from all over India flock there to visit its famous ghats, the stepped stone embankments along the river. There are 88 of these ghats and some of them are sacred places where bodies are burned on large funeral pyres 24 hours a day, seven days a week. There are spots to witness these close up; you can see the fires hissing and spitting orange embers into the sky. You can't photograph them, though; the moment your camera is spotted you'll be mercilessly chased away.

I'm not sure if it was a twist of fate, but my experience of the city was entwined with morbidity. One night, I discovered a narrow, deserted stone staircase in between the tightly-built dwellings. I followed it down from our hostel to the riverbank and one of the ghats. The moon shone bright like an enormous bulb hanging from the sky, illuminating the water. In the distance I heard a continuous, desperate howl so I walked towards it. It came from a dying dog half submerged, utterly ripped apart, seemingly fighting for its last breath. It was still alive but its intestines spread around it on the water's surface. Parts of its testicles had been bitten off, hung on as a chunk of meat. It must have been lying there for a day or two now, fatally injured. I had a feeling that if someone moved it, the poor thing would have just fallen to pieces.

As I was standing there, a man approached me from behind: "Yes, it's been dying here since yesterday," he said. "A pack of dogs attacked it. An old lady came to put medicine on its wounds, but it's too late."

The dog kept howling, seemingly not for help any more but just in desperation and pain, and perhaps signaling its plight before losing all connection with this world. We stood there helplessly, watching its last moments before Mother Ganga acceptingly swallowed it into its dark, holy, nasty abyss.

The scene struck me as an ultimate definition of what Varanasi is: a reminder of the crossover between life and death, with all its raw reality and gruesomeness. To this day, I don't know whether it was my ill health that distorted the city into this infernal environment, or if it was really like that. Perhaps another visit in healthier times would do it justice, but one thing I do know: I have never in my life felt so close to death as when walking around its medieval streets, making my way around shapes on the ground, with lifeless hands poking out beneath filthy blankets.

The city certainly left a lasting impression on me. I felt I'd experienced Varanasi even more intensely, on another level because of my condition. Witnessing up close human bodies burning by the riverside highlights your place in creation. It unmasks mortality and unveils how simply we can perish, with our remains consumed on a funeral pyre stacked up in the middle of just another afternoon.

In a certain way, Varanasi opened the gateway to my traveling years and, beyond that —without wishing to sound like an esoteric guidebook—it was the first step on a long journey to let go and detach myself from the material world, and instead become aware of the spiritual aspects of life.

Even though we were traveling together, Miklós and I experienced Varanasi separately. While I was walking spiritual plateaus, riding high on fever and in a miserable state, he went on a quest to further expand that inner map within himself that connected the dots, relentlessly absorbing cultural references and stocktaking ethnic relations.

One afternoon, while Miklós was out, I was sitting in the patio of the hostel playing around with a flyer on the table when all of sudden, a tall, dark figure towered over me. "That's me, you know?" he said pointing at the paper in my hand. "I'm the doctor here. I must say, you look very sick. Perhaps you should come and see me?"

When you're a white man in India, you're constantly hassled

and followed around; everyone has an offer for you, everyone knows a better deal, or a better way to get to wherever you're going. Such ubiquity makes you immune to this constant nuisance by endlessly waving and hushing people away. In the end, you do it automatically; you just walk along trying your best to ignore them. So when the doctor approached me I did the same; I waved him away, I waved help away. But that afternoon, I just couldn't let go of the thought: "Why don't you just give it a shot?" Meanwhile, I had my doubts: if the doctors couldn't help me in Delhi, what could this man do, having a private practice in a godforsaken hostel?

In the end, though, out of desperation and concern, perhaps, that my condition would become chronic, I gave in and found myself knocking on his door. I laid down on the rattan bed and just waited. "Let whatever may come," I thought. "It can't be worse than I feel now." He sat down next to the bed and started rubbing my feet. I instantly felt a sharp pang of pain. "All your respiratory tracts are congested," he said, "and they need to be cleaned. This will ease them up." He then spent twenty minutes rubbing certain zones on my feet, and when he'd finished he placed tiny magnets all over my soles and my toes.

"Please keep these on for a day, and be careful they don't fall off," he advised. "You'll be better in twelve hours." His words fell flat and I admit I was highly skeptical. I staggered out of his consulting room and headed down to our accommodation to pack for the trip back to Delhi.

"Are you feeling better? I'm glad you saw the doctor," said Miklós, enthusiastically, as we made our way out of the hostel.

It was already getting dark as we walked down the street and hailed a cycle rickshaw. There was confusion in the young but already haggard man's eyes when we told him where we were going, but he took the ride anyway. We didn't know, however, that

Varanasi had two railway stations and he just picked the closest.

Venturing into the evening like two doomed lords, we sat high on the cart, already having doubts. What if we're heading for the wrong station? Worried, we stopped the rickshaw and decided to ask passers-by, but no one could tell from our tickets. Typically, if you ask for advice in India, people would rather say anything, even if it's not correct, and soon a small crowd gathered around us, everyone suggesting different directions. We were running out of time to catch our train, so decided to give up on the crowd and flagged down a tuk-tuk and headed for the nearest station the quickest way.

Finally reaching the station, we rushed through the crowds and then stopped to ask a railway worker which platform we needed. He broke it to us that we weren't actually at the right station, so we slowed ourselves down and, still panting, started walking aimlessly, saying nothing. There was nowhere to rush to any more. Then suddenly, the railway guy ran after us: "Sir, yes, *this is* the right station! You see that display up there? It will show which track the train will come in. Just wait for it because it's only decided the last minute where it pulls into."

Somewhat relieved, we finally had a moment to relax, but kept glancing at the weakly blinking electronic display above us. Miklós looked around, taking it all in; people lying on the floor, or rushing to the tracks, India swirling around us like a human vortex. He shook his head in disbelief with a smile and said: "You'll see, this is not over yet."

Just as he said these words, the generators of Varanasi Railway Station gave out and the power outage plunged the whole place into pitch black. The enormous hall, along with the display that we so badly depended upon, fell into complete darkness. A grumble from the crowd was heard and then flashlights of mobile phones pierced through the gloom.

Minutes away from the train's arrival, we had lost our only source of information, the overhead display, and we had little choice but to make our way towards the platforms. We climbed up to number four, where the railway man said our train was most likely to arrive, and prepared ourselves in case we needed to run to the other side of the tracks.

Then, again, the unimaginable happened. We saw a commotion at the end of platform; we heard screams and saw mobile phone lights, this time moving quicker in the dark. Then, the lights revealed what was causing the panic. An enormous dark mass moving swiftly: a raging bull was at the end of the platform, running around and charging at people! (Cows are sacred to several religions in India and it's not uncommon to see them roaming about freely.) Some people jumped down the tracks, some ran into the waiting rooms to get out of its way. At this very moment, finally, the train, with countless hands sticking out of its windows, pulled into the right platform. Everyone started moving towards it, most trying to clamber on board while the train was still moving. It was just as dark inside the train as on the station, but we pushed through the crowds and finally found our compartment. We collapsed into our seats and burst out laughing. There was relief and exhaustion in that laughter, and it seemed to be the only answer, the only response to the surreality of the day. Soon after, we fell asleep as the train rattled into the dark night, heading north towards Delhi.

The sun was already up when I opened my eyes. Miklós was still asleep. Sleep-fuddled, I staggered up in the compartment. We were stranded at a station. Outside, I saw a man along the tracks, dressed in orange, trying to hang his newly-washed clothes on a fence, while a barrel of monkeys kept tearing them off. The scene was so amusing that I automatically reached for my camera and started snapping away. Then, as the train slowly pulled out of the station, colorful houses and breathtaking countryside vistas appeared and passed by the window, and I was in my element again, photographing everything I could. There's a certain buzz, a sort of image-hungry urge that photographers feel when they get inspired. I thought: "Great, we have a day ahead of us in Delhi and I can spend the day just shooting. Then we can go here, then there, then maybe a few shots at the India Gate and…."; suddenly, the penny dropped: I… felt…. better…! I hadn't even realised it at first but, indeed, I was riding high on newly-found energy. And how else did this express itself other than via creativity? I felt an enormous relief rush over me when it dawned on me that the weight of the fever and debilitating fatigue had finally lifted after so long.

It was as if a miracle had happened. I couldn't help thinking of the healer at the hostel and how skeptical I had been about him. He had told me that I would be better in twelve hours but here I was, just eight hours later, feeling almost as good as new. He *had been* right, after all.

I slipped into a great mood on the train and by the time we reached Delhi I was bursting with energy. Yes, I was still a little shaken from the past weeks' illness, and my sense of smell and taste were still absent, but there had been a drastic change in my condition, literally overnight.

This was my last day in Delhi. I did some shopping and went out to shoot at the India Gate, using my newly-found stamina to take home just a bit more of the city. The seemingly innocent last-minute town visit, predictably, didn't go uneventfully. As I was climbing into a tuk-tuk to go and collect my luggage at the Hungarian Institute, a guy rushed after me. I was already in the vehicle when he shoved a slightly open basket after me right into the car. There was a black cobra inside! I couldn't believe it, I thought: "After all these adventures, here on the last day, I'll get a snake bite."

"Cobra, cobra, cobra!" the man kept repeating as he pushed the basket further forward. I quickly realized that he was a snake charmer trying to sell me his act. Not today, thanks, with one quick push, I threw the basket out of the tuk-tuk and told the driver to drive as fast as he could. I didn't even look back.

I reached the Hungarian Institute safely and after I'd retrieved my luggage, headed back to the small hostel where I said goodbye to Miklós, before heading to the airport to continue my travels alone.

The adventurous trip to India was a milestone for me, giving me a taster of the stark realities of hardcore travel, which would come to dominate my life a few years later. The next day, my wife Barbi and I took a flight to Indonesia where we spent an entire month on an extended, well-deserved holiday. The trip was dotted with hidden coincidences and whispers of the future. We changed flights in Kuala Lumpur — our future home — and, eventually, I recovered my sense of taste and smell at KLIA2, the airport that would become my base when I joined AirAsia. Upon our return, we stopped off in Kuala Lumpur again, and booked a hotel in Kuala Lumpur City Centre (KLCC), where these days we spend our everyday lives; it was on this AirAsia flight that I picked up the inflight magazine that changed my life entirely and led to my career as a photojournalist in Southeast Asia.

I first heard Miklós' most famous song, 'Jaj, A Világ!' (*'Oh, What a World!'*), played on my battered, dirt-cheap acoustic guitar in a downtown Beijing hostel. It was on one of the first days after we'd met and the initial tension still lingered between us. He played it nonchalantly and slightly beer-buzzed, but with such a skill and intensity that it gave me goose pimples. Although I had been constantly surrounded by excellent jazz guitarists in Shanghai, I'd never heard the instrument played with such an elegance and panache. Besides, I'd never seen my old red guitar come alive like that! The irresistible tune filled up the evening as we sat outside the porch on one of the first cold days of November, sipping Tsingtao and smoking cigarettes, and it stayed with me throughout the trip, like some kind of new enzyme spreading inside me, altering my system.

I found Miklós' guitar-playing unique and extremely compelling; even in a dingy hostel, completely divorced from the glare of the stage, it put the listener into a state of surrender and acceptance, like when a surgeon prepares to operate on you—all you can do is let yourself go. Skill and intensity aside, the structure of his music was steeped in the Hungarian folk tradition which, for me, added a magically captivating dimension to it.

Miklós was building upon folk foundations, upon something primal, spiritual even, and it resonated deeply. That's why he could never go wrong with his music. He later said to me, which elucidated my frustration with seventy percent of today's pop and rock music and why I find it so bloody awful: "It's because they themselves are building from rubbish already, so the basic material, the roots are wrong. That's why I use folk elements."

Later, getting to know his entire back catalogue inside out, if I were to search for a downside to his music, it would be that it's so razor sharp, so intelligent, so profound and structurally complex that you can't put it on at just any old time. Miklós' music requires commitment from the listener. It can be emotionally draining, unsettling in a good way, just like a piece of serious classical music.

When he plays live he gives a slight, odd nod of his head, which signals to his band a change in the rhythm, and this very movement defines much of his approach, that every note and phrase has been honed to perfection.

'Jaj, A Világ!' grabbed me unexpectedly, but I didn't fathom its significance in my life until months later. Unknowingly, it had sown the seeds and awakened within me something that I didn't even know existed. At first, I felt a gentle pull *towards* my ever-denied Hungarian roots. This initial, strange sensation would later lead me to entirely ease up on Hungary and turn my frozen emotions into a full bloom of newly-found openness for my native country.

The song's melody left me hungry, and that same evening I asked Miklós if he would play it again and I remember him replying starkly: "It doesn't work like that." The answer wasn't meant to insult me, instead it revealed his self-contained and confident approach towards his art.

While 'Jaj, A Világ!' provided a soundtrack to a cold Beijing autumn, joining three Hungarian guys on a road trip was altogether a refreshingly new experience to me. The chemistry between us was brilliant and I felt truly privileged to be part of the adventure. There was Krisztián, whom I knew from before and considered a friend, although I never really knew where he stood on the matter. He was the singer and guitarist with my favorite Hungarian indie band, Heaven Street Seven. I used to see him occasionally back in Budapest, his natural habitat, but here in China, with his killer sense of humor and in a totally new context, he was something else.

I should spend a moment here reflecting on Krisztián's own music. He was the main reason I was on the trip, and it meant a lot to me when he enthusiastically played me new songs that he later released on his album '*Felkeltem A Reggelt*' ('*I Wake up the Morning*'). Just the opportunity to get to know him better on the road was very special to me. The only difference was that while his music belonged to my past, from another era, Miklós' had already imperceptibly started to shape my future.

Gabor had a sweet, lovable nature. We connected instantly.

He was and still is one of Miklós' closest friends and traveling companions. The two had even ventured into pre-war Syria a few years back, and China was the new addition to their wanderlust. They discussed and argued over Hungarian politics relentlessly, which amused me. Seemingly oblivious to their surroundings, they went on with such passion that their conversations often didn't end until the early hours. Everyone else went to bed and they were still talking.

On that trip, the endless flow of humor, fun, differing views on music, politics, life and Hungary all shed a new light on my own perspectives and presented me with the solid evidence that there was indeed a world outside of my adopted life in China, my own strongly-defended cocoon.

Despite the camaraderie, as the month marched on, the sometimes heavy weight of travel created small frictions within the group. But while the tension mounted—and it did seem significant back then—in the long run, I don't think it scarred any relationships. It was an all-too-natural situation; the kind of strain that bubbles to the surface when people, even friends, are locked together for extended periods. In this case, what became apparent was an intricate rivalry between these two frontmen of successful bands, as they found themselves locked in the often claustrophobic environments of cramped hostels and long-distance transport. I was merely an outsider but, in retrospect, it don't think the angst I witnessed damaged their friendship; instead it outlined their distinct characters and what each wanted from life and their careers. Furthermore, every moment of fleeting disharmony was superseded by a perfect chemistry between them, which remained apparent throughout the entire trip.

Miklós later remarked that my presence "nicely balanced it all out", which helped the group especially during the conflicts.

His comment at last put me at ease and I breathed a sigh of relief that I wasn't just an intruder on their trip after all.

Sadly, I had to interrupt my participation in this adventure as, mid-month, I needed to fly back to Shanghai for a few days to fulfill my monthly editorial duties at *That's Shanghai* magazine. But I managed to shoot the material for the cover of the December 2011 issue quickly and, as soon as I was done, I jumped on a flight that took me back to the heart of the mainland.

I rejoined the group in Guilin. This leg of the journey, cutting through China on trains, buses, boats, basically anything except a donkey's back, remains one of my most memorable travel experiences. I had been living in China for five years at this point, but prior to this trip, I had never travelled much around the country. The unexpected outcome of spending time with the group was that it not only opened up the inner Hungarian in me but also made me appreciate the countryside of China's interior; and visiting other Chinese cities underlined the fact that, for the most part, I had been hermetically sealed inside the often claustrophobic concrete-and-glass confines of Shanghai.

Being one of the boys—more importantly, one of the Hungarian boys—eased me up altogether. I don't think I've ever laughed so much as I did on this trip. The jokes never stopped and quite often we laughed ourselves to sleep. I cannot recall a time, ever—before or since—when I woke up nearly choking in a laughing fit at five o'clock in the morning.

Eventually, when the trip finally ended in early December, we said goodbye in Hong Kong. The last night was bittersweet; everyone was tired, out of energy, out of cash and while sitting out at Victoria Harbour we cracked open a bottle of vodka. When the last drops were gone, we scribbled on a piece of paper and threw the message-in-a-bottle into the waves. I can't recall what we wrote, but all of us signed it and Gabor added his email address in case anyone ever found it. It was the perfect ending to an unforgettable adventure. The next day, the others flew back to Hungary and I returned to Shanghai.

Although the trip had been undoubtedly life-changing, the ultimate bond between Miklós and me wouldn't be formed until the following year, in the autumn of 2012, in Chongqing. This megalopolis in southwestern China is located at the confluence of the Yangtze and Jialing rivers, and the sheer weight of human density is truly felt on its hummocky streets. The wider municipality has a population of a staggering 35 million, but it's not particularly the crowds that make Chongqing so heavy. Its vastness extends like a giant concrete octopus over a landscape that's shaped by hills and valleys and is enclosed by the two rivers, whose waters are of different colors, washing into each other. The city itself is dotted with a sea of seemingly infinite residential complexes and, at ground level, labyrinths of old-style dwellings fill its endless domains. The city goes to the extremes in every sense; here an elevated metro line literally cuts through a residential building's upper floors, there, a half-finished bridge stretches into the misty fog over the river; elsewhere, a small shop peeks out from the middle of an advertising billboard. At night, a colossal glowing halo forms over the city like a living entity, an aura bringing it alive. You can get lost for days walking around and the city still reveals new, jaw-dropping urban landscapes and incredible scenes wherever its small winding lanes take you. Chongqing unveils China to the utmost. In other words, it's a photographer's paradise.

Against this backdrop, I found Miklós on that grim rainy morning in a hostel overlooking the foggy Yangtze River. He'd just finished recording his new album, *Both Miklós Folkside*, in Budapest, but had lost no time boarding a plane to China, effectively escaping the record's promotional duties. He already had other things in mind—taking part in a music conference in Chongqing that sought to unite foreign and Chinese musicians. To say the least, his speedy escape didn't go down well with his fellow musicians and the people involved in his album but, as always, Miklós was one step ahead of the game.

In retrospective, the move made perfect sense. He saw the bigger picture again, and by attending the conference he opened new doors for himself, which laid down the foundations for his next direction. It not only took *him* further, but pushed those left behind who felt let down even further too. What no one could foresee, however, was that the following year would see his band, Folkside, and the Chinese musicians he met in Chongqing merge together into something magnificent. The project was to become a major event that would change his career, finally setting him on the international folklorist path on which he was always destined to travel. But, for now, both the album and the glorious East-meets-West performance in Budapest were still somewhere in the future, shrouded in the thick white fog of Chongqing.

At the hostel, I found him sitting in the bar sipping tea and, as I entered, he rushed to see me and greeted me warmly. Now that we had some history to our acquaintance we had a lot to catch up on. He told me about the conference he'd attended a few days earlier. He said that he'd met an amazing singer and was very keen to collaborate with her. Raving about the way she sang, he described her as having an "angelic voice and an almost witch-like quality".

Back then, the Tibetan singer Yang Ji Ma was almost completely unknown. She was a rough, uncut diamond, a musical nomad, drifting from town to town in Yunnan Province, working with musicians and DJs who were often way below her standards.

By collaborating with her and her ethereal voice, musicians cleverly spotted opportunities to raise their own material above the average. She profoundly and effortlessly echoed ancient Tibetan soundscapes, which carried an otherworldliness about it and, indeed, an almost witch-like characteristic. When she sang in, I couldn't help but picture visions of drifting over misty mountain tops, with clouds billowing over snowy peaks and winds sweeping through open, deserted plains. There was also a great contrast and range to her voice; while her higher pitches truly felt like the sky opened above me, when she sang low undertones she evoked an irresistible unease. Later, in media circles, she even acquired a nickname 'Nushen', meaning 'goddess'. That was entirely justified, given the sacral, majestic quality of her music.

As a photographer, I was often convinced that her features were constantly changing. I'd never seen anything like it before. During performances her face would take on formations, different features and even, when I looked closer, I sometimes couldn't recognize or pinpoint the Yang Ji Ma I knew.

She could do magical things, too. One particular time I recall, backstage at the major show in Budapest that crowned the collaboration between her and Miklós, I was photographing the arrival of the Chinese musicians in the run-up to the finale. No one knew, but I had just had very serious dental work done on my lower jaw — that's why I had returned to Hungary. The operations were major, and took months. I was already healing, but because we were in the middle of a massive schedule, with the media all around us and the rehearsals still in progress, I didn't get any proper rest for days. I was worried that the non-stop, exhausting schedule would affect my healing properly and that this might compromise the painstaking, and painful, dental work. In that particular moment my head was full of such concerns. I was fumbling with my camera equipment backstage at Müpa (formerly known as Budapest's Palace of Arts) just before the show. In the darkness, Yang Ji Ma suddenly appeared out of nowhere, crouched down behind me, slipped her warm palms onto both sides of my lower jaw, just over the site of the deep wounds in my gums and said: "It's going to be OK, you know?" Apart from the momentary surprise, it gave me the goosebumps because I knew for a fact that she had no way of knowing that I had been undergoing dental surgery.

Her looks were utterly mesmerizing; she had long black hair with a fringe turning grey with a beautiful face and hypnotic eyes. In person, she was reserved, kind, full of empathy but, you couldn't help feeling you were in a presence of something celestial.

Yang Ji Ma and Miklós made a striking duo, and whenever they appeared together I just had to take photographs. Miklós was extremely keen on working with her, and was determined to include her as a key element in the Chinese album he was planning to make. It was clear from the very beginning that she had to be involved; in fact, for Miklós she was one of his main collaborators for the project.

As soon as Miklós and I left the hostel in Chongqing, we were taken aback at how the city towered over us and almost swallowed us entirely, as we went around with our cameras snapping photos of locals busy in their everyday lives. Everything I did with Miklós was spontaneous. We never had a particular plan when exploring cities; we just went wherever the roads took us because this was always where we found the best photographic opportunities. We cut through incredible urban landscapes in this monster of a city. We walked to deserted hilltop churches and abandoned houses, and chatted with people at roadside eateries, or else roamed around dense downtown areas, full of photogenic, random life-snippets, which begged for the right treatment of the lens.

After we explored the city we hopped on a train and went to nearby Chengdu, returning to the lovely atmosphere of the Mix Hostel, where the year before we'd spent a few evenings with Gabor and Krisztián. We only stayed for a day this time, as Miklós received an invitation for a performance back in Chongqing, so late that evening we headed back to catch the start.

The other musical nomad—in the truest sense of those two words—whom Miklós found on the same trip was Wang Xiao, or Master Wang Xiao, as he called him. He couldn't have come across a more bona fide vagabond than this tiny man. Endlessly wandering alone in the Himalayas with his lute-like *dombra*, he played songs with an intensity that could shatter stones. Armed with a voice that sounded like he had swallowed a didgeridoo, he masterfully defined and reflected his own state of constant drifting. He reeked of the earth that he walked.

He was a short, stocky fellow and the deep wrinkles on his face reminded me of the winding paths of his native province. His small, bloodshot eyes suggested wisdom and debauchery at the same time or, after a second glance, humor and playfulness. His hair was held together, twisted in a small bun, by a piece of bone pierced through it, and he wore long, timeless attire as if he had come from nowhere in particular, perhaps from another age.

That evening, Wang Xiao invited Miklós to play in the heart of the arts quarter of Chongqing. Wang Xiao called Miklós up to the stage and the music they performed together pretty much outlined the psychedelic folk that Miklós later included on his album *Kinai Utazolemez (The Musical Odyssey)*. They played with an intensity that built gradually, with hypnotic repetition that culminated in a cathartic musical experience that left me dizzy.

Then Miklós took the spotlight alone for a short set in which he played a stripped down acoustic version of 'Jaj, A Világ!' and a couple of other songs. At the end, he looked at me from the stage and said: "This is for you, Tibzi," as he affectionately called me, and played a snippet of music from a classic Hungarian movie from the 1940s that included one of my favourite actors, Javor Pal, doing what he does best apart from acting—singing in a restaurant accompanied by a gypsy violinist, with a bottle of wine sitting in front of him.

It was a simple, lovely gesture from Miklós, because the song became a soundtrack for that trip; he often sang it and knew how much I loved it. It not only meant a lot to me in those days but, once again, it brought me one step closer to unfreezing my long-denied Hungarian roots.

You couldn't avoid culture when in the company of Miklós—it oozed from him effortlessly. Folk songs and all kinds of musical references, as well as great stories, flew in the air around him. He was constantly humming and singing wherever we went, sometimes hilariously to the point of absentmindedness. He absorbed every sound, every melody he heard in the streets like a human sonic sponge. If he caught the sound of someone singing, he could pick up the melody naturally, and follow it confidently to the end. People would look at him in amusement and surprise and, if the person had an instrument with them, his talents would inspire an impromptu street performance.

One of the most important things I learned from him, something that stayed with me and grew even more significant, was about the scourge of noise pollution. Miklós had an extremely sophisticated ear and picked up easily on any unnecessary sounds all around us. It was something I didn't quite understand back then, but it became a major annoyance in my life.

It started with a seemingly minor incident. Back then, all the mobile phones in China had an irritating default ringtone. When you called someone and were waiting for an answer, the system played an annoying Chinese pop song. Miklós had me on speed-dial, and he called me quite often. One day he had this strange request: "Tibzi, can you please change that terrible default song? I can't bear to hear it one more time."

I burst out laughing, thinking he was joking. But he was serious, and looked concerned: "No, I mean it. Please, please do that for me." I did, and thinking back, I often smile about this strange request. I didn't understand it, but it came back to me after I turned 40, a few years later. Few people are aware of the noise pollution that plagues us. You know those No.1 songs that you don't even know who they're by, but they're already in your head? I hear them in taxis, airports, restaurants... They're in the ether. It's those stupid pop songs that constantly fill our environment, infiltrating our world. The older I get, the more I feel like shouting out loud: "How dare you! How dare you invade my private space!"

These days, whenever I ask taxi drivers to turn down the radio, in doing so risking losing points in Uber's customer loyalty program due to my 'unpleasant' behavior, I think of Miklós — he was the one who brought my attention to this problem.

Miklós constantly introduced subjects that I found fascinating into our conversations, and by the end of 2012 he had completely captivated me. I found myself stripped of my former musical tastes centring around British and American bands. Now, I began to listen to folk music, even *Hungarian* violin gypsy music, as I entered a new phase in my cultural consumption. And not just in terms of music, either. Miklós drew my attention to details in the visuals too, that was rooted in him. He was changing me without me even being aware of it.

We parted ways again in Chongqing, but this time Miklós was adamant that he'd be back within a few months. Upon returning to Hungary he didn't waste any time, and quickly set about recording an album that brought together the contrasting styles of the musicians from his band, Folkside, who provided the Hungarian gypsy elements, with an overlay of traditional Tibetan and Chinese influences. It was inspiring to see just how quickly he brought such monumental projects to life by simply acting on impulse.

Dániel Gryllus, a famous musician from the legendary Hungarian band Kalaka, took on the producer's role, via his Hangzo-Helikon publishing company; he'd produced Miklós' two previous albums. Everything was moving fast and things quickly began to take shape.

A trip was organized back to Yunnan, China, to record the songs live. Miklós, Gryllus and his son Samu were accompanied by one of the finest musical engineers, the surprisingly down-to-earth Hidasi Barnabás — Miklós' confidant — who'd produced albums for famous Hungarian bands such as Kispál és a Borz, Quimby and Tankcsapda.

Miklós' new team was set to return to Yunnan Province, to the cities of Dali and Lijiang, and team up with the Chinese musicians whom Miklós had already approached. Wang Xiao and Yang Ji Ma were lined up, along with the excellent He Brothers, a duo Miklós had found on his first trip; they, in a way, had been the very beginning of it all.

These preparations for the album finally silenced everyone who had initially criticised Miklos for walking away from the promotional duties of the Folkside record. Now, instead, he assembled a new band to focus on the project that would put him on the map as Hungary's — if not Europe's — most significant folklorist of the new century.

The early morning traffic of Shanghai was at a complete standstill. It was still dark as torrential rain pummeled down onto Pudong's jammed highways. I was convinced that this time I'd definitely miss my flight, and I was almost right. I ran through the enormous new terminal of Pudong breathlessly, passed the few duty-free shops, and just managed to board the plane before the door was closed behind me. I sat back panting heavily and looked out as the aircraft ascended into the heavily overcast Shanghai sky. Within a few hours I had touched down in the sparking sunlight at the tiny airport of Lijiang, heading straight to the old town where Miklós and his team were already loading up equipment in one of the small hotels, getting ready for the recording.

I was about to meet some Hungarian legends. Producer Dániel Gryllus was one of the best-known figures in Hungarian music. The Gryllus name was a trademark for popular folk music in Hungarian circles. His band, Kaláka, which he formed in the 1960s, was deeply rooted in the country's culture. Some of their material, especially the music they wrote for children's TV shows, had been tattooed into the brains of an entire generation from a very early age. Dániel and his son, Samu, were friendly to me from the very beginning.

Miklós was in a different frame of mind already, focussing fully on the album, so needless to say it wasn't the time for the kind of laid back, no-direction vagrancy we'd shared while traveling together. This was a serious working environment that had taken a lot of organizing. Nevertheless, we still had a lot of fun, especially when the Chinese musicians arrived.

For me, visually, it was like striking gold. I loved documenting large projects with so many interesting people involved, and I was having the time of my life. There was so much to appreciate. The nature of the entire project excited me, as did the personalities behind it and, as with anything involving Miklós, the scale and the quality of it all. I knew I was filming and photographing something that would last.

The recording process was very spontaneous, which I found fascinating. Everything was unpredictable. Hidasi practically brought a whole mobile recording studio with him from Hungary, which was to be set up anywhere—mostly in private guest houses. Apart from Yang Ji Ma, Wang Xiao and the He Brothers, several musicians were still to be recruited on the go; there was a constant search for contributors, and nothing was set in stone. One of the most astonishing things about the album was that when the time came to press the record button there wasn't much discussion of what to play; they just continued with their rehearsals and this on-the-fly approach brought unbelievable results. I'd never seen musicianship on this level and just to be a part of it sometimes left me breathless.

By the time I arrived at the sessions, a few tracks had already been laid down, but I was lucky enough to film the most important one, Yang Ji Ma's unforgettable collaboration with Miklós. It was recorded in the Dali Mint Inn, a small home-style hostel in the old town.

Miklós was understandably nervous. Yang Ji Ma was an untouchable entity, who somewhat unpredictably appeared and disappeared throughout the days of the session. Miklós was very much aware that if he lost her, the album would be significantly poorer. He referred to her as his "golden bird" and confided in me that if she didn't see the sessions through, the very album itself was at stake. She turned up one evening but was visibly put off by an unpleasant jam session hijacked by some of the local musicians and left without saying a word. Miklós disguised it well, but I'd never seen him so upset. As I was only filming and photographing the project, and wasn't an official part of the production team, he often called me aside to talk to me, releasing some of the pressure.

But his moment did arrive when Yang Ji Ma returned the following day. Miklós took the necessary precautions and banned everyone from entering the building, allowing only me, Hidasi, Yang Ji Ma and the musicians to be present. We prepared in complete silence: we placed a few chairs against a staircase where the musicians would sit, found a corner for Hidasi's recording station, and we were ready. Miklós and Yang Ji Ma exchanged a few words before Miklós nodded at Hidasi to begin. It was completely silent; then Miklós' crystal clear guitar sound filled the room.

That half hour was the single most intense musical experience of my life. The quiet start, in which Yang Ji Ma began singing mantras over Miklós' guitar, built slowly into a monumental track with a fierce, hypnotic ending. It was utterly spellbinding. No music I had ever listened to possessed such power. The room seemed to transfer into another dimension.

There was one critical moment, though, of which I was especially happy that Miklós wasn't aware. In the middle of the recording, the house owner's dogs, a small foxy type animal and a larger Labrador, appeared at the top of the staircase that curved away to the upper floors. They hesitated at first but then started trotting down slowly, step by step. Miklós, Yang Ji Ma and the percussionist were practically in a trance among the intricate system of cables, stands and microphones set up around them. I watched in horror as the small dog ventured further down. If they decided to run down—as dogs do—it could have been disastrous. The musicians had already been recording a unique, improvised take unfolding for over fifteen minutes, and if the two four-legs decided to bound into the proceedings, tumbling over everything… No, I didn't even want to think about it. I just stared at them, holding my breath, as the smallest one stopped and hesitated at the last turn of the stairs. And then perhaps because they themselves felt charmed by the music—or possibly the opposite—both dogs stopped at the last second and turned back up the stairs.

I sighed with relief, and by the end of the session I felt sure I had some fantastic material on my hands. Later on, when Miklós was still high on the joy of a successful recording, I told him about the dogs but he just laughed it off. He was so happy that he didn't even entertain the possibility that such a masterful take might have been ruined by a couple of canines.

When the recording was finished, everyone took a deep breath. The magic subsided and we returned to the mundane reality of the Dali Mint Inn. All agreed that they'd nailed the most important track of the album. Now it was my turn to get to work. Miklós didn't know it yet, but I had already planned to make a short film about the sessions, and since the Yang Ji Ma footage had turned out so well visually, I couldn't wait to begin. This track would become my first significant music video.

The sessions continued as the musicians commuted between Dali and Lijiang—wherever Miklós found collaborators—and I hung around for a few more recordings to gather extra material.

I returned to Shanghai the following week and started working on the edit of the short film, A *Musical Odyssey of Both Miklós*, until events things took an unexpected turn. A few days later I got a call from Miklós and he informed me that he would like to come to Shanghai to spend some time there.

As soon as the recording sessions wrapped up and the Hungarian musicians returned home, Miklós flew to Shanghai with his girlfriend and future wife. This time, the circumstances were different, and little traveling was involved. My impression was that he just wanted to spend a little more time in China, to get to know Shanghai and experience life in one of the big cities of the Middle Kingdom. By the time they arrived I'd managed to find them accommodation with a good friend of mine, a French jazz guitarist called Marc de Vivies. Miklós discussed moving to Shanghai permanently, but in the end stayed for just three memorable months.

Back then, my photography and video production business was going well, so I was able to help keep Miklós afloat financially by occasionally offering him jobs. These consisted mainly of helping me out on shoots, or with editing or post-production processes when I was pushed for time. When running my own business specializing in visual media, I have found it extremely hard to find, let alone trust, someone to help out when it comes to handling my creative material. If clients like my style, I tend to stick to that style, and to find someone able to reproduce that is nigh on impossible. But I seemed to find the perfect person in Miklós. His precision, finesse and eye for detail came in handy when I found myself overwhelmed in a sea of projects. He was a tremendous help and took a huge workload off my shoulders; and it suited him too, as he was able to earn some money — an essential factor in order to survive in Shanghai's expensive economic climate.

We had a pleasant spring ahead of us. For me, it was a breath of fresh air having him around, and the times we hung out together revitalized my routine. I found him a cheap scooter, on which he happily rode around the city, where he took his own photos, attended my shoots and frequented late night jazz clubs.

Miklós spent most of his days editing my work in a cafe near my house on Anfu Road. We usually met at midday to talk through the projects, had lunch and often planned things for the evening. His Shanghai sojourn, however, wasn't musically driven. Despite the city's lively music scene, Miklós rarely played on stage in Shanghai. It further highlighted for me just how different his approach was to music. He very rarely played for fun, and he never allowed himself to dip into the city's vibrant performing landscape. His focus was on my projects and his own, and he only very occasionally navigated between both, never letting his quality-control ethic slip one bit.

There was one memorable show, however, when he did join Yang Ji Ma on stage at the MAO Livehouse. She was on a short tour of venues in Beijing and Shanghai and, initially, didn't even know that Miklós was in town. Her live set was usually backed by a Russian DJ but, to my ears at least, this was thankfully interrupted by an acoustic interlude in which she was joined by Miklós. They played tracks from the Yunnan recording sessions from just a month earlier, and the event once again highlighted the crystallized brilliance of their collaborations. Almost topping that, Miklós then played a completely unrecognizable version of his signature song, 'Jaj, A Világ!'.

While in Shanghai, Miklós thrived on his anonymity; he enjoyed not being recognized and savored every bit of foreign territory in his new, temporary life. In contrast, there were times when the very same thing put a strain on him, and this I found understandable.

While working with me, the job sometimes required him to adopt the role of sideman, taking care of B-rolls on certain shoots. He embraced this willingly and handled our working relationship very well, even if the sometimes humiliating positions that photographers find themselves in was hard on him. Having to document party idiots arriving at pretentious venues can be soul-crushing for *any* photographer, let alone to one whose day job is as an internationally acclaimed musician. Working in a coal mine would have been more dignified; the kind of hired paparazzi work we sometimes had booked was definitely the Siberia of photography, and one needs a strong stomach to handle it.

This was also true for our editing and post-production work. I don't remember one job when a client didn't request adjustments of the first cut; it happened over and over again. At first, being used to his own working practices in which the final product was always his own flawless creation, Miklós took such demands personally. When I reminded him that he needed to detach himself, as our product was simply a company's output that needed to satisfy clients' requirements, he understood and began to relax. My advice disabused him of the mindset that the end product was his and his alone. I witnessed his inner struggle over this acquiescence, and I admired his guts as he eventually overcame such obstacles one by one. He swallowed his pride, which led to a greater working relationship between us.

Miklós' brief Shanghai sojourn was eventful and, thankfully, uneventful at the same time. There are so many things I could say about those three months but when such time is spent with a friend, in reality very little takes place apart from the unfolding of everyday life, and that's what made it special to me and seemingly uneventful if committed to paper. So I choose to stop writing and leave the rest blank.

That July, Miklós and his girlfriend made their way back to Budapest and our airport goodbye was really emotional. I couldn't help but think back to the first time Miklós and I had met in Beijing years before, and it was amazing to see how far our friendship had come.

That month, just after Miklós left, I founded my own production company in Hong Kong and decided to name it Almasy & Both, in honor of our collaborations and mutual appreciation. Technically, Miklós had nothing to do with it, but as the workload increased I found that including his name served as a fitting tribute to the months we'd spent together in Shanghai.

Our lives parted ways for a while. I was focusing on building the new company in both Hong Kong and Shanghai, while he went back to Budapest to put the finishing touches to his Chinese album. For the time being we didn't have any plans for teaming up together. But of course, as always, he was one step ahead.

The idea of taking the entire Chinese project lock, stock and barrel to Hungary was conceived sometime at the beginning of 2014. The project, with all its glory and success, must have been a logistical nightmare. He had to get used to this, however: in the future he'd repeat the process on a much larger scale. The idea was to bring all the musicians who'd been involved in the recordings over from Yunnan to celebrate the album release with a major concert in Budapest's prestigious arena venue, Müpa.

It was a mere coincidence that I was in Hungary at that time to document the events running up to the final performance. I never spend long periods in my home country, but that year I was undergoing considerable dental surgery over a period of months, one in the spring and one in the autumn. As luck had it, the concert coincided with my stay for my second appointment. I was especially fortunate because the event took place during my convalescence, when I could finally speak again after the operations.

This time, rather than coming from abroad, I traveled to Budapest from my home town of Debrecen, where I'd been recovering. Miklós picked me up at the central station, and we greeted each other with the usual "Zhege difang," and our usual laughter signified the irony of our meeting in Hungary, of all places.

Again, there wasn't much time to hang out. The Chinese musicians arrived the following morning and I went with a small entourage to pick them up, while Miklós waited for us in the hotel. As they exited the arrival hall, I saw the He Brothers first, with their ever-contagious smiles, followed by Wang Xiao and the rest of the musicians. We were all in for a small shock though when Yang Ji Ma appeared at the exit gate; she'd shaved off her beautiful trademark hair and approached us virtually bald. It was a drastic sight and took us a while to get used to. We found out the reason behind it a few days later. She was pregnant and she explained that, according to Tibetan tradition, women have to cut their hair because wearing it long saps energy from the embryo growing inside. However, later placing the mosaics together, I realized that there was also another reason. She was planning to retire from public life and this was her first real effort to shatter the *Nushen*, her media image as a goddess, before she could disappear into private oblivion.

We took the ensemble to the hotel, and four days of madness started with open rehearsals and press conferences leading up to the stage preparations at Müpa, where the show took place on the last day of their visit.

Meanwhile, with Miklós' agreement, I decided to post daily YouTube videos on the preparations leading up to the main event. I was staying at his place on the western, Buda side of the Danube (which divides the city into two, with Pest on the east), so whenever I was free from running around filming the musicians, I spent the mornings in his kitchen, editing the footage.

Finally, the day of the show came, and everyone was excited but jittery at the same time; some of the musicians terribly so. They were simple people, mainly from mountain villages, and now, facing a full auditorium in the heart of a sophisticated European capital city, with all the attendant press and TV attention, plus the prospect of their performances being recorded live, they became extremely anxious. The pressures exerted a particular strain on the He brothers; dressed in their traditional attire for the performance, they paced around the backstage area with uncharacteristically concerned expressions on their faces. This was indeed a big production, and they had confronted nothing on this scale before. I guess this was the moment when they truly realized Miklós' inappeasable ambitions.

At 7:45 that evening the curtains went up and Miklós' *Chinese Odyssey* suddenly came alive in all its magnitude in front of an enthusiastic 1,500-strong audience. The set-list, which mainly consisted of the Yunnan material, was brilliantly interwoven with Hungarian elements from Miklós' Folkside album. The show was simultaneously elegant and charming; Yang Ji Ma and Wang Xiao's songs elevated the event to majestic heights, while the He Brothers provided the most amusing moments. The show was the toughest on Miklós; not only did he have to give an immaculate performance, but he also was the only connection between the almost entirely Hungarian audience and the Chinese musicians. But the magic worked and for nearly two hours the interior of Müpa was magically transformed, with all vestiges of the modern world swept away by the musical evocation of the stark reality of the Himalayas.

Just before the finale, Miklós stepped forward to thank everyone who made the production happen. Suddenly I heard from the stage: "And, finally, I would like to thank Nicky Almasy for accompanying us on this wonderful journey, documenting it all from the very beginning."

He pointed me out, standing there with camera in hand, half-submerged in the shadows. The Budapest audience turned to me as I froze in sudden shock. Only a few people in the whole building—the musicians and the production team—knew who I was.

This was a pivotal moment for me, the one when I realized how everything had turned around. Miklós might have previously thanked me for accompanying him on his Chinese journey, but in those few seconds with the entire audience staring at me, I realized how far he had actually brought me, ripping me out of my Shanghai cocoon. Delegations from the Hungarian cultural milieu, with which I was so unfamiliar and from whom I had distanced myself for years, now looked at me curiously. All the local photographers in the media pit turned and glanced in my direction, wondering who Miklós was talking about. That same week my name was everywhere in the national press, mostly name-checking me for my Chinese short film. In the maelstrom of this moment, for a split second, I recalled what he told me back at Shanghai airport just before he was leaving: "Thanks for all the help. You'll see, I'll return this favor to you one day."

It seemed this was my day, my time, the one that turned it all around in the unfamiliar climate of my own country, bringing me full circle: back home.

But the evening wasn't only a turning point for me. Despite all the success, the *Both Miklós Musical Odyssey* show was in a way Yang Ji Ma's final moment to shine in the glare of the spotlight. Unfortunately for the rest of us, soon afterwards she sank back to the relatively mundane scene from which she had emerged, and all that could have been just slipped out of view. With her triumphant performance in Budapest and on the album serving as high-water marks in her musical life, it felt such an unlikely move that she had chosen to let it all go.

The concert was a fitting end for a phenomenal collaboration, but also seemed to me to be the swan song of a promising career. Soon afterwards, she moved to Shanghai with her husband and got subsumed back into the local, mediocre underground scene, her voice lost against the backdrop of slightly out of tune guitars, programmed DJ beats and lazy musical structures, all of which gradually but entirely demystified her.

For any artist who worked with Miklós, there was certainly

the option to seize the moment and make something out of it. Sadly, Yang Ji Ma certainly didn't, and instead remained in the lukewarm scene in which she'd been before they crossed each other's paths in Chongqing.

Rumours circulated that she became a target for the Chinese government because, after all, she represented Tibet, one of China's sensitive issues, and that she'd been advised to hold back on her career to prevent drawing unnecessary attention to herself. Whatever caused her to withdraw from the limelight, in my opinion, it led to the waste of an exceptional talent.

That evening, once the hustle, bustle and ecstasy of the show had subsided, Miklós and I jumped into his car and he drove us back to his place in Buda. It was early autumn, the weather was still mild but I could already feel the first bites of winter's chill arriving. The windows were down and a cool breeze swept through the interior of the car. This moment was so surreal, somehow even cinematic; the aftermath of the show reminded me of those scenes in old black-and-white movies when the stars sit in a stationary car in the studio while images of the road outside are projected behind them. After a few minutes' silence he asked me: "So... how was it?" It was the most precious moment in all the time I'd known him, and has remained so ever since — nothing could beat the weight of having no answer to his question.

When we got back to Miklós' place he needed several hours to come down from the show, so we opened a bottle of wine and talked long into the night. A sense of closure lingered in the air; everything that *was* China, *began* in China, and had come to a grinding halt right there and then. It wasn't sad, not even bittersweet; it just simply marked the end of an era, giving a sign to the times and to both of us to move on. So we did.

To Miklós, it was certainly the end point of an enormous

project, but it was also the very beginning of something grander. The stage lights were still warm at Müpa but, as always, Miklós was already one step ahead. I didn't know where exactly his thoughts were leading him but I was sure that he was headed somewhere new. This was his first giant leap towards becoming the fêted folklorist he is today and, as it transpired, he was about to embark on a journey that would eventually take him further — to India, to Africa and to his beloved Ukraine. I was proud and grateful to have been there and to have been able to capture it all in both pixels and memories.

Cities present you with a constellation of people, shooting stars from which you must recognize and connect with those who display exceptional validity in your life and help you move forward. It could have been anyone, but oddly and randomly, Beijing gave me Miklós Both, a man whom I believe displays regal integrity and rare authenticity. He is an artist who constantly dragged me into the unknown. He rendered me fearless of uncharted waters and made me immune to physical distance. And while he pushed me further to explore foreign lands, he also somehow managed to pull me closer to my long neglected roots. Through Miklós, I went back home, not just geographically but also in my heart. So that, thanks to this Hungarian Prince of art and life, I rediscovered the *real* unknown territory: my own country and, through that, my forgotten self.

Red Icons – The AirAsia Run

To put it very simply, I landed my photojournalist job at AirAsia thanks to the legendary airline boss Tony Fernandes, but perhaps this is making it sound too easy. The long process to become an Allstar (AirAsia's internal name for its employees) was rather an intricate affair that precipitated the biggest crisis of my adult life, almost costing me everything I'd built up over a decade beforehand.

My long-winding journey with AirAsia, the biggest low-cost airline carrier based in Southeast Asia, started with an innocent holiday trip to Indonesia, after an exhausting year and decade working in Shanghai. I was a busy freelance photographer working in China for local and international publications and it was part of my annual routine that, when I felt burned out with work, I hopped on a plane to vacate the claustrophobic Chinese metropolis. For many Shanghailanders — an old term for foreigners living there — who were living in the city's concrete-glass-steel jungle, AirAsia was a synonym for an easy way out, an escape route to Southeast Asia. It is a connection hub to dream destinations, sinful tropical cities and exotic islands scattered endlessly over the region, but just within reach.

When you're a Shanghailander, the windows of respite open twice a year and close again quickly before you know it. Freelancers may get to skip town more often, but as Shanghai is completely sealed off from any green areas, it takes too much organizing to escape to any appreciable degree. So instead, city dwellers hold themselves hostage to the urban rhythm and make excuses to stay.

When there is a need to get out, there are two options. Chinese New Year arrives in the freezing cold, and for foreigners presents itself as a second holiday season just after Christmas. But as annual visits home have only just been taken, the choice is to remain in China or else choose a nearby destination, preferably somewhere warm and remedial away from the bone-chilling temperatures.

At this time of year, the urban engines of Shanghai completely shut down. As the migrant workers return home there is an exodus from the city—the only time when Shanghai, shedding what seems like at least half its 25-million population, becomes an eerie ghost town, albeit a huge one. This is the best time to get away for a week or so. The second choice is the National Day Golden Week, inaugurated by the government at the turn of the 21st century to commemorate the establishment of the People's Republic of China on 1st October, 1949. This holiday of seven (occasionally eight) days is not as dramatic but, as most companies take a break, it provides another opportunity to retreat from the city.

Especially in winter time, to board an AirAsia flight is an experience in itself; a sudden sobering slap, in demonstrable contrast to the rigidity of the Chinese metropolitan mindset. An atmosphere of carefree nonchalance hits you instantly as you board the plane. The airline's distinct, red-uniformed cabin crew greets you, as you squeeze into your seat among the hordes of lightly-dressed tourists, seemingly already in holiday mode. Right there as you embark, you realize that you're suddenly, instantly somewhere else, somewhere more relaxing; the easy-going ambience is enchanting. The tight legroom and the limited in-flight menu hardly matter; it's only for a few hours anyway, and it's part of the budget airline experience. Instead of seeking fleeting airborne comfort, the focus is already on the destination.

It was under this cheerful get-away spell sometime in the second half of 2015 that I took a pivotal AirAsia journey. I leaned back in my seat, picked up the glossy inflight magazine, *Travel360*, from the pocket brushing my knees and casually flicked through it. I was instantly impressed. I noticed its great quality: the articles were insightful, the quality of the writing was high, the photography both on the cover and inside was stunning. It wasn't the usual perfunctory rag stuffed full of ads with a few filler articles. This was a proper magazine, a great, informative read; a great specimen of printed media. I read it through from cover to cover. I studied each article, not even suspecting that I was holding my very future in my hands. Although it was a pivotal moment that changed my life, unknowingly and imperceptibly, for the time being I didn't pay too much attention to it. However, after reading it through, I slipped the magazine into my bag rather than replacing it as you're supposed to.

That's all AirAsia had meant to me until this point; a means of escape, a holiday facilitator, a cheap and affordable way out of a seemingly never-ending, hectic schedule. I knew nothing about the company's operation, its history, or its background — it was just an airline I liked and used regularly. Least of all did I suspect that one day this corporate entity would not only become my home in Southeast Asia, but that I would turn out to be its only foreign photojournalist, and that my ideas and my stories would inspire not only myself but hopefully the magazine's numerous readers with a wanderlust that embraced thousands and thousands of square kilometers. I hardly imagined that the team behind this supposedly disposable inflight publication would become *my team*, and that I'd become part of its system, delighted to nestle under the wings of its iconic red livery.

Tony Fernandes, the founder of AirAsia, is a legend in his own right and a genuine one at that. Hailing from a simple working class Malaysian-Indian background, owning one of Malaysia's most famous and most successful companies qualifies him as the ultimate self-made man, someone with whom common people can easily and rightfully identify. He's an embodiment of dreams coming true, of working hard and taking those dreams to the extremes.

His story is well-documented; back in 2001 he bought an unloved, debt-ridden, once government-funded airline called AirAsia for the token price of one Malaysian ringgit (25 US cents) and under his jurisdiction the company finally took off. He began with two aircraft, and within a year he was turning a profit. Building an airline from scratch in the immediate aftermath of 9/11 was challenging but, astonishingly, he turned the ailing business around within just a year. Tony's trick was that while the company grew from cheap tickets, he connected together some of Southeast Asia's unlikeliest destinations and slowly but surely brought much of Asia within reach thanks to his growing fleet. By the mid-Noughties AirAsia had become Southeast Asia's biggest airline, now running a 250-strong fleet of airplanes. In short, he revolutionized aviation in the region.

And the man hasn't stopped ever since: he's relevant and hands-on as ever and hasn't decamped to an ivory tower. His approach is direct to the extreme; to get to the bottom of the company's inner operations and challenges, he works the flow on a monthly rotation at the lower levels of the AirAsia employment system; he packs the baggage, serves food on flights, listens to and accepts suggestions. Thus, he meets any problems first-hand and not via memos or reports from thrice-removed executives.

His creative force is as strong as ever, the company is constantly changing with innovations. Being an employee for

AirAsia oftentimes feels like working on shiftings sands, making it a challenging, adventurous and yet ever-inspiring ride.

Tony Fernandes is also known for his generosity when it comes to recognizing talent. His leadership nurtures creativity and innovation among the Allstars. Many stories circulate within the company about him giving out major opportunities, even top positions, spontaneously. Once, he was waiting for a flight to Singapore and he got into a conversation with a young guy. Tony admired his enthusiasm and it convinced him to offer the boy a top position in AirAsia's Singapore department.

My encounter with Tony that eventually led to my being on the receiving end of his generosity was still further down the line, but when it actually happened it turned around my situation entirely, lifting me out of the difficult times I was going through in Southeast Asia.

At first, my brush with *Travel360* magazine didn't seem that big a deal to me. I was comfortable in my Shanghai life, the photography and video business I had been running on my own for a decade was going great. I had my own Hong Kong company, I had assignments and jobs coming in from all directions. I was secure in my position and, frankly, I didn't even need any extra work. So, when I got home from the Indonesian trip, I threw the magazine down on my desk and I casually dropped an email to the editor attaching my portfolio see if there might be an opportunity of some work in the future. It was just another freelance option and I didn't really give it a second thought.

To my surprise, the editor's response was prompt; I received an email the very same day. She suggested an assignment in Shanghai straight away and informed me that she'd send a writer to work with me on it. I agreed to the shoot—it was Shanghai's Museum of Glass, in Putou district. I already had material on the museum but I didn't mention this. It seemed a good start, to get to know each other and if a writer was coming anyway, what harm could it do to shoot the place for the second time and get to know the people behind the magazine?

It turned out to be the right decision: the new visit to the museum gave me my first cover for *Travel360* just five months later, and this kickstarted a whole new chapter in my photography career and cemented the first cornerstones of my new direction in travel photography. Meanwhile, I also offered my recently-shot photos of the then up-and-coming Myanmar, and they accepted it for a pictorial in the same issue. As a result, I ended up with almost 20 pages of my photography and the cover for my very first issue of *Travel360*. The potential for continuing my life in Southeast Asia was slowly rising out of the future's mist.

The importance of AirAsia and its inflight magazine only became relevant when, in the meantime, I decided to leave Shanghai after 10 years. The aim was to find another livable metropolis while moving further into Asia's tropical zones. After months of mulling it over and examining the region, my choice finally fell upon Bangkok, Thailand. The Thai capital seemed to be the next logical step; it was still a metropolis but a more laid-back one, less rigid than Shanghai. Somehow, it seemed to present the right balance. Within weeks, I'd paid a visit to the busy Sukhumvit district that spreads out like the pulsating arteries of this vibrating city, just to map it out and gauge what opportunities might lay before me. It felt enticing enough to make the move. It was time to shake things up and start a brand new chapter.

I'm simply incapable of looking at things other than from an artistic prospective. I view every step I take, every action, every city I move to as an art project, and this is how I usually make decisions too — it's something I can't shake off.

To leave Shanghai after ten years was a conscious decision

to get out of my comfort zone. I'd established myself as a photographer there, I was a well-known choice with a steady clientele and so, ultimately, it was a pretty hard decision to let it all go. But I felt I'd started to outgrow the city. I'd hit a certain ceiling work-wise, and I began to get bored with what I was doing, and the ten-year mark seemed to suggest a full circle and presented a good opportunity for me to move on.

The move to Bangkok was a reality check, a self-imposed test. I wanted to see whether the Nicky Almasy brand name I'd built up so strongly in Shanghai would work further afield, would stand the test outside the bubble I'd created it in. Would it only work in Shanghai? I often wondered. Would it work somewhere else? I had enjoyed some international success over the years — my photography had been published in the UK's *Financial Times* and *Daily Mail* newspapers, in the design and arts magazine *Wallpaper*, and in the *Where Singapore* travel monthly, and I'd won two Best International Architectural Photography awards — but I knew I needed a real, drastic transformation.

I wanted to see if I could jump up a level. Every relatively successful artist should do this now and then — as soon as they get a little too comfortable. The idea is not to destroy your customer base entirely, but close a chapter and start again from square one. Looking back, it was my fantasy Berlin-period that David Bowie made after his first flush of success in the 1970s. But instead of Berlin's divided urban landscape, I chose the palm trees, the swelteringly hot streets, the noisy traffic and the mighty temples of Bangkok as my new backdrop. Only later did I realize that the move was a very dangerous reality check, a game of Russian roulette with my career that involved many risks, both financially and personally. But my mind was already made up. And I recognized AirAsia as the suitable vehicle to help carry it all out.

At that point, I didn't have a clear vision or direction in my head, but the signs and the move to Southeast Asia suggested that I should gravitate towards travel photography. The *Travel360* editor's keen interest was a promising lead, coming from such a high quality and well-known inflight magazine. It was something I'd never done before. This was a totally different world from the glass and steel of Shanghai Tower, miles away from the sweat and smoke of the jazz and blues musicians I had so eagerly documented in my once beloved city, and all the other work I'd taken on in Shanghai for lifestyle magazines. I could see some common elements: there'd be strong portrait-shooting opportunities, diverse architectural choices, old and new; and the vivid colors I was working with in my photography all seemed to fit the new direction perfectly.

But there were other challenges to face on a personal level. After 10 years of constant success and recognition, with my name regularly in print, supported by a loyal client base, to arrive in a new city where no one knew who the hell I was, was rejuvenating but occasionally depressing. Although I knew this was exactly what I needed and felt prepared for its hardships, it was still demanding. Leaving something so sure behind to trade it in for anonymity, especially at the age of 41, was a strange choice I admit, but I knew this was the only way to test myself professionally.

Needless to say, I wasn't at all inconsiderate to the views of my wife regarding the move. The decision was mutual and it suited her own aspirations as a professional yoga teacher; Southeast Asia being renowned as the most authentic hub for yoga training fitted her direction perfectly.

There were ups and downs to our decision, however. I experienced some ups instantly, during my very first days in Bangkok, and they were simply inspiring. My newfound anonymity filled me with comfort and I felt great being invisible after the relatively small and claustrophobic community of Shanghai, where so many people knew who I was. I saw it clearly: I needed a new chapter in my life and this was it. But I didn't quite yet know how challenging the downsides would be, the real hard part which crashed down on me later on, sucking me under to depths I'd never experienced before.

Once I found myself on new ground I came to one crucial realization — that photography itself just wasn't enough any more. Leading up to the mid 2010s, I came to the conclusion that the profession was becoming increasingly swamped by opportunists who just happened to have picked up a camera, printed their name on a card and called themselves a photographer. There was nothing wrong with this, of course; I had been just such an opportunist, except that I did it a decade earlier. However, by now I couldn't help but feel that masses of people were being converted to the seemingly easy-going and attractive lifestyle of the freelance photographer.

Let's overlook for a moment the question of who has talent and who hasn't. With the arrival on the market of cheaper and better quality cameras in the second half of the 2010's, it seemed that anyone could snap photos for a living (or so they thought), turning the profession into what I perceived to be an overcrowded ship that was slowly but surely beginning to sink. And I decided to be one of the first to head for the lifeboat.

When the *Travel360* editor, Beverly Rodrigues, suggested that I should write my own stories, too, along with photographing them, I jumped at the chance. I had never capitalized on it but I did have some experience in this field; I had begun writing while I was living in London in the 1990s. I got my first opportunity in freelance journalism from Andy Davis, my friend and then-editor of the British music monthly *Record Collector*, and I regularly contributed to the magazine with articles that mostly concentrated on my favorite acts. I had two major features under my belt, one on the Huddersfield rock band Embrace, and another on the American rapper Eminem, but I also wrote short book and album reviews. Andy gave me a chance because he saw that insatiable enthusiasm in me towards my favorites and was reassured of my abilities as a writer from the book of my poetry that I'd given him that included some English verses.

After ten years, I resumed writing music features again, for *That's Shanghai*. The editor gave me the music editor position where I had to fill eight pages each month with articles and reviews on local, Shanghai and international music acts supplemented by my photography. Producing regular features chiseled my skill further by the years but ultimately and surprisingly, nothing prepared me for the level of professionalism I had to rise to in terms of writing for *Travel360*. When I read the editor's feedback about the first article I submitted, I realized that it was certainly time for me to buckle up and knuckle down, because I was suddenly facing the toughest editor I'd ever encountered. Against her standards, my efforts were still the clumsy but ever enthusiastic scribbles of a self-made writer. But I was there to learn and accepted the challenge from the very beginning.

As I settled into my new home in Bangkok, I was compelled to update my work ethic entirely. Although photography was my forte, I had to refigure it into being merely one of the tools in my kit. Instead of just running around encumbered with heavy equipment as any typical photographer has to do, I now had to do much more legwork in my mind—I buried myself deep into online research on the subjects I had been commissioned to write about. There was a genuine bonus here: the heavy burden of the Chinese Internet straitjacket no longer applied. Thailand had regular, Western-style freedom-of-speech access to YouTube,

Facebook and, crucially, Google's otherwise ubiquitous search engine—all the sites banned in the inwards-looking Middle Kingdom were now available. I found it liberating both professionally and personally. Only those with experience of living in China can understand this kind of relief. Chinese residents suffer from the country's unrelenting clamp down on foreign sites. The only solution was to use VPN (Virtual Private Network) services to get beyond the so-called Great Firewall of China, but now in Thailand it was finally possible to do a simple online search and instantly connect with anyone, or any idea, that I fancied. The lights had turned green and everything was up to me now.

When informed about my move to Thailand, my new editor provided me with some sample AirAsia destinations, so I began scanning through Thai cities and provinces, on the lookout for engaging cultural angles. Upon reflection, the new direction totally suited my skills; I loved connecting the dots by tracking down the people behind the stories, lining up the photo shoots and interview opportunities. Even during my Shanghai years, instead of snapping photos randomly, I was always looking for the stories and the personalities behind them, and this new direction took that approach to another level. It suited my style of focusing on one subject for weeks at a time, or even for a month. In this respect, Southeast Asia provided me with another revelation: instead of chronicling hectic city life, my attention now turned to small communities in swelteringly hot villages, hidden deep in the Thai countryside. My focus shifted from sky-high buildings to tiny, humble settlements and the people they contained; modest wooden houses with walls decorated with photos of their King Bhumibol the Great—revered at home and renowned elsewhere as the world's longest-reigning living head of state.

I searched for stories through a photographer's eye, what might work visually in a magazine while paying attention to what would pique the interest of the editor and through her, the readers. Striking, colorful, rich in detail, dipped in history and tradition; these were the priorities and they proved to be compatible with the magazine's wanderlust-inspiring angle. I was looking for material that instantly lured the readers in with enticing imagery, and from there I unfolded the details in the article. My propensity to idolize a certain subject—as I did previously with up-and-coming musicians— came in handy. Throughout my life, if I found something interesting, I focused on it almost to the level of obsession. I dissected it, examined it and through that came to portray it naturally. And now, suddenly, this was my job.

This was how I approached my first cover story for *Travel360*, 'The Indigo Dye'. Through my research I came across indigo dyeing in the northeastern province of Thailand, Sakon Nakhon, and I instantly imagined this dark shade of blue spreading over the pages of the magazine. Indigo is deeply engrained in Sakon Nakhon's past, and there were many vendors selling dyed clothes, but I wanted to find the source, where the tradition had begun; how the dye was made, what was the process and who were the people behind it. I wanted to cover everything from the sowing of the indigofera plants—the distinctive color is extracted from its leaves—through the dyeing process right down to the products reaching the shops. That's how I discovered a local woman named Praphaiphan Daengchai, who had resurrected the indigo dye tradition with her mother, Khun Teeta, around the beginning of the 1990s, and had established the company Mae Teeta, trading solely in original indigo products. Not surprisingly, no one spoke English around the villages, so I hired an up-and-coming exclusive tour company, the Very Local Trip, to get me close to locals and help me to conduct the interviews. Meanwhile, I came across some Hollywood connections too. The production company behind *Troy*, a Brad Pitt blockbuster, had ordered thousands of blue costumes from Mae Teeta. This discovery gave a contemporary twist to my story.

The feature made it to the cover of *Travel360* and before I knew it, I had yet another cover story, featuring the colorful street art around Chiang Mai, the former capital of the independent Lanna Kingdom, in mountainous northern Thailand. I first came across the city's murals on a personal trip—I found that the streets of this well-known holiday destination were adorned with random murals of Kurt Cobain, elephant-art and the work of local artists, whom I tracked down through online search. The new success gave me yet another dose of optimism, and confirmation that travel writing plus photography was the right direction to take me forward.

Just a year before, I'd been flipping through the magazine on a random flight, and now three of their issues featured my writing as well as my photography. While I was still freelancing for *Travel360*, the office had the nonchalant habit of failing to inform me if a photo of mine had made it onto the cover. There was nothing fishy about it; they paid me, of course. But I realized later that they were just too busy to keep their contributors informed. Without any prior knowledge therefore, if I happened to come across a photograph of mine gracing the magazine cover sitting in its seat pocket right in front of me, it had an electrifying effect on me. Five million readers! I'd had several magazine covers under my belt by that time, so I was used to my photos being on display throughout an entire city; however, unsuspectingly discovering that I'd made it to the cover of *Travel360*, and witnessing my article being read by passengers sitting right next to me, was a totally new experience. Such scenarios assured me that my new strategy was indeed working. I'd tapped into something great, I felt, and I was inspired to apply myself yet further into this exciting new venture.

While my ties with AirAsia strengthened further, Bangkok turned out to be only a temporary solution. The unfavorable job climate in the city left little to build upon. I was hungry for new, local projects. I tried to forge ahead constantly by emailing magazine editors at various publications based in the city but, after being used to super-fast Chinese responses, I realized rather quickly that such speedy communication just wasn't the same here. I even descended into the excruciating world of networking events, but it didn't take long to get the measure of the city's limitations in this regard, and the penny soon dropped that this approach wasn't working. Bangkok is an odd city like that; to the outsider it appears to be a modern metropolis bustling with energy, but once you spend a few months there, and especially when you're looking for freelancing opportunities, the cold realization dawns that, in fact, it's just a terribly overgrown holiday town. Its enormous main road, the Sukhumvit, the one that actually runs straight into western Cambodia, is sprawling, but its arborescent *sois*, the side streets that lead into semi-rural areas, mark its urban limits. Even for locals this is where employment openings close. It's an unbelievably diverse and fascinating city. But for a job seeker, it's a desolate environment.

First and foremost, in Thailand all work is strictly prohibited for foreign photographers—there is a special law that forbids it. I learned this a little too late. As a tourist, you can walk around and take photos anywhere you like, but even a half professional-looking shoot in the street with, say, an assistant holding a reflector, can get you arrested, or at the very least, questioned. This was a big change for me. In China, its own many restrictions notwithstanding, I could walk about and do whatever I wanted in Shanghai or Hong Kong, even stop the traffic for my own convenience. But in Thailand, as I discovered, employers prefer local lensmen, to protect their own professional infrastructure. The result is that any unsuspecting foreign photographer based in Bangkok goes grey waiting for the phone to ring. To outsiders, the Thai market is a closed shop, almost completely sealed off. To put it bluntly, the locals just don't want your services, no matter how high the quality of your work. You won't even be considered. There is simply no demand. It was a huge blow in terms of my day-to-day existence, let alone my future plans. This was the first real obstacle against my intended artistic and personal transformation, and it gave me sleepless nights.

Despite this scenario, by some unbelievable twist of fate, I ended up living in a compound that was home to a small group of Russian and Ukrainian photographers and models trying to make a living in Bangkok. From the relative security that my AirAsia assignments abroad afforded me, I got to witness their day-to-day struggles first hand, as they tried to made ends meet under the dire Thai conditions, not to mention the rapidly changing photography climate as the new Instagram and hashtag generation gatecrashed the scene around the mid-2010s.

The compound I moved into, Regent Home 22 at the end of Soi 85, was near the skytrain station On Nut, close enough to downtown but far enough to keep a safe distance from hectic city life. The quiet soi, branching off from the Sukhumvit Road, reached deep enough inside the grid of houses to be a cozy, if only temporary, home. I would awake to birds chirping, to the distant sound of the skytrain whizzing by along Sukhumvit and, occasionally, to a car passing outside the window—but it was still a refreshing change from the bustling urban existence I'd come from. The compound, built only a few years previously, was clean, new and well-equipped with a gym and an outdoor swimming pool—something I hadn't been used to. The rent was unbelievably cheap and the location was very convenient. I could choose not to leave the compound for days, even for weeks on end and I was still OK there; there were plenty of shops and cheap eateries around, so if it wasn't necessary to go to town, I could just hang around and immerse myself in the local *sabai-sabai*, the Thai holiday state of mind. This was the ideal place to contemplate what to do next, which I felt I needed sorely after leaving China.

In fact, the whole city of Bangkok itself is like this; it affords comfort and time to think. It's the perfect place to park your life down for a few months if you're at a crossroads and don't know which way to turn next. It's an affordable place; I discovered that I could live there for very little, eat great food every day and still maintain a high-quality and relaxed existence.

To watch the Russians and Ukrainians in Bangkok hustling for jobs was a case study itself for any freelance photographer struggling within the same insular Thai environment. Indeed, their expat community was tight-knit too; they helped each other out by working together, borrowing each other's equipment, and passing on jobs to one another. The roof of my compound was used as a photographic studio, as it provided a constant source of natural light, a substitute for the lack of opportunities down at street level. Given Thailand's weather conditions, the light was always great; you just needed to be familiar with how the sun moved around the building in order to pick the right time for your artistic preference. The photographers constantly took models up there to practice their skills. It was a mutually beneficial arrangement, as the models used the photographers when they needed head-shots or additions to their portfolios.

Through the introduction to the community by a very kind Ukranian guy called Vova Andriichuk who later became my friend, I soon got fully involved too. I also had a lot of equipment they could use, so everyone got excited. Besides, we all got on together very well. They advised me on how to get up to the roof and how to use the 'studio'; and it wasn't long before I began working on small photographic projects, which led to collaborations. Stepping out of my comfort zone and finding myself among these expat photographers, who at first didn't even know that we shared the same profession, was definitely a right step ahead for me, and I found it a liberating experience. It was the first time that I'd started to feel a genuine degree of distance from Shanghai.

In all aspects, it was an inspiring milieu. The expats explored every avenue of the urban opportunity. Some of the male models sold their sperm to Chinese tourists for a few thousand dollars a time. As infertility was on the increase in China and unmarried women in particular were barred from accessing sperm banks at home, would-be mothers came to Thailand. Westerners' 'donations' were quite popular, especially if the fathers-to-be had blue eyes. It was easy in Bangkok; all the donors had to do was register, upload their portrait to a sperm bank catalogue, deliver their samples, and wait for a call.

Photography, modeling and the booming sperm business aside, the Bangkok community masterfully played visa games with Thai authorities. They were aware of every slight rule change, they knew every backdoor trick of how to stay afloat in Thailand. There was so much information passed on by word of mouth, foreigners didn't even need to search online. Every little change in the visa situation echoed through the compound the same day. From just in front of the local supermarket there were regular buses traveling across the border to neighboring Laos twice a week, for visa runs disguised as simple holiday trips.

Back in Shanghai, my wife and I had steady work visas for

the entire ten years we lived there, and we therefore found it excruciating to get used to the unstable immigration situation in Thailand. Although we knew we were on the right track, we felt utterly stateless. My wife is also Hungarian, and as European Union citizens we had a relatively good position in Southeast Asia, but only up to a certain period of time — we could survive for eighteen months if we pushed it, but staying any longer was just asking for trouble. The authorities tend to be very well informed as to which overseas visitors are playing the living-in-Thailand game, and after our safety-net period had expired we expected to be stopped at every passport control point and bombarded with awkward questions. Even if we weren't deported, the threat of it shook our tiny, fragile world to the core, and was a constant, bitter reminder of our uncertain future.

Although living in Bangkok was cheap, I was beginning to struggle financially. Not only were the costs of regular cross-border runs to neighboring Cambodia and Laos to get updated visas eating into our reserves, but the terms on which freelancers were employed at AirAsia were far from ideal — payment wasn't due until three months after each completed job.

My wife and I made a cosy home in Bangkok for almost a year, but with each passing month it became more apparent that our stay there was only temporary and that we would have to move on again eventually. It was just a matter of time. So, drifting towards further uncertainty we came up with a solution: the next logical step seemed to be moving one step closer to AirAsia's headquarters — Kuala Lumpur, Malaysia.

I had never overcomplicated moving to a new city. I just packed my bags, moved and then figured out the rest later. And it always worked. Earlier in my life, riding on the breezy gamble of youth, each new territory was somehow easy to conquer. I was more flexible, easy-going too and, in a bizarre way, I felt as if I had actually made an art out of it. I guess I could have been lucky as well, although it rarely seemed like that at first. After London, New York, Shanghai, and Bangkok, by the time Kuala Lumpur was on the horizon, it felt as if yet another emigration was just part of my life's routine.

But there was something else to consider now. I had just turned forty-one and I knew that the next place we chose to live had to be the right one. We were running out of time, money and energy. It was our second fresh start in a new city within a year after Shanghai, and I knew this time it had to happen. The risks and the possible consequences of failing began to get incredibly stressful. There was no way back. With no money behind me there was no Plan B, other than to return to my small town in Hungary. And I would have rather died.

Thus, short of other options, I targeted the biggest goal, the longest shot, the one that over-reached every previous ambition I'd had in my profession. Even though, on paper, success seemed an unlikely and distant chance, I felt I had to officially join one of the biggest companies in the region. I decided now was the time to finally set my sights on my dream job—to become a full-time photojournalist for AirAsia.

Upon arriving in Kuala Lumpur to start our new life, we took a small Airbnb apartment in the city's suburban Serdang district. This wasn't anything like our romanticized relocation to Bangkok just a year before, when we still had some security in our lives. This was deadly serious. We undertook this major move with no visa and without knowing anyone in the city apart from the magazine team. The heavy pressure of starting from scratch again now bore down on us with full force, and it was a strange situation to put ourselves in after a decade of seemingly bulletproof stability. Even by my adventurous standards this was a bold move.

Therefore, I instantly set my plan in motion. There was no time to waste. I requested a meeting with my *Travel360* editor. It was easier now that we were both in the same city, after all. One of the main difficulties we had encountered previously was communicating solely via email, and the move to Kuala Lumpur finally dispersed that. I suggested that I could take on more frequent commissions, two stories per month, in fact. I did hint that I would eventually like to join full-time but, for now, I figured it was better to take it one step at a time.

At this point, I had been freelancing for AirAsia for about eighteen months, and I knew that I was a good asset for the magazine. Otherwise I wouldn't even put all my chances on this one card. My stories and ideas almost always ended up on the cover, my style clearly seemed to fit the magazine's, they liked my work; and by then I had already developed a great working relationship with the team. I assessed my own worth and banked that I wasn't building upon empty dreams. The magazine was used to sending out two people for each job, a writer and a photographer, so I presented myself as two-in-one. Actually, as three. As AirAsia was moving towards digital, video content was becoming important, and when I brought up that I was already making films too, my skill-set looked even stronger. Over the following months, as my ideas became regular features in the magazine, and as cover stories too, I carefully made the suggestion that I'd like to join them full time. This was my only savior. I felt the constant hassle of freelancing was behind me; I wanted something solid, reliable and secure. The only way to turn my situation around was to join a big company, to fall under the saving grace of something major. But if truth be told, no one really wanted a full-time photographer on their books.

As I've said, by the mid-2010s, it seemed that every chancer with a new DSLR hanging around their neck was brazenly infiltrating the supposedly glamorous profession of photography. However, there was one major flaw in their thinking. While this glorified vocation seemed very attractive to the uninitiated, there was absolutely no one willing to employ them full time. The rapid rise in the numbers of photographers plying their wares brought a quick and easy solution for anyone looking for imaging services. If a company needed someone to do a shoot, they were spoilt for choice, and it wasn't hard to find a newbie willing to undercut the cheapest quote, which all too often was itself then also undercut, and so on. There was a surfeit of photographers out there whose dream was to turn their hobby into their profession, and they didn't mind working for just a few bucks to get started. Thus, if you chose this line of work you were easily doomed to the freelance lifestyle for an eternity, always without security. A company would never pay taxes or provide insurance; they would choose another freelancer from the thousands on offer rather than take you under their wing with all the costs involved. So when I realized that I actually had an all-in-one package to offer AirAsia — writing, photography and videography — I wasted no time presenting it to them.

Luckily, the editor felt the same; she wanted me to be part of the team but there was a major issue to deal with — AirAsia had temporarily frozen hiring due to over-employment. We both wanted the same thing but we were stuck. But then Beverly had an unlikely suggestion, which sounded odd at first: why didn't I approach Tony Fernandes, the boss of AirAsia, personally? It had happened before, she reassured me. He had been known to randomly embrace talent, so I might as well give it a shot. At first, I found the suggestion utterly ridiculous and, frankly, I didn't think it would work; why would a man who owns 250 airplanes care about my problems? Why would he even bother? And how would I go about approaching him?

Tony's autobiography, *Flying High*, had just been published, and as the book's editor was the very same editor I was communicating with, she suggested that I go along to a book signing event at the brilliant Kinokuniya bookshop at KLCC—the Kuala Lumpur City Centre commercial complex—meet the man himself and then follow it up with an email. All I had to do was to appear at the event with her and get introduced so that, "he can at least put a face to the email." I was nervous at the suggestion, but as my options were limited, I agreed. I attended the event and bought his book. As he signed it for me, I quickly mentioned that I worked for *Travel360*. He smiled and asked: "Oh really?" before adding something to his signature along the lines of "Thank you all for your hard work at *Travel360*."

The encounter was brief but I discovered later that Tony had a great memory and remembered me well. Back home, I immediately started to read *Flying High*, and was struck by how much his true personality came across in the book. His story was similar to mine, only on a much grander scale. He took chances and worked hard; and if he failed, he stood up and got back to work again. All his achievements had been built up from unlikely little coincidences. When I came across the line, "I read every single email carefully that lands in my mailbox," I paused for a second and thought to myself, "This could actually work." I turned on my laptop and composed a letter to him, telling him that I was a freelancer for his company but I would really like to work for AirAsia full time, not just as a photographer, but as a videographer and a writer too. I was honest and to the point and, in the hope of making an impact I wrote in the subject line, "The tall white guy from the book signing". And then clicked 'Send'.

There was no immediate answer. I drifted between believing and not believing that he'd ever get back to me. It seemed unlikely but somehow I felt he would. Instead of obsessing about it, I just went on with my life and tried not to think about it for the time being.

Weeks later I was on assignment, traveling across Iran, another country (like China), in which Western websites are blocked, so I rarely had internet access. In Tehran, I eventually got the news I'd been waiting for — a message from my editor saying, "Nicky, Tony responded, he said yes." When I finally regained access to my emails I saw Tony's reply to me personally. He was concise, but the news was definitely good: "Thanks for your message, Nicky. If she's agreeable, yeah, let's do it."

I was thrilled. I particularly loved working in Iran, but it became an even more memorable journey as, upon my return, my professional life took a sudden upwards trajectory, with all its promise of regular work and job security. Until then, I'd been constantly roaming around in foreign lands, and my work was becoming more difficult. I felt as if I was drifting about without a home. It's easy and fun to travel when you have somewhere secure to return to, but without it, travel can be a dark, soul-searching experience. After receiving the email, I sensed a small ray of light piercing through the gloomy skies. I felt a touch of belonging, and it filled my days with joy in the cool, autumn-stung streets of Tehran.

I had been working on stories about Persian carpets and the old, traditional *hammams* — public bathhouses — and I now began enjoy this fascinating country in a new light. On the way back from Tehran to Kuala Lumpur, the flight was almost empty. It was quiet, apart from the engine noise. There were only a few passengers on board, some women in their hijabs at the back, and a few men, already sleeping. I seemed to be alone with only the cabin crew passing by for company. It felt like a private, celebratory moment with AirAsia, the airline that I finally appeared to have conquered. After spending two weeks in alcohol-free Iran, I particularly enjoyed a cold beer, as I relaxed with soothing thoughts of my impending employment security in the cool cabin of the night flight heading back to my new home.

It all looked positive. However, what I didn't know was that there was a still an awful long way to go. Tony had said yes, but there were several layers of upper management at AirAsia I still had to go through. It wasn't as simple as, "Tony says yes, so you're hired." In actuality, all he'd done was give the green light to over-ride the moratorium on hiring new stuff. Now I had to go through the process of compiling formal proposals, explain in writing why I was fit for the job, prepare a portfolio and make a CV—I hadn't needed one for the last fifteen years. And these were only the first steps.

Luckily, I met most of the conditions. First and foremost, you had to be well-travelled. Now, a couple of years back, when I was mostly locked in China, this might have posed a problem, but for the two previous years I'd been expanding my horizons with regular trips to India and Indonesia, Myanmar even; and with the ongoing freelance assignments my geographical checklist was only expanding. I could have chanced it, and just said that I knew all about jetting from one country to another, but within AirAsia, travel is their language; it's so embedded in their daily interactions and communications that anyone would have sussed me out soon enough. I had to know what I was talking about. I had to have an opinion on almost every place I'd been to or might be asked to visit, especially in Southeast Asia; otherwise I'd have been lost. As it turned out, it helped tremendously that I'd lived in China for a decade and that I had learned to speak a bit of Mandarin.

But progress was slow. My email reply from Tony had arrived in November but by January I realized that my application had become mired in the minutiae of the company's bureaucratic system. The process stretched out for so long that months went by in which nothing happened. It was an excruciating wait. My time — as well as my wife's — was running out in Malaysia. With our European Union passports and tourist visas we could survive for about a year-and-a-half in pretty much in any of the ASEAN countries, but after that, every time I re-entered Malaysia I was quizzed as to what I was doing in the country. I'd never wanted to reach this point. In those eight months, I'd established a life in Kuala Lumpur, and tricked myself into believing that I had good base to build upon there. But in fact I had nothing. If just one attempt at re-entering the country was refused everything would be lost — my home, my belongings, my so-called life. And as there were two of us, the risks doubled. We were seriously approaching that point, and it made me increasingly nervous each time I returned to Malaysia after an assignment, armed with fake hostel reservations and half-baked lies about being a freelance writer traveling the region. AirAsia had issued me with a note confirming that I was indeed freelancing for them, but even that could have got both me and the company into trouble as, without the appropriate visa, they were employing me illegally. I was terrified each time I approached the customs desk at the airport.

Meanwhile, our move to Southeast Asia plowed into our savings. And still, the process dragged on and on. I knew that joining AirAsia would solve all these problems instantly, but for days and weeks on end seemingly nothing was happening. It had started out as a superb idea, but as time wore on, it became a serious business, and then a desperately urgent one with very high stakes — our very existence was on the line.

The biggest mistake I made was that although I kept my eye on the ball, I only considered one ball, AirAsia, and had begun to let go of everything else. One of my strengths throughout the Shanghai years was that I had many projects on the go simultaneously, so I always had something to fall back on. This time around, the only way to get the dream job was to concentrate upon it with every single pore in my body. I really don't think it would have happened otherwise; it was too intricate, too unlikely, with so many strings to pull. It demanded my constant attention and nurturing. I felt every slight movement of the process. I do believe that if you keep applying yourself, almost forcing it into practice then it finally will happen; thus, the first steps in my transformation already existed in emails and in meetings, when I introduced myself as 'Nicky from AirAsia'. By already freelancing for them I was halfway there, but I still needed to validate my position and become an official employee. The red of the airline's branding that once signaled merely holidays and trips, now took on an entirely other meaning. Everywhere I saw it, in ads, on billboards or at the airports, the anticipation cut deep—I was just inches away from joining. It was so close, yet still out of reach. I went to bed and woke up with AirAsia and *Travel360* tattooed in my mind, an intersection of hope and obsession.

I was concentrating on it so much that with the move to a new country I suddenly realized I didn't have anyone to talk to any more. All my friends were scattered around the world. I became lonely and withdrawn with thoughts of AirAsia constantly in my head. It was only my wife Barbi who kept the spirit in me, and her constant presence was the only support that I had. Apart from that, my social life outwardly was simply reduced to zero. It was a painful realization: in Shanghai, I had always been the centre of attention; it had been me who'd formed the communities that surrounded me. I was leading the way back then, and now, all of a sudden in Kuala Lumpur, I felt totally lost. The city's structure didn't help either. I had admired cities all my life. I enjoyed exploring and conquering them, making them mine. I always found enjoyment in discovering a new city for myself, learning how we'd work together and I did this with each of them. However, Kuala Lumpur was the first one that I couldn't properly embrace. I just couldn't get a handle on it.

Kuala Lumpur is predominately a driving city, an Asian Los Angeles; it spreads out with its highway system that looks like someone dropped a giant plate of concrete spaghetti on the tropical terrain. Between the roads there is thick jungle, full of dangerous snakes and spiders. My wife and I used to go shopping on foot and once we discovered a dead python on a path about twenty meters from our modern condo. This made it obvious that cutting through the vegetation was something we shouldn't do, not even for photography or walks of discovery.

Even the structure of the city is impenetrable. It's a string of villages connected by long motorways and, if you have no particular business in these villages, you shouldn't go there. It's a city that's just impossible to explore on foot. People simply don't understand walking here. As a pedestrian, you're in no-man's-land, constantly running into obstacles. Once I tried. I knew that the station I was heading to was close by, as the crow flies, and decided to walk across a bridge to get there. Predictably, I soon ran into a patch of jungle and the safe option would have been to turn back. Instead, I marched on, but the forested area only gave way to the hard shoulder of a thundering motorway. I was dehydrated by the end of my naive trek, which was only redeemed when a random driver took pity on me, picking me up from the side of the road and driving me to the station. At least I had my 'white-card' which marked me out as a foreigner, to explain my foolhardy adventure!

Even if you dare to set forth into these enclaves of nature, you have the enemy of the constant, intense heat that exhausts you within an hour. Thus, even the one thing I loved and kept me going when moving to a new city, my walks of discovery, were denied me here.

As the months wore on, there was really nothing else to turn to and I was ready to give up. AirAsia's editor did send some encouraging messages, but I was so fed up and tired of it that I was seriously considering letting it go. I figured that if I forgot about this whole AirAsia ordeal and turned my attention to something new, things would change.

This period exposed me to the darker side of Asia. Until then, I had only been exposed to the glorified Southeast Asia, as a popular destination for Westerners' holidays, when you dip your toes into the region for a few weeks for a break. This aspect of Southeast Asia is mostly associated with carefree getaways, promising rejuvenation against the backdrop of palm trees, sunshine, beaches, islands and the like. Such sojourns, even if spiced up by a few obligatory scams and troubles along the way, leave the traveller with an impression that's mostly pleasant; it's the safe side of Southeast Asia and the one with which most visitors are familiar.

One level deeper is frequented by adventurous types, who go the whole nine yards, wandering from country to country for a few months, sitting at their laptops in hostel canteens and carefully adjusting their photographs before broadcasting them to the outside world on social media. In extreme cases, they get lost in an Alex Garland-esque *The Beach* fantasy world, living as temporary nomads; they get tattooed and braid their hair, before eventually returning to their lives with an experience that they'll remember for a lifetime.

Beyond that there's another Southeast Asia that's known only to a tiny clique. Those initiates have already swum too far from the shores of so-called normal life and hurtle fearlessly down paths that, despite the region's enticing, seemingly laid-back way of living, very few dare to follow.

These are the real self-declared outcasts of Western society, who voluntarily choose the riskiest routes, gambling on uncertain futures. For them nothing else remains in life except for the unpredictable allure of this region, rich in beauty, short in opportunity. In more tragic cases, these consist of casualties from broken marriages and wrecked careers; running from never-ending mortgages or sometimes just the relentless uniformity of their ordinary lives. But, more often, they are adventure-seekers with a lust for life, who have decided to take their existence into their own hands and place it against the backdrop of a dream holiday that can be extended permanently. They are the ones who are willing to speculate on shifting sands, accepting a life without a home; daring the stormy seas of visa regulations, and hanging on to freelance ghost jobs with late payments that never seem to arrive.

This Southeast Asian battlefield is the antithesis of the one with which average travelers are familiar, and those very same aspects that make it enjoyable as a holiday hotspot are liable to turn against you. When you visit places such as Thailand, Indonesia or Malaysia for a getaway, it's easy to tap into the laid-back nature of the locals, the slow pace of life, and the curious local customs. These factors only add to the relaxation that's required. But when you want to make a living in these very same places, the easygoing—often amusing—approach that at first seems attractive, seemingly only strives to thwart you. Local in-built nonchalance becomes your grief. It seems as if nothing is really happening. You're an outsider who doesn't fit in. And, ironically and most annoyingly, everyone calls you 'boss', while you're the only one who doesn't have a job.

While I was casually frequenting the *Travel360* office while freelancing, I don't think the team ever knew how much the magazine meant to me; it was a long, thin safety line stretching from China to Southeast Asia. If it broke and I fell, I felt there would be huge consequences. It was the mother of all tightrope walks, a year and a half in the making, perched precariously above the smoldering ruins of my previous life in Shanghai. I spent the last months of 2017 totally depressed in our Central Residence home in Kuala Lumpur, which seemed like a luxury prison—I had nowhere to go, no friends to meet up with and no reason to venture beyond the front door.

Then, suddenly, in the first few months of 2018, everything sped up. AirAsia lined up a string of new assignments for me, which drew my attention away from the endless wait for a full-time position. The first one was in Perth, Australia, to cover the Ultimate Fighting Championships—a brutal mixed martial arts tournament in which both men and women from around the world kick and punch the hell out of each other in search of glory. AirAsia was sponsoring the event, which took place in the Perth Arena.

Accompanying their team, my job was to cover the preparations, the press conferences, the weigh-ins, the open workouts, leading up to the final event on the last day. The shoots were intense, and introduced me to a new aspect of being a snapper, to the hitherto unknown realms of sport photography where capturing every unrepeatable second mattered. I was struck by how much the blood that splattered all over the ring, staining the canvas, matched perfectly AirAsia's corporate red branding; a portent, perhaps, of how the event brought on one of my most painful, but in retrospect humorous, photographer's stories.

Despite all the prior meetings and preparatory emails,

everyone forgot to inform me that AirAsia was actually fielding its own fighter for the contest, and that I had to pay special attention to him. It must have been so obvious to all concerned that they assumed that I already knew. But in the rush that led up to the event, no one actually told me—and there was no indication in the brief.

On the day of the fight, I was documenting every single minute of the action going on inside the ring. I captured each fight meticulously, but as I hadn't been to the toilet since 6am, at around 11am I decided to visit the men's room. As it turned out, I chose the very moment when the AirAsia fighter came on. In fact, although I still had a few minutes before the battle commenced, security at the Perth Arena was so tight that the security guard wouldn't let me back in—not even a member of the press—until the fight was over. I could do little but watch the brief, two-minute fight from a distance, and glance over at my camera resting redundant on the ledge outside the ring. The bout ended with an extremely quick knockout. "Oh well," I thought to myself, "I missed one fight. No big deal." However, my stomach soon turned when I heard the winner, Tai Tuivasa, shout from the ring in his moment of glory: "…and thanks to my sponsor, AirAsia." Once I was allowed back into the area, I hurried to the stage, where the freelance sports writer I was working with, Matt, ran up to me saying: "Great fight, wasn't it? Need the photos ASAP!"

I was devastated. The assignment that had gone so well up until then, had turned into a nightmare within minutes. Just when I was on the doorstep of AirAsia, traveling with the AirAsia team, I missed something so important to them, and all because of an over-zealous security guard. I needed a solution quickly. I had to resort to something I've never done before or since in my photographic career, ever. I approached one of the other photographers nearby, explained the unfortunate situation, and asked if he'd be willing to give me a few shots of the fight. Luckily, he was a nice guy and was happy to share his work. Once the event was over, I ran back to the hotel, waited impatiently for the kind photographer to send them over and then quickly passed the images onto to Matt.

There was something else, something unprecedented, that happened within the same twenty-four hours. I guess, with the amount of travel I was doing it was bound to come sooner or later. That same evening, after the UFC's stage lights had dimmed, the AirAsia branding team went out to a nightclub. High on the thrill of their man's victory, they decided to stay up all night and catch up on their sleep during the return flight, which was scheduled for 6:50 the following morning—always a critical time to catch a plane. They asked me to join them, but I found the no-sleep idea a bit too much when there was a flight to catch, so I opted to stay in the hotel instead. Waiting for the dawn, I tried to stay awake and foolishly consumed three bottles of Australia's fine XXXX beer while watching TV. I must have fallen into a deep sleep in the early hours. So deep, in fact, that I didn't even hear the alarm.

That panic of waking up knowing that it's too late, that no amount of rushing will make up for the time, is something hard to experience. There were many missed calls on my phone and messages saying: "Nicky, where are you?" I didn't know if I should answer them or use the last precious moments to try to do what I already knew was impossible: to get to the airport hoping against hope that I could still catch the flight. I knew it was impossible: it was 5:40 a.m. I wasn't even ready, my chargers were still plugged in, my clothes scattered around the hotel room, my suitcase only half-full. I knew there wasn't enough time but I tried my best regardless. I called a taxi and asked the driver to go as fast as he could. Needless to say, by the time I got there, the check-in gate was closed. There was one member of staff from AirAsia still in departures and she jokingly said: "Oh, so you're the photographer we've been waiting for."

There was an unexpected, bizarrely positive, aspect to missing the flight; from the breathless, desperate running, the extreme, high level stress, I suddenly found myself in the position of having all the time in the world. Annoyed, yes. Angry at myself, of course, but there's nothing I could do about it. The situation turned into a pretty relaxing early morning spent at Perth Airport. I bought a coffee, ordered breakfast and started working on my laptop.

There was something else that made this experience slightly bearable; when I sat down in the waiting area and somewhat calmed down, I glanced down on my phone and there was a message from the deputy editor of the magazine: "Nicky, AirAsia finally started to process your papers."

At once, relief fell upon me and I didn't care any more about missing the flight or having to busk the photographs for the assignment. I phoned my wife and asked her to book another flight back and, in the saving grace of the good news I'd just received, I tried not to think about how much it cost.

Finally, things had started to progress, but the last stage was still ahead, and it was the one that proved to be the toughest on me. A further three months went by after receiving the message at Perth Airport. Following preparations of my work visa, AirAsia transferred my papers to the Malaysian immigration department for inspection — and they informed me that there were cases when they rejected foreigners, and that if that happens to me, AirAsia cannot make an appeal. They shouldn't have told me this! It turned my world upside down. Being so close, the possibility of my bid failing at the last minute, and due only to Malaysia's internal bureaucracy, weighed down on me with what felt like a thousand tons of pressure. It was like walking on the edge of a razor. On one side, my dream job, security, salary, insurance—it was all there, just waiting for me. On the other, there was just nothingness. A dead end from which I didn't know the way out. It was eating me alive. From there, if I was rejected, I knew no one could save me, not Tony Fernandes, not AirAsia, and I would instantly tumble back to square one; only now I'd have no visa and most of our savings had gone. My wife and I would have to find yet another new city in yet another new country, and search for a new home without the funds to pay for it. The thought of it cramped my stomach.

Over the previous two months, the stress had produced seemingly endless psychosomatic symptoms; my abdomen hurt, the feeling of frayed nerves in my stomach was constant. I was lethargic and highly stressed at the same time. I was incapable of doing or thinking of anything else. My lifeline is constant creativity, but now even that was gone. I was so on-edge all the time. The situation totally paralyzed me, and just dragged on and on. Malaysia has an awful lot of public holidays—fifty-two days per year—and we were entering a major holiday zone. This is a predominantly Muslim country, and Ramadan—an entire month of fasting, prayer and reflection—was upon us; and upcoming elections would bring on even more hold-ups. Delay after delay. Six months had passed since I'd written to Tony, and it had been another four since the authorities had begun to process my papers.

The night before I finally got the news, something strange happened. I was alone in the apartment. It was a time of high stress, as had become the norm, and everything was getting close to a tipping point. Although not in a traditional religious way, I do pray each day to a higher power, and that evening I prayed even more intensely and desperately for the end to this nightmarish waiting game. For about eight years I'd been wearing a silver medal of Ganesh, the Hindu god of success, wisdom and the removal of obstacles, and it had come to mean a lot to me. The same month that I'd acquired the medal from India coincided with my first magazine cover, and ever since then I seemed to be on a lucky streak, securing fifty covers with various international magazines, not to mention the awards I'd won. I strongly believed that my prayers to Ganesh bore some relation to my achievements in photography. I was genuinely certain that the medal had helped change my life. But that night when I felt that my stress was its highest, and the unprecedented pressure was sweeping over me, the medal broke. I found it on the bed next to me when I woke up, snapped into two pieces.

The same morning I left for the airport as I had an assignment in Beijing. I was queuing at the immigration counter at Kuala Lumpur International Airport when I opened my emails. The first one began, "Nicky, we're glad to inform you…".

I felt the world shifting around me. It wasn't only the great news—finally!—it was that the huge weight than had been bearing down on me for months on end suddenly slipped off my shoulders. An incredible sense of relief swept over me. The email continued: "…everything is confirmed now, immigration finally granted your work visa. Please give us a starting date." I stepped up to passport control and the officer was bemused at the irrepressible smile on my face. More than a year's worth of stress had finally come to an end.

I went on an uncontrollable emotional rollercoaster. I was extremely happy, the next moment I felt like crying; I guess this was how my body dealt with a sudden relief and the release of a tsunami of emotions. I thought about having a celebratory shot of whisky at the airport bar but I was already naturally high enough on happiness. It suddenly dawned on me; now I understood why the medal had 'chosen' that particular day to break into two—and no one could convince me otherwise that it was just a coincidence. Ganesh had taken a hit on my behalf, while dealing with the magnitude of overcoming the particular obstacles that stood in my way. This had been my toughest challenge yet, and he'd helped turn around the biggest crisis of my adult life.

By the time I arrived in Beijing, I was a new man; confident and full of plans. I took a room in my favorite hotel near Tiananmen Square and I went for an evening walk. It was one of my best assignments. The subject was 'Beijing in Love' and as I wasn't writing it, I found it easy work. AirAsia had booked a local freelance writer so I was relatively free, taking photographs and enjoying the city in my new, secure status. The fight was finally over. I'd won. I was an AirAsia staffer, an Allstar.

To work for AirAsia in the 2010s meant prestige and chic, especially in Malaysia, where Tony Fernandes was renowned for revolutionizing aviation and travel across Asia. My situation wasn't only turned around at last by having some security behind me, but on the surface, in my everyday life, too. Once I started to wear the recognizable bright red AirAsia ID card around my neck, like every one of the Allstars does, people's perceptions instantly changed; it sparked interest wherever I went. While commuting around central Kuala Lumpur, where foreign tourists constantly swarm the busy central area, I noticed that people looked at me differently. As a foreigner, I stood out among the hordes of travelers and backpackers roaming Southeast Asia. The badge suggested that I'd undergone an initiation to the region, that I was there for a reason over and above tourism. I was an AirAsia staffer, and yet I was evidently not Asian. I was something else, and it was therefore assumed I was a well-traveled connoisseur of the region. I started to notice how constantly it caught people's eye. Malaysians were even more eager about it. Many times on the subway, still now, people approach me and ask if I can pass their CV on to the hiring department. They strike up random conversations with me. The guards at my apartment compound—most of them from Bangladesh or Sri Lanka, and speaking little English—had seemingly already made up their own minds before addressing me.

"Sir, you work for AirAsia?" went the ubiquitous question.

"Yes."

"Sir, you're a pilot?"

"No, I'm with the inflight magazine..." I would answer, often stopping mid-sentence, noticing the certain glint in their eyes that showed they were happy and felt privileged to greet an AirAsia pilot on a daily basis. I soon realized it was pointless to try and convince them otherwise, and shatter their illusions. Fuck it, yes, I was a pilot.

At the beginning of the following month, I began work at RedQ, AirAsia's nexus—a pun on "headquarters" (i.e. RedQuarters). As I expected, it ushered in enormous changes. At last and at once, it dramatically pulled me out of my hermit status. I became part of a great team. We already had a working relationship but now, instead of running in and out of the office, fleetingly, as a peripheral cog in their inspiring machine, now I could walk in with newly endorsed corporate confidence and take my seat alongside them. I was an Allstar, with all the benefits. From the hopeless situation into which I'd slid, dangerously close to the edge, all of a sudden I found myself in a position in which the future seemed bright. I had a salary, insurance and security. Not only that, I was now part of a dynamic team in the inspiring world of magazines, based in the building at the heart of the airline.

It didn't stop there. It was as if, for all my suffering during the previous year-and-a-half, I'd been awarded a prize. The company bought me the latest Apple Macbook Pro laptop, plus brand new camera equipment worth US$15,000 — for which I was most grateful, as my existing gear had been eroded by the damp and dirt from shooting in the tropical heat over the last couple of years. And via my working visa, I acquired my Malaysian driving license and got my own car — thanks to that particular perk of the job I finally managed to conquer Kuala Lumpur. Life had indeed changed. Joining AirAsia felt like winning the lottery.

The energy of RedQ was incredible and was further boosted with the unique qualities you can only find in the building of an airline. The building's human traffic is not just local Allstars. As they fly in and out of KLIA2, all pilots and cabin crew are required to register at RedQ, therefore the distinctive red uniform is a ubiquitous sight as they commute on the company's internal buggies, between RedQ's twin buildings, situated two hundred meters or so from each other joined by a pathway. The windows overlook the massive runways of KLIA2; virtually every minute an aircraft lands or takes off, their roars filling the atrium, shaking the entire building with the mighty power of their engines. Plane tails like giant red shark fins cruised outside the windows as we sat at our desks. The sight had an empowering effect on the work we did and was a constant reminder that we were working for something grand. The atmosphere was almost tangibly electrified.

It's easy to disappear within RedQ. I often did. When stress was high and I'd had enough of sitting at my desk, I strolled down to the artificial grass circles in the vast arena-like space in the middle of the building and lay down on one of the multicolored beanbags, or else sat on repurposed furniture salvaged from construction sites, and just relaxed. Every airline should have sleeping capsules like AirAsia's. These giant futuristic red coffins are placed at various locations around RedQ — with 'Please take a rest, really, the boss doesn't mind' written over them. In this environment, pilots and cabin crew arriving from all destinations, magazine staff jetting back from assignments, and ground staff who work on site around the clock, are all entitled to take a break, and I often saw shoes placed outside, as their owners snoozed inside, lying down comfortably on company time.

From the start, one of my favorite aspects was walking the AirAsia dogs. When the company moved to RedQ, there were four stray dogs occupying the grounds. Anywhere else, the strays would have likely been evicted, but Tony decided to adopt them and house them on site instead. Their kennel, located on the side of the building's parking lot, was affectionately known as DogQ. As soon as I joined full-time, I offered to walk and feed them on a daily basis. Because of the Muslim majority in Malaysia and an Islamic distaste, sometimes actual fear, of dogs, it was no surprise that no one else among the 2,000 employees at RedQ volunteered. I jumped at the chance. What better way to interrupt your computer screen-dominated day than popping outside for an hour to walk the dogs by the runway? The animals were named after AirAsia's flight codes: AK, D7, QZ and FD. Since then, after walking them regularly I still find it hard not to associate these codes with the actual dogs: I think of my favorite one, the cute QZ, every time I see those letters printed on a boarding pass.

And then there was the presence of Tony, of course. Months after I joined, I saw him walking through the office aisles of our floor, talking and joking with the staff. He spotted me, and walked towards me. "I know you," he said. "You're the one who wanted the job." He was eating something and still half-chewing. After a momentary pause, and with a tone indicating that everything is possible at AirAsia, he added: "See? We made it happen."

Little things like that do more to boost work morale than any pay rise. Having him around seemingly inspires people. I'm extra sensitive to bullshit, and I can tell you that this man has zero. He's one of those bosses whom you just don't want to let down, as you know he's done incredible things. While you're having a serious meeting, he's biking around the building, and staffers watch in awe as his silhouette passes by the glass wall of the meeting room. He holds the most spontaneous meetings, just turning up at the office to announce some major change, or else he just comes by to say "Hi", for no particular reason. As he offers staff members a fist bump, it energizes them for a day.

As an AirAsia staffer, apart from your regular assignments on your duty travels, you receive the ID90 code, the ninety percent employee discount that's valid for all the airline's flights. This means you can pretty much hop on a plane to anywhere in Asia, or even Australia. In addition, you even get an e-coupon, which entitles you to even more free travel. It means that you can go wherever you want, whenever you want. Their world is your world.

To work for an airline as a photojournalist was truly a honor. It was my dream job. Because of the sudden contrast, coming from an utterly lost, desperate situation, to now finding myself part of the dynamic RedQ set-up, I couldn't wait to get to the office in the mornings. In fact, I was always one, sometimes two hours ahead of the team arriving. My lengthy commute wasn't even an issue; I felt privileged and happy to wake up at 5:30 on those cool KL mornings in our Sungai Besi home, just to get to work, just to belong somewhere, finally, and in a still relatively new country too. I felt my life being transformed in a matter of days. It was justified, finally; AirAsia and my workaholic nature was indeed a perfect match from the first minute. I think this is what my editor recognized in me when we began working together and harnessed it accordingly. Tony might have given the company the green light to hire me, but it was Beverly Rodrigues who helped me to get there and for that I will forever be thankful.

While working regularly for magazines in Shanghai I adopted the 'you're only as good as your last issue' rule early on, so I understood the game, and the dynamics of the magazine world. On my first official day, the team was closing the next issue, which meant I was instantly thrown into deep editorial waters; waves of press checks, color corrections and last minute text changes all washed over me. I was placed within a chain of people to whom the completed articles were being passed around to check for mistakes; I was treated as if I'd always been there. Also on my first day, while I was showered with "Welcome aboard!" greetings, there was even talk of shooting Tony for the cover that same morning — with a birthday cake smeared all over his face, as the airline celebrated its 18th anniversary. The shoot was actually cancelled at the last minute, but I remember quietly surrendering to the tsunami of unpredictability that I'd brought upon myself — and wholeheartedly welcoming the fact that being given random tasks at a moment's notice was a massive improvement on the uncertainty of being a freelancer, and not knowing where the next pay cheque was coming from.

Witnessing how the team at *Travel360* operated within AirAsia's giant, corporate machine was another notable aspect of my new position. Now part of this team, I had to make the most of it and be seen to be contributing. I might have invested an enormous effort into joining the company, but the hard part was still ahead. I had to adapt to the full-time office environment, which was entirely new to me. The field work was already there; I'd been used to that for years. However, daily office life was a challenge that I couldn't fully fathom at first. To adjust to an already set system of team dynamics was something I had to learn.

Astonishingly and ironically, I found out at my very first editorial meeting that AirAsa's intention was to shut down the magazine by the end of the following year, 2019. My heart sank. Why had I endured all that stress to join a doomed publication? What's going to happen now? Such thoughts raced through my mind. Initially, it worried me, but surprisingly, the whole thing didn't cut as deep as I feared it might. Later, I figured that I had no option but to go with the flow, and so I made my peace with it. Whatever happened was going to happen, regardless of my own personal concerns. After all, I was now fully on board at AirAsia and this was the most important thing.

The plan was that *Travel360* would still continue as a title, but only digitally in PDF format on AirAsia's new inflight ROKKI wifi system. The physical magazine had to go. We were assured that editorial jobs weren't on the line, but we had to be part of the digitization process that the company was undergoing. This was Tony's new vision and so everybody accepted it. I thought this was a surprising move, as he was always proud of *Travel360*, or so I'd heard; it had been his idea in the first place, when the airline started, to create its own in-house, self-published inflight magazine.

Without wishing to rub up against one of Tony's decisions at my very first meeting, I did voice my concerns from the consumer's perspective, as a regular AirAsia passenger, that if *Travel360* was reduced to a mere file on the entertainment system, competing with a choice of movies and games, no one would read it. Apart from being well-written and engaging, one of the reasons the magazine had become so popular among its five million readers was because prior to take off everyone had to switch off their phones and all electronic devices. It was clear that the digitization would kill the interest, and the magazine would lose all its advertisers, which was a major source of income.

However, while the months whizzed by at the usual editorial speed of light, as 2018 drew to a close, the magazine managed to survive. There was too much money coming in from advertisers to ignore, and upper management couldn't bring themselves to actually flick the switch. I was amazed at how professionally the chief editor and the regional manager defended the magazine and the small team behind it. Like a true first-defense line, they fought back constantly against AirAsia's corporate machine and, while under tremendous pressure, continued to produce the magazine and at the same time maintain its high quality.

I found a new home within this exciting microcosm, circling in a whirlpool of contradicting energies. While the higher powers pressed down upon us from above, we marched on with a productive and inspiring workflow. I just love the atmosphere of an editorial office; the dynamics of it, how we always work months in advance of the issue date, how information constantly changes hands, how ideas ceaselessly float in the air, communicated at short spontaneous meetings, which form and then dissolve just as quickly. Cover images are decided within a shockingly small timeframe, born within half an hour and then living with us for months. I was fully aware that it wasn't enough just to be an employee of the company; I needed to improve all the time, to get even better and better each month, to adapt to new things, to learn new techniques, which I do to this very day. Working for AirAsia was like walking on shifting sands. Departments constantly changed; they were dissolved before being resurrected and reshaped. I remember during one troublesome time, when one of the bosses called a meeting which he began by announcing: "This is like *Game Of Thrones.* Anyone can fall, anytime." I found the comparison a bit banal, but the company did shift its shape endlessly, forever keeping its employees on their toes.

There is something truly fascinating about working for an airline. The issues, the problems the company has to tackle, are much bigger than an average company's, and are on a different scale. To put it simply, they are more interesting. The number of issues that trickled down to my humble world, in which I was tucked away at my desk in the magazine department, never ceased to amaze me. One of the most interesting was the status of Taiwan, the island off the south-east coast of China that, since the Chinese Civil War in the late 1940s, had been separately ruled and which the Chinese Communist Party has branded a 'breakaway province.' We had to refer to Taiwan as part of China, both in print and online, or China had threatened to ban AirAsia from all its destinations, which would have been an enormous loss to the company. We could only mention Taipei, Taiwan's capital. This meant that in the rare articles that appeared about Taiwan, we had to tiptoe around the subject.

Writing about religion was always a thorny issue and, for someone to whom it is not important, I ran into difficulties a number of times. Thankfully, sharp editorial eyes always watched over me, but it was easy to make grave mistakes and upset someone, somewhere, getting the entire publication into trouble in the process. In the ASEAN region, in which so many different religions brush up against each other, I had to tread lightly. It was guaranteed that at least one of our five million readers would take umbrage at something and make a complaint. I remember being corrected several times when writing about Sikhism, over things I'd assumed were perfectly innocuous. Just mentioning a particular conflict that took place hundreds of years ago, raising a sensitive subject such as the Mughal War and who won it, could be problematic. Passions run high, even after several centuries.

I watched with awe how the editors maneuvered within these cultural confines, how it had to strike a careful balance when, for example, the Chinese calendar came round to the Year of the Dog, in a Muslim country where canines are traditionally considered unclean and impure. Upsetting Muslim in India or China could have led to flights being pulled, affecting the entire company.

Thus, I began omitting all religious references from my articles, because I had learned that, all too often, it just led to trouble, even if I was super careful. I would never be offensive to any religion in any way within my writing; on the contrary, living in Southeast Asia – especially Malaysia, where three ethnic groups, Chinese, Malay and Indian, live under the same roof — made me understand and appreciate the role of religion more. To invoke a religious pun, the devil is in the detail, and as a European it was sometimes hard to grasp the subtleties.

The number of my assignments at *Travel360* doubled after joining full-time. Before, I had usually chosen my own subjects and pitched them to the editor, but now I was sent out to shoot on fam-trips (familiarization trips) — educational assignments organized exclusively for media partners or travel agents — to sports events, gala dinners, award ceremonies and company functions. If Tony was attending a gala dinner in Bangkok, I had to fly there over the weekend and document it, then jet back home by Monday morning. On one occasion I flew to Singapore and stayed at a fancy hotel, just to take one single photograph. There was no limit to the subjects I was asked to shoot and write about. I saw my life transform at maximum speed from humble freelance living into a full-blown jet-set existence, covering no fewer than 135,000km, roughly three-and-a-half-times around the Earth, in my first official year at AirAsia.

Bangkok and Kuala Lumpur became hubs, jumping-off points that I used as flying doors into rooms that I entered and left just as quickly. I got to know their airports inside out. I became so familiar with Bangkok's Don Mueang, KL's KLIA2, Bali's Ngurah Rai and Hong Kong Airport that I had my favorite bars where I could catch up with work, where even the waiters knew me. There were also familiar faces among AirAsia's ground staff and cabin crew. I could easily predict layovers, work during delays if I was in a particular hurry, or else extend my stay, spend a weekend and visit friends in whichever city I found myself on any given day.

The time I spent on the road, or in the air, and in the office during a calendar year was perhaps thirty to seventy percent of my waking life, with the emphasis always towards more travel. Being on the road you're pretty much in your own world. In my case, this is where I feel comfortable and even though I'm on duty, I love disappearing in my beloved cities. But office life back at RedQ was another matter entirely, and I began to feel its stresses and strains very early on. While on assignments, troubles tend to revolve around the weather, unreliable contacts, miscalculations, all-in-all manageable difficulties, but adversities of the office environment are real beasts against which I had to establish a new defense. Not that AirAsia had many tough, strict rules. On the contrary; staffers weren't required to arrive until 10 a.m., the general atmosphere was, as I've said, very relaxed and my colleagues were usually great to work with. I rarely ran into a real asshole and, even when if I did, everyone knew who they were and so any errant behavior was relatively easy to dismiss.

By the time the Covid-19 pandemic hit and so astonishingly and unexpectedly swept away all the traveling aspects of my job in the beginning of 2020, I was already an integral part of the company. In fact, this was the point when I realized that I didn't know the company at all. Covid, or rather being grounded by it, ensured that I became a genuine, core AirAsia staffer. Rather than being forever out on assignment, out of touch and probably out of mind, I got to know the day-to-day office workers better, and became familiar with many more internal departments of the company.

The pandemic had its upside for me. I got to meet Tony Fernandes more often, accompanying him as a photographer to press events, as AirAsia was forced to adapt under the tremendous pressures of the virus. I watched first hand how he tackled the challenge of reducing his operational fleet of 247 planes to just 80, even then with most of them mostly flying only domestically; and how inspiring he remained even during these worst of times. I was inspired to see how he faced such problems with a sense of humor. During 2020, the entire tourism industry was forced into suspended animation, and most airlines suffered greatly. AirAsia was no exception and lost its long haul fleet, AirAsia X. As destination countries such as Japan, India, China and South Korea remained closed at the end of the year, AirAsia X itself became redundant. AirAsia Japan closed first. The problems trickled down through the entire company and, sad to say, after twelve years of existence and in spite of Tony's earlier decision and his managers' efforts to keep it going, my precious *Travel360* magazine was suddenly gone without a trace, its staff disseminated throughout the company into different departments.

Tony's presence remained as electrifying as ever, however, giving everyone hope through the darkest times. While the company lost hundreds of employees, he fought back by rehiring as many as he could; pilots became ground staff, some even became waiters and managers at his new AirAsia restaurant chain, Santan. By the end of 2020, I was braced for the worst; my role as a globe-trotting photojournalist was gone and I was certain that the company would have to let me go. I felt it was inevitable and mentally prepared myself. And yet, against all expectations, my work permit was renewed for 2021, and when Tony came up to me shortly afterwards in RedQ and greeted me with a fist-bump, I felt his gesture energizing me for another year. It may have been a casual deed on his part, but for me it meant the world.

There is little time for nostalgia working for an airline, perhaps even less so now, but whenever I look around me in RedQ and think back to the day when I randomly picked up a copy of *Travel360* on a flight somewhere between Indonesia and China, I can glimpse the engines of fate turning in my favor, of how just one seemingly insignificant moment can turn our lives around and how enough persistence can make you achieve anything. Indeed, as another AirAsia motto says, 'Dare to Dream'.

Travel 360

"Where would you like us to park the tram for you on the island — where would you like to shoot it?" asked the head of Hong Kong Tramways in all seriousness in the morning rush hour for the cover shot of a magazine. "Central Market would be great," I answered hesitantly in slight disbelief that this was actually happening and indeed, hours later, the operators parked the tramcar there and held up the swarming traffic for me downtown in one of the greatest cities of Asia. I had a a ten-minute window, just to find the right angle and to click the shutter release button on my camera in the sweltering morning heat.

Rolling along in a car that meanders along the coastline with breathtaking ocean vistas and picturesque landscapes, under the deep blue skies of Morning Peninsula, Australia, sampling the finest vineyards, wine tastings, breweries, restaurants and museums. An entire suite for a week in Marina Bay Sands in Singapore, Novotel in Brisbane, Park Hyatt in Melbourne, The Westin in Perth. Treated as a VIP wherever you go, in cities where I never even dreamed of being; Seoul, Nagoya, Melbourne, Brisbane, Bangkok, Tehran, Imphal, Yangon, with all doors swinging open upon landing with permission to shoot, everything at your own mercy — a seemingly endless inspiration for a photographer.

Meeting the master of dough figurines in the great city of Wuhan, China and getting to be friends with him, discovering small martial arts communities in India, meeting and interviewing the last ninja in Japan, sailing soundlessly upon the surface of the Kinabatangan river in a tiny boat at an arm's reach from a four-meter crocodile as it silently swims in the early morning sun in Sabah, filming a Jultagi rope walker troupe just outside of Seoul.

These are some of the most rewarding moments that the photojournalist job threw me over years but as always, there's another side to this, when you get to run into the reverse of these experiences and meet the inevitable.

"Sir, if you don't leave the premises immediately, I'll put you in jail and everyone here around you! Am I understood?' barks the strict Sikh policeman angrily in the blinding midday heat of Chandigarh, northern India as I look around me and my companions: a dozen kids aged ten to twenty, all armed with swords and knives of traditional Gatka the local martial art uniforms. Minutes later, I am jamming them all into two rickshaws to find another location within a limited time frame.

Getting the wrong visa stamp at Amritsar airport in Punjab, which throws you into instant illegal status and because of it you are unable to check in to *any* hotel in town, with endless of paper work, wasting time in immigration offices while your schedule is tight anyway. Sleeping at receptions, arriving after midnight in Tokyo finding that they messed up your reservation. Getting that tap on your shoulder, with an armed soldier towering over you before questioning in the streets of Tehran the very tap every photographer fears around there. A security guard trying to tear the camera off your neck while another rips the equipment from your make up girl's entire set and empties it in the nearby bin. Collapsing in your hotel after traumatising events and reading your editor's urgent note: is the write up ready yet? Being regularly pulled out of queues at immigration and visa centres because the job title in your passport is 'photojournalist'. Missing flights, sleeping at airports.

Things will go wrong despite meticulous planning by colleagues, tour agencies, local helpers, because of the frequency of the trips. But then seeing people looking at your cover photographs right in front of you, smeared all over Asia regularly on flights and in waiting rooms and recycled over and over in advertising campaigns. Seeing the joy in people's faces when they see themselves on the cover and in the articles.

Indeed, it's all the full rock'n roll treatment, a taste of the fifteen minutes of fame you always dreamed of, or at least a smaller, portable version of it. Enjoy it while it lasts but get ready to crash and burn eventually.

To work as a photojournalist for an airline is as fabulous as it sounds and it seems to be the subject of everyone's envy. I never met anyone from any walk of life who didn't comment on the exceptionality upon hearing what I do. You're always on the road, living an exciting life, with a constantly changing environment around you, and you not only have direct access to the most incredible places, to dream destinations and the perfect getaways but get to observe these through the filter of their most remarkable aspects: their own culture, art and heritage. As these visits are mostly official, usually initiated by tracking down the best available contacts, thorough access is always granted whatever the subject is. Thus, upon landing at the given destination you're already treated as a VIP, an insider. The photography, the interviews you do, bring you in close contact with your subject; you're granted an entry way beyond what any tourists or visitors can dream of. With the help of special local guides, you're allowed to have an intimate encounter with what you're writing about or shooting, and these opportunities are constant reminders of what a privileged position you're in.

The frequency of the assignments is also something worth contemplating. I often felt a strange kind of embarrassment by cutting my way through three or four lifetimes of travel dreams, bucket lists of the average person within a given month: jumping from busy downtown Tokyo photographing cosplayers, to rural Punjab shooting Sikh martial arts, or one week exploring the hidden gems of Bali and Lombok, the next cutting through the thick jungles of Borneo with 4x4 off-roading over a week, then heading to experience indigenous whale watching in Australia.

Aside from the places you get to, what makes all this even more rewarding is the diversity of the people you get to meet along the way. It's impossible to properly explain how many extraordinary characters and personalities you make brief, temporary acquaintances with: artists, journalists, sportsmen, artisans, community leaders, politicians, and then I haven't even mentioned the guides, drivers, the people along the line of your work or even beyond that, the random strangers life just throws your way on a train or in the airplane seat next to you to make your travels even more unforgettable. All in all, being a traveling photojournalist creates incredible human traffic around you and leaves a rich trail of contacts.

But ultimately, the real beauty of the job is the ability to momentarily elevate people and communities, their individuals and leaders, to exposure and to recognition. When the articles I write and shoot eventually came out, being read and seen by millions and millions of passengers each month, the joy when they see themselves on the cover or over the magazine spread through my photography and writing was simply priceless and ever so gratifying. I often felt like I left a trail of small families behind everywhere I went. And through these families, by embracing their cultures, by highlighting their efforts and hard work, anywhere I went I created small distant homes to return to.

Needless to say, the free travel privileges job even more enticing. On top of your work travel, you can basically hop on any plane, anytime, practically for free and go wherever you want. Hundreds of destinations are within arm's reach, which gives an incredible sense of freedom. But this already brings up the first interesting question: does anyone really need *that* much travel on top of what they already do?

Through these enticing aspects, the photojournalist lifestyle is endlessly glamorized as one of the ultimate dream jobs. Travel *and* photography. What an irresistible combination, right? And to do that for a living? You must be the luckiest person alive! I remember once, on assignment somewhere in Sakon Nakhon in northeast Thailand, I was walking out of a restaurant sitting on a lake when someone shouted after me with a strong English accent: "Long way from home, right? Not many foreigners out here. What are you here for?"

"I'm shooting and writing a story for an inflight magazine."

"You mean, you travel the world, take photos and getting paid for it?"

"Yeah ... pretty much," I told him, half-looking back at him while walking.

"You lucky bastard," he said, each word sounding like a full sentence, as I made my way to the car with a faint smile on my face. This unknown stranger pretty much nailed down perfectly the perception of the job. But as with everything else, there's a flip side.

Traveling 150,000 km a year, the equivalent of roughly four times around the world, it's easy to get jaded. Constantly locked in the grid of hardcore travel schedules, long journeys, flying across different time zones through program-heavy itineraries, losing hours, gaining hours, missing sleep, criss-crossing countries in the most random succession while not being grounded at any time for weeks or even months is equally damaging to your psyche and health. As you gradually become immune to distance, it can have long-term damaging side effects. It can also lead to a total loss of self by dangerously distorting one's reality. To put it simply, nothing can quite rip you to pieces like frequent travel does. And what it does to your relationships or to your marriage is yet another story; I'm truly blessed that my wife so understandingly and patiently adjusted to my peripatetic existence, using the time in my absence to build her own yoga-instructor business in Kuala Lumpur and by this preserving our relationship, which with this much travel could have easily been derailed if handled the wrong way

Most often, people use the word *jetsetter* as something to envy. It always carries a sort of jealous connotation. There's an escapism attached to travel, a universal fascination that makes its dark sides look insignificant simply because it just doesn't happen to that many people. But truth be told, the word *jetsetter* only sounds fabulous until you really, truly become one.

The airbrushed image of work travel that is often portrayed in the media, the businessman in a sharp suit, laptop open in front of him, being served a drink by a smiling cabin crew member, is a total misconception. That sharply dressed man could well be in deep trouble, with his personal life in utter shambles due to his never-ending travel.

When I was younger, I used to read about rock stars waking up on tour and not knowing which city, or even country, they were in and I remember how I was in awe of that kind of lifestyle. But when you get to that point and experience it yourself, it's neither funny nor glamorous. One time, because of a rescheduled flight, I ended up being in four different countries within the same weekend. It took days to recover from it and had a domino effect of totally ruining the travel and the experience ahead.

Worse, when you're working you're always expected to hit the ground running, whether it's an assignment with a full week's packed schedule ahead or you land from a long trip right into an editorial deadline. It's like being teleported to a different dimension; you don't quite know where you are, and you need to function immediately with results. It was taken to extremes in my case; my job description included three criteria when on the road; I had to conduct interviews, absorb the essence of the story and write a well-researched 2,000-word article; I had to take high-end, magazine-quality photographs, always aiming for a cover shot that would be stared at by millions; and I had to bring back video material and edit a five-minute mini-documentary out of it. That was my original deal with AirAsia, that's how the company saved money—instead of sending three people, I went alone to bring all this material back. Thus, the assignments were mentally draining because I had to concentrate on three entirely different things, while also carrying heavy equipment and planning it all on my own with multiple stories on each trip.

Excessive travel can make you feel utterly lost. Once, I remember after a month and a half of hardcore work travel, I woke up somewhere in a hotel room with drawn curtains without the faintest idea where I was or why I was there. The curtains were closed, and I looked around the dark room. I saw my luggage on the floor, magazines, brochures scattered everywhere, Converse trainers lying by the door, cameras, lens, used boarding passes on the table. A life that apparently everyone envies. But nothing registered. Questions flickered through my head, and I couldn't even venture a guess at why I was there: Was I late from somewhere? Had I missed my flight? But most importantly: What city is this? Where the hell am I!? Minutes can feel like an eternity in this kind of situation, so in blind panic I eventually ran up to the window and drew the curtains. The traffic of Bangkok was flowing slowly underneath like a river of steaming metal in the scorching hot morning rush hour of the city, dotted with its characteristic purple and green taxis, and the steaming urban vista reminded me that I was there to take photos of Tony at an event.

According to Native American philosophy, with each trip your soul needs a few days to arrive in your wake. The problem I had was that my soul couldn't quite catch up with me: at times switching countries twice a week at one point landing in Tokyo, my soul must have been still hanging around in Amritsar near the Pakistan border and by the time it was ready to join me I'd already moved on to somewhere else. This frequency of travel creates a domino effect, a strange sense of absence, a void that always follows you around.

Aside from the worrying physical and mental effects on health, the fact that you're always just a corner away from being totally burned out, there's an even more concerning aspect to the hyper-mobile lifestyle: losing the one thing considered the ultimate escape. To most of us, travel is the all-time, number one go-to. When monotony pollutes our everyday and we feel the need to get away, travel seems to be the best answer. Getting away from our routine offers a fresh perspective, an opportunity to recalibrate our psychological compass. It's the object of everyone's desire, the most rejuvenating of recreational activities, seemingly the answer to all problems.

But the moment anything is done to excess, it's ruined. It's the same with travel. When getting away becomes your routine, that's when real problems start. Extreme traveling robs you of this one thing and turns it against you in the most cunning ways. Once you get tired of it, there's simply nowhere to escape anymore. At its worst, when it's married to a vivid, ultra-happening, adventurous lifestyle like photojournalism, you become immune to beauty, to excitement, which exiles you to the devastating hinterlands of utter indifference. You burn out to the level that nothing really interests you anymore. And believe me, that is a scary place to be. For example, there's something worrying about your state when six giant humpback whales circle around your boat off the coast of Stradbroke Island in Australia and are met by your apathy. Right there, you're living one of the most magical experiences a human being can go through: the whales, first as giant dark shadows, move under the surface before suddenly jumping out of the ocean with their mighty weight, then crashing back into the waves. As they move the boat around, their massive bodies are a reminder of your own human existence and—I say this rarely now—it is really something to see. When this beauty is utterly lost on you, you know you truly have something to worry about.

Once I was sitting at Jakarta airport after weeks and weeks of assignments, waiting for a flight. We had done a marathon twelve days in Perth, Australia, as guests of a tour company, experiencing everything there to see in and around the capital of Western Australia. Within those two tight weeks, we went through a non-stop schedule of the city's aquatic attractions, including glamping, a visit to the sights of Rottnest Island, barbecues on houseboats, a wild seafood experience while dolphins swam around our boat, crab scooping, night cruises with dinner, a ferry ride around the city, kayaking against Perth's cityscape and even swimming with the dolphins in the end. But it didn't stop there; we ventured into experiencing and shooting the best bars of Perth, sampling their selected food and specialities, then visiting distilleries, breweries, vineyards and chocolate factories around the region before heading to Yanchep National Park, photographing kangaroos, visiting the Crystal Cave, diving down to the Freemantle Underground Prison, then Araluen Botanic Park, then Tree Adventures, then a twilight spent abseiling and ordering pizza, and finally a trip to the top of the cliffs overlooking the city of Perth as airplanes landed in the sunset. The visual spoils never seemed to end.

Sounds like the dream, doesn't it? But in fact, within those weeks when we didn't have a break, I had seriously managed to overdose on travel experiences and all I wanted was to be left alone and stare into space without words for the following days. Those waves of emptiness, the disillusionment with pretty much everything, crashed over me sitting right there at the airport and it was almost unbearable.

Little things used to make me happy. I remembered when I used to love just being at airports; it was that simple. The anticipation before a trip when you don't even mind waiting, you just buy your favorite magazine and flip through it, read a great book in the waiting lounge—this used to give me great pleasure. But this time I wasn't interested in anything. I felt this enormous, gaping hollow emptiness and felt utterly let down by my own self: "Other people would kill for this lifestyle, why don't you appreciate it? What the hell is wrong with you?" That is what I kept asking myself, while a strong and unfamiliar sense of guilt overwhelmed me.

Luckily, I was with a colleague, another frequent travel writer who had been in the travel business longer and was used to this jaded state of mind. She pointed out that it's not me, it's the exhausting process of constantly being on the move. Only then did I realize that in fact, I was so overloaded by experiences, I'd seen so many things in the previous few weeks with such rapid frequency, that I just simply wasn't able to digest anything anymore. My mind was still busy dealing with what had happened weeks ago in another country, processing it while again and again a fully booked day of new things washed over me until the enjoyment was entirely bleached out. When in this state you're obliged to dip into yet another trip, yet another different experience. Once you reach your limit, you begin to lose yourself altogether.

When you're on the road, your temporary homes, the hotels, meaninglessly click and switch like projected images one after the other behind the shadow that is you. Marriott, Crown Metropol, Park Hyatt, QT, Novotel, Hilton, Wyndham, you name it, are all just repetitious, ever-changing but never-changing artificial backdrops, mere empty stages to dress up your solitude as a traveller. I often find that the more luxurious the hotel, fine art hanging on the walls, their one-of-a-kind décor, the more it enhances a sense of loneliness. There is a lack of human connection. Besides, they isolate you from the essence of your chosen destination with their ostentatious comfort-bubble and cut you off from reality altogether.

I used to love hotels. That anticipation of arrival, the clean, untouched rooms, even small things used to get me excited; even discovering what's the view is like. You're ripped out of your frame of existence and you're finally on the road; it's so rejuvenating. I adored them for their concept just as an environment; one can disappear in their anonymity and get lost in the Escher-esque revolving grid of their carpet-cushioned, silent corridors, with identical doors leading into identical room-arrangements equipped with sterile single-use sets of toothbrushes, shaving kits and beverages, all compressed into a frame of temporary privacy. Everything was exciting about them; the randomness, the facelessness of your next-door neighbor, the noises that filter through the walls from guests who might not be the same as yesterday, the empty trays left on the corridor floors and the strange phenomenon that no matter how big a mess you leave behind, it always magically gets rearranged to the same order by the invisible hands of hotel staff.

But when these momentary shelters become your everyday

reality, if this is in fact all you have to fall back on each evening, when you live in them for weeks on end, these very same magically self-cleaning units are nothing more than bitter, blank reminders of just what an ungrounded life you're living.

Any hardcore business traveller would reassure you that beyond the dazzling luxury decor, the exaggerated reception smiles that only last strictly until checkout time, nothing awaits but a dark reflection of your inner emptiness. It hangs over you like a sinister pendulum, and it intensifies at night as you sigh into the empty room before falling asleep. A traveller's loneliness knows no distance, sneaks under your door, finds you in your fancy bathtub, stares back at you from the bathroom mirror, and it's already there under the nicely creased bedsheets with the carefully folded towel swan on top before you even climb under the clean, crisp blankets. Endless business travel is like jumping through different dimensions as city skylines revolve outside your window; Nagoya, Osaka, New Delhi, Seoul, Guangzhou, Beijing. As exciting as they are to be in, from the hotels, these cities are all shimmering mirages of a seemingly projected reality.

Hotels go hand in hand with luxury, and luxury is one of the things I can't tolerate around myself. Unfortunately, as a photojournalist I was more exposed to it than I wanted to be. A common cliche rightly associates a person who cultivates a flashy appearance with a shallow personality, but even beyond that there's something deeply troubling when someone is attracted to opulence. Even more so when one is dependent on it. I regard luxury as an exterior extension to the hollowness of the people who seek it. It's a passage to a world of unnecessary needs, a desperate escape from reality. What's so shocking and unfathomable about it is the level of naivety needed to buy into it. It puts on display the self-importance of the person who enjoys it.

When you enter the world of hotels, affluence is almost inescapable, you unwillingly slip into its ugly, multi-layered realms. Chef Nicolas Freeling notes in his book *The Kitchen*: "The better the restaurant, the more your food has been prodded, poked, handled, and tasted." And this is what happens when you're exposed to luxury in the service industry. But instead of the food, it's you who'll be constantly prodded, poked and handled. And through the jaded filter of a traveling, over-worked photojournalist, endlessly stuck in the media game, you are constantly subject to that.

For instance, there's certainly a sense of honor being a special media guest of Singapore's truly stunning Marina Bay Sands for a few days, but your stay comes with a price. With a suite overlooking the majestic Gardens by the Bay and a breath-taking view over the city, you also find yourself in an invisible prison, at the mercy of the service industry, caught in a web of obligatory appearances such as dinners, lunches, visits where there's no room for anything else apart from pretending to be in awe at all times. The pretence is on such a high level and frequency that once you're in it, it's demanding on the face muscles to keep an agreeable smile on all the time.

You're entitled to partake of the clinking glasses of bubbly at the high-end morning buffet and be a witness as the cream of the service industry play to the selected media's gullibility by simply spoiling them. Often, an event scheduled for the end of a busy day after being already swamped by media appearances and photo ops can be the very thing that robs you of the last tiny shred of privacy on such trips; you retire to the hotel room in the evening to get a good rest before it starts again the next day.

An opening of a chic new burger joint in the Marina Sands springs to mind. The event was at nine o' clock in the evening and I was expected to appear in smart casual, forcing on an already worn out smile.

After making and appearance and fulfilling my photographer commitments, with a glass of wine in hand, after I clinked my way through the crowd making sure everyone saw me, that it will be remembered I was actually around, I escaped the free flow of classy wine and craft beer and edged nearer and nearer to the exit. Then finally I disappeared around the corner with the wine glass left by the decorative plants.

There is of course nothing wrong with indulging in a 5-star cocktail party in the heart of Singapore wonderful food and wines, partaking in sparkling conversations making new acquaintances and invaluable contacts. But when you're so overdosed on travel that you can hardly hide your fatigue and the overflow of emotions uncontrollably start bubbling to the surface, the cracks begin to show, jeopardising a truly unique position.

Constantly traveling in a surfeited state of a mind, caught in a dizzying whirlpool of experiences, can distort reality entirely and corrupt your outlook on otherwise innocent things that surround you. Tragically, often even kindness is taken the wrong way. Simple customs like staff bowing and acknowledging your presence, a kind gesture that's been embedded in some Asian cultures for centuries, can easily trigger your irritation and you won't even notice how it backfires on you. Staying in luxury hotels in Southeast Asia, you find yourself surrounded by constantly bowing hotel staff, who are instructed to stop and greet you — worse for me, if they knew my name.

I recall a particular, two-week media trip through Bali and Lombok, Indonesia, where was no escape from this. Anytime, anywhere I went, no matter how early, how late, everyone called out on my name, every single employee, even the guy watering the grass at 6 am: "Good morning, Nicky! How are you this morning?" On one of the early mornings I popped down to the cafeteria and asked for a cup of coffee to take up to my room to do some work before we were about to embark on a day full of activities. I was still sleepy, not even properly dressed and I wanted to get it over with as quickly as possible. Soon, people gathered around me, instead of handing me the very simple thing that I asked for, a coffee, they showered me with questions: "What kind of coffee? How about breakfast, Mr Nicky? Shall we call the manager? We have very special Lombok coffee for you. But you can have any kind, why just a simple coffee? Or would you like English tea? Or you just prefer the coffee?" Thus, eventually, from merely wanting to get a cup of coffee in the morning, I was escorted back to my suite by three servants balancing silver trays rattling through the garden path behind me.

Otherwise insignificant verbal expressions of satisfaction or awe such as "amazing," "delicious," "wow" and "unbelievable", the words mostly used as an exchange for the kind service, become tainted by their overuse. It's something you wouldn't ever notice on your average two-week holiday, let alone be bothered by but surrounded by members of the media spoilt for a month and jammed with events, these become your most dreaded words, the ones you get most tired of; as everywhere you go all day, everyone tries to charm you with everything from wine tastings to kitchen tours. You hear them so often that by the end of the week every "wow" is painful.

In retrospect, the saddest thing in all of this that you lose your sense of humour, your patience over people who are probably in the same boat as you, caught in the very same media game as you, at the mercy of the service industry, who are instructed to do that by their bosses, under as much pressure as you.

All in all, looking back now and a two-year break later, I do find it ridiculous how I've spent all those years in this, kicking and screaming against all this luxury, enjoyment and comfort and I never allowed myself to enjoy any of it even for a single moment.

On the same trip, we flew over to the Wyndham Bali Dream Resort. I've been to Bali many times and I have a personal connection with the island. The hotel is nestled within a complex of a group of high-end hotels wedged between luxury beach clubs and an "award winning" golf course, entirely cut off from the surroundings. It was my first business trip there and the occasion cast a rather unusual perspective on my beloved island. It was as if I saw it through a plexiglass of luxury, a towering invisible barrier that completely isolates you from the essence of this wonderful region. To each their own, but a resort like this is an odd choice for a holiday when really, it's the simplicity where Bali's essence lies, in immersing yourself in its traditions, passing by houses each morning as residents place their offerings in front of the houses, talking to locals, sampling the local cuisines. I always found it almost magical waking up in the heart of the cultural centre Ubud, or in one of the wooden bungalows in the nearby rice fields. Therefore from a personal point of view, I was shocked that such a holiday choice even existed around here and I often pondered why would one go for it.

However, the resort did give me an unexpected surprise. Coinciding with our media trip there was a music festival on one of the beaches and its headliner was Suede, the band that inspired my move to and love of London in my youth and basically triggered the life I was living. The band stayed at the Wyndham and although we saw them having breakfast at the next table on one of the mornings, I never managed to approach them, which was odd considering how much personal connection I had to them; hanging out in Camden bars with various members back in the day and also staying right next door to singer Brett Anderson at one point in Notting Hill. But right there, caught in the travel machine of AirAsia, there was no time to reminiscence.

After being showered by media gifts by the hotel, I made my way deeper into the complex, to find my suite somewhere in the west wing. I sat down on my bed and thought: Now what? Instead of venturing right into the exciting grid of side streets, as I usually would do, I was totally separated by the long-deserted avenues leading into the complex — it would have taken at least 45 minutes in the scorching heat to reach one of the main roads. I couldn't get out because as soon as they saw me at the reception, my presence would create a commotion among the staff: "Where is Mr Nicky going alone? Does he need a chauffeur?"

On the very same trip, one of the most horrible experiences in Bali was OMNIA, a swanky, oceanfront club offering a swimming pool, three bars and DJ events in a "stylish," open-air setup. I never thought Bali could be interpreted in such a wrong way and as it was for work I couldn't just walk out. It was almost a traumatic experience. The shoot I had to do there, of people wriggling, grazing up against each other in swimsuits while snapping selfies, was possibly the worst few hours of my photojournalist career, ever. To make it stop – and I think it was the first time I ever did this — I told everyone to nail down the shoot quickly because I was not feeling well. Typically, they sent a driver for me and on the way back to Wyndham I asked the driver to take my equipment back to the hotel, to the pull over and drop me by the road. Making my excuses of buying medicine, I could finally, secretly disappear and indulge in my beloved grid of Bali streets for a few hours.

This all inevitably brings up the question that you could rightly ask—whether this level of Karl Pilkington-esque cynicism qualified me for being the right person for the job at all. It was my relentless contempt for luxury that I clashed with most of the time and instead of projecting it outwards, I just scribbled notes endlessly on these trips that resulted in what you're reading now. I did love my job as a traveling photojournalist and on these assignments I remained fully professional, I was fully aware that I was at work and the whole experience wasn't for my personal entertainment. But OMNIA was the one occasion where the repulsiveness was so intense and so direct that I almost let it slip.

Fam trips were the hardest part of the photojournalist job. These are when travel providers, tour operators, tourism boards, hotel chains or other DMOs representing a destination invite members of the media with the purpose of educating about their products and services and promoting them. They are frankly the most testing aspect to the job, so devoid of pleasure that no right-minded journalist looks forward to them. Fam trips are loaded up with extremely schedule-heavy programs usually from early morning to late evening and they normally take three full days to work your way through, but I've been to ones that lasted an entire week. It's straight-out business; travel providers are trying to jam as many things into a certain time frame as possible, often aggressively without any regard to whether you can take in anymore or whether you're exhausted.

The main problem with these organized trips is that they defeat their own purpose. By the end, it's so dense and overdosed that you end up hating the destination itself and more importantly, they completely derail you from the sole purpose of being there in the first place. Because the fast-paced schedule cuts you off from the natural human interactions—such as meeting artisans of a certain trade—which stories are based on, it's just impossible to come up with a narrative and you are officially allowed to invent one.

To me as a photographer, fam trips were even more mentally straining because I was locked together with this new breed whose name alone sends shivers up the spine: influencers and Instagrammers. These people exist only in a vision of their projection in the social media platforms, they live entirely in the reflection of their accounts and it's just painful to be around them.

When you come in close contact with them, especially when they are in action on fam trips, they seem transparent, like those exotic fish whose spines can be seen through the light. They run around seemingly in a trance and absorb anything that's instantly postable and only see the world that surrounds them through their phone-screens by opportunities to be exchanged for likes or followers. Taking away their phone would grind their lives to a halt.

Airports might be associated with the excitement of travel and holidays, but they are stressful and unhealthy environments to pass through when getting from A to B, often during ungodly hours. It's where you're the most vulnerable; crowds are locked together in their most agitated, tired state, joining one queue after the other, caught in-between worlds, unprotected against the germs in eateries, corridors, lavatories while being forced to buy overpriced, bad food. These are mostly the acceptable collateral of travel; the one thing I find the most annoying about airports is that you're at the mercy of their very often dysfunctional operations, and in the end it's you who has to suffer and tolerate the results of their shortcomings.

There are some airports like New Delhi and Beijing that are enormous and chaotic enough to make you miss your plane, but it can go the opposite way too. Sometimes its efficiency that wastes all your time, which can be even more irritating than chaos itself because you're not prepared for it, so you don't expect it. In Osaka's Kansai airport for instance, the airport staff are so overly efficient that it constantly leads to congestion and long queues. Once, also in Kansai, I nearly missed my plane back to Kuala Lumpur despite being at the airport five hours before departure just because the staff were doing everything so meticulously with so much attention to detail, even quizzing me about where I would go after Kuala Lumpur. A friend of mine at the same airport missed his flight because he purchased souvenirs and by the time the security had opened the decorated box at the baggage check, then nicely packed it back up, his plane was gone.

But it's always good to see an airport that relaxes that travel anxiety to a certain level and if there's one that truly rids you from this stress, it's Bangkok Don Mueang Airport. There's no airport that compares to the laid-backness of Don Mueang; the atmosphere is relaxed, everything is reasonably priced; it's just living proof that an airport can be a great leisure experience without becoming an over-the-top theme park, like Singapore's Changi.

As an ultimate escape, when I was utterly drained of energy, I headed to my favorite hangouts, the airport bars. Just to disappear into these godless oases of distorted reality floating between different time zones, utterly out of context of the real life, the normal human rhythm of day and night, is a very special treat of traveling. They are the only places where I discard my two rules of "no drinking during the day and don't buy overpriced drinks." With the time zones changing so rapidly around you, it really doesn't matter anymore.

I knew these wonderful oases far too well. In Hong Kong

International Airport, my favorite hangout was the Velocity Bar and Grill. In Kolkata it was that nameless bar right in the middle where they pour overpriced Kingfisher like there's no tomorrow.

Practically living your life at airports with intense traveling schedules, the joke is that you always have time on your hands, with delays and endless waits in airport lounges and airport restaurants but you're too burned out to focus on any work. I always found it funny how before a month of travel I loaded up with stacks of books and by the end I ended up watching *Family Guy* on my laptop because that was the only thing my brain could process.

One of my favorite things through all this travel was what I called the haunting game. Amid work-related travels, when my trails led through cities I used to know as home — Shanghai, Bangkok and even Hong Kong in a sense — I always took some time off and went back to the places where I had lived or worked.

I called these occasions hauntings because whenever I revisited my former homes, I felt like a ghost walking around, in the very same surroundings of the life I once had there, now totally evaporated, the friends and acquaintances that peopled these places all gone. Just to walk into these former living environments sent a shiver down my spine as they were mere shells of what they were once: homes.

Thus, whenever I was in Bangkok my way took me to the area of On Nut, where I spent most of 2016 before I got the AirAsia job. I walked down Soi 85 where our apartment used to be and sampled my favorite eateries. In Shanghai, where I spent ten years of my life, this haunting game was perhaps the most intense. The level of nostalgia was almost unbearable once I immersed myself in the long-forgotten details of the past, in the ever-mesmerizing French Concession; looking up at our old flat's window where we lived for years at the corner of Wulumuqi and Wuyuan Lu.

I returned to my favorite restaurants and ordered what I used to eat. If the owner or the staff was the same, I could see that momentary confusion running over their faces as they tried to place where they knew me from. Even if I was extremely busy, while on assignment in these cities, I always made sure to make time for these exceptionally interesting and somewhat eerie visits; sometimes I would even extend my stay for an extra day to do my haunting.

By work travel and these little personal indulgences, I'm glad I did use every single moment. Little did I know that there were changes just around the corner that would irreversibly transform everything that surrounded me: the aviation, the tourism industry with all its privileges, would soon be washed away.

The COVID pandemic was fast approaching and meanwhile, the exhaustion from the constant travel was catching up with me and I was burning out quickly. I was utterly neutralised by travel and sadly, I had become fed up with my passion, photography. It felt like I didn't have a home, a private life anymore, I was becoming cynical and totally indifferent to any excitement coming my way. My world revolved around boarding passes, hotel rooms, airport bars, waiting halls, tight schedules, deadlines and so on. Even when I was off-work, the boundaries between travel, work-travel and holiday blurred and shifted. Outside work, I became an unbearable travel-companion, even to my wife. I refused to leave the hotel rooms on private holidays, I didn't want to see anything and visiting any tourist sites was out of the question, based on shooting about seven of these daily, while I tried to minimise minimise human contact and talk to as few people as possible. I felt like I didn't belong anywhere, and only later I realized I didn't even know the apartment I was supposed to be living in in Kuala Lumpur. By then I'd been on the road for five consecutive years and my lifestyle had spiraled into an unbearable speed.

What I didn't suspect, however, was that it would all end naturally, that my travels would end abruptly and I'd be grounded in a way never thought possible, that I would succumb to a bigger force that would tower over me, something unprecedented, something entirely different than I had ever known, that it would be mightier than any obstacle known before, an obstacle more impenetrable than any Mexican-American border wall. It took time before I could fathom that it would bring five intense traveling years to an abrupt grinding halt while transforming and polarizing the world like only wars before had been capable of.

I was just about to venture into a yet another month-long assignment starting out in Varanasi, focusing on the culture of the mysterious Aghori Babas, the *sadhus* who cover themselves with finely mashed human bone dust, who are associated with the post-death rituals and cremation, engaging in all post-mortem rituals. While in Varanasi, there was another feature to cover: the festival of Maha Shivratri that celebrates the wedding of Lord Shiva to Goddess Parvati. From there, I was to travel to Kolkata to catch perhaps the most visual celebration on lens, Holi, where paint is thrown around in festive crowds, marking the beginning of spring and the harvest season across India.

From Kolkata I was about to head to Thailand, first to the Lan Na Kingdom of Chiang Mai to cover local flag-making traditions, then to do two stories in Bangkok: map out the waterways that criss-cross the city and photograph the city's pet-cafes. All shoots and interviews were scheduled already; yet again, I was venturing into another marathon, another jetsetter round spread over a month.

I remember that very last week I was busy searching for a

camera cover, a protection from the paint thrown around in the Holi celebrations, while planning my routes and arranging the tickets when the news of the first wave of COVID was emerging and becoming more real with every passing day. With my usual kamikaze approach, I tried to ignore it, to block it out. But the decision wasn't mine; my editor suggested postponing the dates because word was getting around that a two-week lockdown was coming. As this editorial order stopped me in my hurried tracks, I was extremely annoyed at first, with all that planning and future photo material going to waste. But once I accepted it, it became easy, not even knowing that my acceptance would entirely change my life and mark the end of an era.

At first, the arrival of COVID felt like redemption. As lockdowns and new terms like social distancing and MCOs (Movement Control Orders) were slowly creeping into our everyday language, I took comfort in my newly found spare time and immobility. Suddenly, it was like jumping out and landing safely from a dizzying carousel going faster and faster. I remember how grateful I was to be away from travel for two entire weeks to catch my breath. Little did I know that these two weeks would eventually turn into three years without even being on an airplane or leaving Malaysia at all.

Over the following years, the boundaries of travel shifted dramatically. Travel and tourism as we had known it was transformed entirely and to some extent forever. Southeast Asia was under strict lockdown; cities became ghost towns, flights were grounded, airports were empty. AirAsia, was reduced to a local food delivery business and an Uber-like taxi service, with major layoffs, trying to repurpose its enormous customer database to local needs. Tourist sites froze in a moment, just like in an apocalyptic movie. In Kuala Lumpur, thanks to a seven-month lockdown in 2021, our world shrank to the apartment we were living in. With these changes, the AirAsia job was gone and I didn't mind it at all. I welcomed the new chapter in my life. I was tired of constantly moving around, perhaps aged out of the lifestyle too, and found a new comfort in just staying in one place and get to know the country I eventually chose home; to get familiar with its people, its culture. And last but not least it was time to come to terms with the life choice I made: living so far away from my home country, in the process losing almost all attachment to it.

The break stretched through entire years and provided me time for a long-overdue retrospective not only on my hyper traveling years but on how far I had come overall through the decades from the time I planned my escape at the music library in my hometown some thirty years before. The never ending, self-inflicted exile, the self-searching chase, running from continent to continent, from country to country, from city to city, never seemed to cease over these years, had consumed my youth as well as most of my adult life. I suddenly found myself myself in my late forties living in Southeast Asia in a tropical climate. How on earth did I get here? — I realised I had never had a chance to look back properly and things had happened at such speed that I needed to trace back my steps. There was an awful lot to digest and contemplate. And all of a sudden, I had all the time in the world.

In general, people who consciously made the life choice to settle where they were born, or in a city nearby, betting on a safe home with kids, usually have an ambivalent view on the life of a constant drifter or someone who moves permanently abroad. Like many of us, I've been the object of this curiosity far too many times and in reverse, I always study people while they're pondering whether they could live this way or not. On the one hand — because a healthy dose of wanderlust is inherent in human nature — they tend to envy it, but they are also aware that they wouldn't be able to keep up with it. Torn between being fascinated by your lifestyle and also a bit terrified of it, they tend to take a step back. Without meaning anything bad, they — even friends — consider it a rootless existence. They look at you like you don't belong anywhere really, especially when they don't have a clear concept of the foreign land you live in: Malaysia? China? India? How can a westerner spend a lifetime in those places?

But what they cannot fathom is that your friend is the unknown, it's the unpredictable that you have signed up for, that shifting sand is your main drive. That there's a twisted balance in all of this, a method to what appears to be madness from the outside. Decades of drifting taught me that the further you move, the closer you feel to your own roots. It's a magical feeling, really. Any person who has spent a lifetime abroad can tell you about that unique and exceptional perspective they have on their country of origin; it gives you a crystal clear sense of judgement and orientation often wrapped in a healthy dose of romanticism. All in all, in some ways, to us drifters, this is our way of coming full circle in life.

All of us go through this experience and digest the past differently. Mine is probably an image of my hometown faded, frozen in time somewhere in the early 80s, with that small newspaper kiosk standing around the corner, still existing in another dimension. It might be a distorted image, yes, but it's certainly something to return to; it's a milestone, something to measure how far one has come.

When I return to Hungary, rarely now, occasionally I find myself momentarily touching the houses, the trunks of old trees around the places I grew up, the stage sets of my childhood, as I'm walking along the streets. And I know how it must look from the outside. But what appears to be a forty-something halfwit in a long coat touching walls is actually an almost sacral ritual in real time, possibly the closest one can come close to time travel. To pick up that building's, that tree's or that ground's energy that once gave you life; that reminds you this was once home.

But however comforting this is, you can't stay for too long; you succumb, you give in to that pull, that choice you have made, to be away, your pact with the unknown calls you, the quest that drives you further and further away. If this is what rootless means, I'm all for it, I exchange it for any earthly possession. To be an outsider, a sojourner everywhere I go. And paired with that workaholic fuel that takes me so far from home, that armed me in the first place; risking my life in Mexico or in the jungles of Borneo; if London is not far enough, then New York, if Hong Kong is not far enough then Shanghai, if Bangkok is not far enough then rural Cambodia, if Kuala Lumpur is not far enough, then up to the haunted misty jungles of the mountains of Frasers Hill. Further and further away.

There seems to be no place to rest. Well, maybe one. And I can even name it: it's Farquhar Street, George Town, Penang. This was an unlikely discovery. Frankly, I didn't think there was one more city in me. After the COVID lockdowns when I started to rebuild my life I began frequenting George Town every month. This historical UNESCO site is known for its multicultural background, its eclectic architecture and as a cradle of Peranakan, the Straits-born Chinese heritage. George Town developed over hundreds of years of trading and cultural exchanges between East and West in the Straits of Malacca. It is a goldmine for someone who likes to document people and buildings.

I have slowly started to find friends here, work, new projects and just generally, new potentials. After leaving AirAsia, I started my own company, MonoMark Studio, with an ex-AirAsia colleague, the art director of *the magazine of Travel360*, and George Town with its potential and culturally fetid ground, became the centre for my business. I also came across yet another spectacular human story entwined in architecture. I met Chris Ong, a former banker of the world and a similar drifter who, in his fifties, after a lifetime living abroad, returned home and used his fortune to enrich the area he grew up in with Peranakan-style mansions and boutique hotels, rebuilding his family's cultural heritage. It was Chris who made George Town home for me with a unique privilege of being allowed to stay in his Peranakan residences while helping him document his heritage and his remarkable structural transformations around the area.

It's George Town where I eventually seem to find peace, a certain sense of ease, a touch of discontinuity. And this street, along which I often walk, maybe because its particular location dividing land from sea, running like a barrier along the coast, is a special one. When I stop on Farquhar Street, facing the horizon, only my thoughts and my gaze run over the surface of the sea, further rushing towards the unknown, This is where I take a breath, where time seems to stop at last, where I eventually run out of kilometers and feel I have perhaps have come full circle. There is no distance left to run.

Acknowledgements

My great thanks first and foremost to my wife Barbara Bogos for her support and patience throughout the years this book was conceived. Thank you for my family, my mother, my beloved grandparents and my brother Zsolt. An eternal thanks to my dear friends Andy Davis, JFK Miller, Ned Kelly, and Aelred Doyle who went through the book's manuscript and helped to tidy it up and correcting it along the way. Thanks to my former editor Beverly Rodrigues for often mercilessly pushing my writing abilities to the maximum and helping my initial career in Southeast Asia and also my former team at AirAsia for inspiring me.

Also a big thanks to Graham Earnshaw for giving me a final direction with the book, a clear sight and good advice.

About the Author

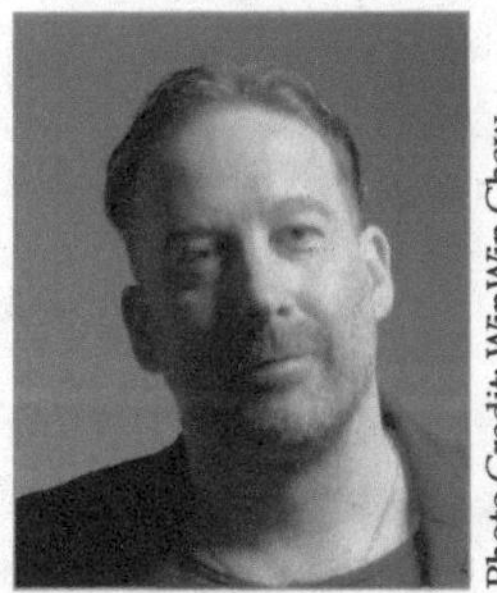

Award-winning photographer and filmmaker **Nicky Almasy** has been living and working in Asia since 2005, concentrating on architecture, culture, art and heritage. In Shanghai he was commissioned to shoot the second tallest building of the world, the Shanghai Tower, and was the construction photographer on the project for five consecutive years. His first book, Hudec, on architect Laszlo Hudec, was published in 2017 and was followed by a biography of another Hungarian architect, Karoly Gonda, published in 2019. His work on architecture won two photography awards, one for ENR and in 2012 and 2016 for Arcaid. He has also worked with various international publications such as WHERE, The Financial Times and the Daily Mail, and his photos have been featured on the covers of over fifty magazines. Nicky was the photojournalist for AirAsia for five years working exclusively for the airline's inflight magazine, Travel360. He lives in Kuala Lumpur, Malaysia shooting documentaries on culture and heritage.